The Emergent Gospel

ORBIS BOOKS

Maryknoll, New York 10545

THE EMERGENT GOSPEL

Theology from the Underside of History

*Papers from the Ecumenical Dialogue
of Third World Theologians,
Dar es Salaam, August 5–12, 1*

*Edited by

Sergio Torres
and
Virginia Fabella, M.M.*

The Catholic Foreign Mission Society of America (Maryknoll) recruits and trains people for overseas missionary service. Through Orbis Books Maryknoll aims to foster the international dialogue which is essential to mission. The books published, however, reflect the opinions of their authors and are not meant to represent the official position of the Society.

Library of Congress Cataloging in Publication Data

Ecumenical Dialogue of Third World Theologians, Dar es
   Salaam, 1976.
   The Emergent Gospel.

   Includes bibliographical references.
   1. Church and underdeveloped areas—Congresses.
2. Theology—Congresses. I. Torres, Sergio.
II. Fabella, Virginia. III. Title.
BR115.U6E36   1976   291.2   77-22134
ISBN 0-88344-112-8
ISBN 0-88344-113-6 pbk.

CONTENTS

LATIN AMERICA

CONCLUSION

Introduction

This book is the result of a conference. Its contributors seek an alternative to the present dominant theology and suggest hope for the future. The conference was held in Dar es Salaam, Tanzania, in August 1976. Twenty-two theologians from Africa, Asia, and Latin America and a representative of black North America met to reflect upon the significance of theology in the countries of the Third World.[1]

The meeting grew out of an intuition that was increasingly felt by Third World Christians who considered the division among rich and poor as the major phenomenon of contemporary history. This very division challenges all Christians in our dual capacity as actors in history and as disciples of Christ.

The power and decision-making centers of the Christian churches are still located in Europe and the United States. Their organization, their norms, their theology—all have been greatly influenced by the philosophy and values of these countries, which have been considered the center of "western Christian civilization." According to many contemporary thinkers, there are signs pointing to the impending demise of this civilization. However, many leaders as well as rank-and-file members of these churches remain unaware of this erosion and continue acting, thinking, praising God, writing theology, dictating policies, etc., as if their countries were still the center of the world. It has been repeatedly said that, toward the end of this century, the center of the Christian world will have moved toward Africa and Latin America.

Third World Christians have begun to look at history from their perspective as citizens of poor and dominated countries. Their judgment and outlook is different from that of European and U.S. Christians. The Dar es Salaam Conference was one such instance. The principal objectives of this conference were to scrutinize the "signs of the times," to listen to the Spirit amid the division between the rich and the poor, and to examine the two distinct perspectives operative in theology today.

DAR ES SALAAM AS PART OF A PROCESS

It is difficult for me to write this Introduction with complete objectivity. From the start I have been associated with the conference in both its preparation and its implementation. After some informal sessions theologians from the Third World, together with groups of Christian thinkers from Europe, Canada, and the U.S.A., became convinced the time was ripe to initiate a more systematic dialogue that would contribute to their mutual enrichment. The opening address that I delivered at the beginning of the conference on August 6, 1976, contains the background history, the objectives, and the importance of this theological endeavor.[2] In the same address, I pointed out that if we wanted to affirm our identity as Third World Christians, we needed to maintain an honest and ongoing dialogue with our brothers and sisters in the First World, with the hope of uniting our efforts toward the building of a new creation and a new humanity under God.

Tanzania was the ideal site for this conference. There the difference between the rich and poor nations is starkly dramatized. Tanzania has a per capita Gross National Product of $127. Its arid regions, its droughts, and its poverty are a challenge to the whole world. This country identifies with its leader, President Julius Nyerere, and with his program of *ujamaa* to combat underdevelopment. This program, which combines elements from both the Christian and the best African traditions, constitutes a real source of attraction and admiration for all those who ask questions about the future and the role of Christians in the developing countries.

The conference was held on the campus of the University of Dar es Salaam, a symbol of the country's aspiration toward progress and self-reliance. The theologians from the three continents of Africa, Asia, and Latin America had a unique experience. The integration of the group was at first a difficult process. The participants came from various Catholic, Protestant, and Orthodox backgrounds and traditions as well as from different races and distinct cultures. It was hard work to come to a mutual understanding. But through dialogue, discussion, and at times even confrontation, we achieved a significant degree of unity. Despite the difficulties, the conference was a success. After intense days of work and prayer together, the Final Statement is a testimony of our acceptance of the various points of view and of our search for the best expression of our common purpose.[3]

THEOLOGY OF THE THIRD WORLD

A book is different from a conference. This book that we now present to our readers is a reflection of what we wanted to realize in Dar es Salaam. A book records an event in a permanent way but it fails to transmit all the richness of personal encounter and the experience of being together. Some of the authors included in this book could not attend the conference but submitted their papers just the same. On the other hand some of those who presented papers at the conference will miss seeing them printed in this volume. Editing a book is not an easy task. Because of space limitations, one is obliged to leave out articles equally important as those included.

A book or a conference is a link in the chain of human and scientific progress. In recent years, many books on Third World theology have been published.[4] Orbis Books has made an appreciable contribution in this area. This volume does not pretend to be superior to those already published. Rather it endeavors to be different.

The concept of Third World is, in the first place, not limited to geographical space. It is not enough to live in Africa or Asia to share what we understand by theology of the Third World. There are people who live in Hong Kong or Bolivia who do not identify ideologically with the Third World. Their hearts, their interests, their futures are linked with the dominant classes of the world. The same can happen in a book on theology. It is not enough for authors to live in or come from poor countries for their theology to differ basically from the theology of the rich countries. Herein lies the originality of this book and the emergent theology it represents. It proposes to develop scientifically a theology that speaks with the voice of the poor and the marginated in history. As the final document states:

The theologies from Europe and North America are dominant today in our churches and represent one form of cultural domination. They must be understood to have arisen out of situations related to those countries, and therefore must not be uncritically adopted without our raising the question of their relevance in the context of our countries. . . .

We reject as irrelevant an academic type of theology that is divorced from action. We are prepared for a radical break in epistemology which makes commitment the first act of theology and engages in critical reflection on praxis of the reality of the Third World.[5]

There is always a gap between what we aspire to and what we actually accomplish. The quality of the papers included in this book is varied, but what is important is our working hypothesis and the intention to formulate in a defined way what *should* be a Third World theology and what distinguishes it from other theologies.

One point was discussed at length in Dar es Salaam. Some of the participants felt that North American blacks did not belong to the Third World, so they should not be included in the process. However, the Africans claimed that for them, there was only one black world, whether in Africa, in North America, or in the Caribbean. The future will show whether this statement proves true or not.

The participation of women was not seriously considered until the Conference itself. It is unfortunate indeed that until now this project of Third World theologians has had the weakness of not having an adequate representation of women. Though the Organizing Committee asked each continent to send women participants, once more the result of discrimination against women in the churches became evident in Dar es Salaam: Only one woman participated. The Committee recognized this deficiency and made the firm resolution to correct it in future conferences.

METHODOLOGICAL CRITERIA

Professor Ngindu Mushete, in his article, "Unity of Faith and Pluralism in Theology," explains how it is possible to speak of different theologies that represent the universality of revelation and the unity of our faith.[6] "One Lord . . . one baptism." Although his arguments follow the traditional European model, he opens the way to counteract an objection that frequently arises.

Carlos Abesamis moves a step ahead when he affirms that the so-called "indigenization of theology" does not necessarily mean moving toward an indigenous theology. "I hope we are beyond the stage where 'indigenizing theology' means translating the western theological works written in Latin, French, German, or English into our dialects. 'Indigenization of theology' is not a question of translation of language to language. Neither should producing an indigenous theology mean 'applying' the theology of Athanasius, Ambrose, Pannenberg, Rahner, or Vatican II 'to the local situation.' "[7] This is very important, because most of what has been called "indigenization" or "contextualization" of theology is simply a translation or application of traditional theology.

Allan Boesak adds another important element when he says that theology should neither be a "cultural theology" or a "religion of culture." When we speak of searching in history or in traditional culture for the symbols and language to reformulate the biblical message, we are stating part of the truth. However, the theology of the Third World is not merely a "cultural theology." As Boesak says: "A contextual theology, like black theology, clearly is, must be authentic. It must not yield to uncritical accommodation, becoming a 'cultural theology' or a 'religion of culture.' An authentic situational theology is prophetic, critical, not merely excavating corpses of tradition, but taking critically those traditions from the past which can play a humanizing and revolutionizing role in our contemporary society."[8]

The relationship between theology and ideology is critical in this effort. James Cone, among others, makes this point when he speaks of the difference between white theology and black theology. In his book *God of the Oppressed*, he dedicates Chapter 5 to the theme of black theology and ideology.[9] His question is valid for us: "How do we distinguish our words about God from God's Word, our wishes from his Will, our dreams and aspirations from the work of his Spirit?"[10]

Orlando Carvajal responds from his point of view, stating that in our methodology of theological reflection it is important to discover how our language in general and our theological language in particular are very much related to the economic and social context in which we live.[11] This aspect has been generally disregarded by western theologians, leading them to assume uncritically that theirs is the universal and unchangeable theology.

The article which directly addresses the difference between the two theologies is written by Gustavo Gutiérrez. Well known for his book *A Theology of Liberation*,[12] he presents a very solid and well-documented study on the two distinct theological positions. He assumes that in our times there are three theological tendencies: the traditional theology of the Establishment, the political theology of Europe, and the theologies of the Third World. Although his paper attempts to establish a comparison between the political theology of Europe and the theologies of the Third World, his argument can be applied accurately to the First World in general. His paper is, at one and the same time, a genuine challenge to the theology of the First World and an apt description of the Latin American theology of liberation. In my opinion, this document is one of those that best express what we attempted to do in our meeting in Dar es Salaam, that is, to use the scholarship of academic theology to express the aspirations and sufferings of Third World Christians who are struggling against all forms of oppression.

The main criticism against this endeavor has been that our theology is not systematic, that it is not articulated according to the prevailing norms of academia, and that there are no books that explain this theology. Our critics are right; we have not yet been able to express in books the lived experience of specific people. But this does not mean the rejection of the scientific tools of theology. Moreover we feel a continuity with the theology of past epochs. If we claim something different, it does not mean we have relinquished being Christians or rejected the richness of our Christian tradition. It is precisely because we acknowledge our link with our religious heritage and social environment, with all of their prejudices, that we recognize the shortcomings of the dominant theology. What we reject is the presentation of this theology as universal or eternal when it proceeds from a particular culture and a particular epoch. This is the difficult task of discernment, which should be done in obedience to the Spirit and in communion with the church.

At this juncture, we should try to define in a precise way what we mean by a *different* theology. It is necessary to present a brief historical description and critical analysis of western theology in order to point out how it is possible to believe in the same Risen Lord and express, live, celebrate, and transmit the same faith but from a different starting point.

WESTERN THEOLOGY IN THE EIGHTEENTH
AND NINETEENTH CENTURIES

For many centuries the theologians' task has been to explain and interpret for each new generation God's revelation as found in the Bible and Christian tradition. But this grounding of theology on authority came under sharp questioning during the eighteenth and nineteenth centuries, as the modern scientific picture of the world took shape in the human imagination and the Bible was subjected increasingly to close and critical historical analysis.

What occurred in those centuries was the development of a worldview very different from either classical or medieval culture. From the point of view of Christianity this new modern epoch can be characterized as a culture emancipating itself from theological domination. Underlying this whole movement is a renewed awareness and trust in a human being's capacities, an appreciation of human life on this earth. Reason supersedes revelation as the supreme authority.

Centered on rationalism and individualism, this new worldview in the eighteenth and nineteenth centuries was the result of two important economic and political phenomena: the Industrial Revolution and the French Revolution. The Industrial Revolution was a revolution on the level of production: a new dominant class—the bourgeoisie—was born, and a new mode of production started—capitalism. The French Revolution was a political shift from the former system.

As a result, theology faced a choice of either adjusting itself to the advances of modern science and philosophy and, in so doing, risking accommodation to secularization, or resisting all cultural influences and becoming largely reactionary and ineffectual in meeting the challenges of life in the modern world.

Protestant theology in general, and particularly in Germany, tried to face this challenge. The names of Kant, Schleiermacher, Hegel, Strauss, and Ritschl are well known. Catholic theology, with the exception of liberal Catholicism[13] and Modernism,[14] both of which had little influence, did not accept this challenge and became closed in on itself.

But the theologians who accepted the challenge of the Enlightenment entered in dialogue with the ideology of the bourgeoisie about the incompatibility of Christian faith and modern science. However, they did not dialogue about the incompatibility of Christian faith and the new mode of production that was shaping western civilization in a new way.

THEOLOGY IN THE TWENTIETH CENTURY

By the beginning of the twentieth century it had become very clear that radical reconceptualization of the foundations of the theological enterprise was required. Then came World War I, the crisis in western culture, and the rise of neo-orthodoxy.

Today, it is not difficult to understand why in that situation of crisis there was a return to the security of the Word of God. This movement was the neo-orthodoxy whose best representative was Karl Barth.

Other subsequent theological efforts have to be mentioned. Christian Existentialism,[15] Christian Realism,[16] Political Theology,[17] and the movement that culminated in Vatican II[18] are the most important.

What is happening today? There is a crisis in theology. That crisis is almost universally recognized. The explanations come easily: secularization, lack of community participation, crisis in the culture, the absence of theological giants such as Barth, Tillich, and Bultmann.

The theologians of the Third World have their own interpretation. We can summarize this interpretation in this way: There is a crisis in theology because there is a crisis in the culture of western scientific rationalism. And there is a crisis in the culture because there is a change in the economic mode of production, which has not been able to resolve the injustices of the world and overcome the different forms of oppression.

When there is a crisis in the mode of production, the whole social organization suffers and quakes. But it is difficult for people who are enjoying the benefits of the system to understand the crisis and to discover that the promises of the liberal system and the economic organization of the West have not been fulfilled.

There are some voices in the Third World who remind us of this failure. Some nations in the world, some classes in society, and some races that western society has marginalized in the process of its expansion have begun to emerge from their captivity, rejecting the conditions that their masters have imposed on them. They have started their "long march" that nobody will stop.

They will create a new culture, a new mode of production, a new age for themselves and, unavoidably, also for their masters. Among those races, classes, and nations, there are some people who live their struggle, their hope, and their projection of a new age in the faith of Jesus Christ and the power of his Spirit.

They are reading the Scriptures in a new way, from a different perspective. They are engaged in a new way of doing theology. Western theology has read the Scriptures from the point of view of the dominant classes. The new theologies of the oppressed and the poor are looking at the event of Jesus Christ from their oppression and poverty, from the underside of history. This is the difference between the two ways of doing theology. The break is primarily political and only secondarily theological.

AFRICAN THEOLOGY

It is necessary to state a few words regarding the participation of the different continents represented at the Dar es Salaam Conference. We begin with Africa.

Africa is a continent rich in its multiplicity of cultures, complex in its process of political independence, and insecure in its economic and social development. Patrick Masanja, professor of social sciences from the University of Dar es Salaam, presented a synthesis of the socio-economic and political realities of Africa which provided the context for the discussion that ensued.[19]

In discussing African theology, the other African participants offered insights according to their varying backgrounds. Some emphasized the content and spoke of African culture as the raw material for this theology; others preferred to offer methodological criteria for this effort.

The two theologians invited from South Africa, Manas Buthelezi and Allan Boesak, could not attend the Conference but sent their contributions for publication in this book.[20] Their writings express the level of maturity that some sectors of the Christian communities in South Africa have reached.

Dr. Buthelezi is a prominent figure in the Lutheran Church in his country. In his article, he brings out a significant distinction for African theology—between the "ethnographical" and "anthropological" approaches—showing how the latter is more relevant for the present African situation.[21]

Allan Boesak is a young theologian who finished his doctoral dissertation only recently and is fast becoming one of the leaders in the field of black theology in Africa.[22] His paper serves as a complement to Buthelezi's work. He introduces two new dimensions in the debate: the relation between African theology and black theology in the U.S.A., and the consideration of African theology as a theology of liberation.

In recent years, there have been attempts among North American blacks to trace their "roots" to Africa. Gayraud Wilmore's book *Black Religion and Black Radicalism* is a fascinating history of the continual nostalgia for the homeland and of the efforts toward dialogue and rapprochement.[23] There have been consultations among black theologians from the U.S.A. and Africa to seek out the common features of their race, their history, and their future. In the past three years, with the events in South Africa, there has been a new consciousness among members of the black communities in the U.S.A. to return to their roots and establish a more active solidarity with their African brothers and sisters.

Boesak speaks of black theology in South Africa, but his views are applicable to the rest of Africa. "It must be abundantly clear by now that black theology cannot be easily divorced from African theology."[24] A further contribution from Boesak is his concept of "an ethic of liberation." In dialectical dialogue with black theologians from the U.S.A., he develops a black liberation theology in a form both novel and appealing.

Boesak brings out one final important aspect of black theology. It springs from love and not from hate or violence. The ultimate source is the reconciliatory love of Christ himself. "Black theology takes love very seriously, opting for agape, which stands at the very center of God's liberating actions for his people." And in relation to white society, he adds: "Black theology, by offering a new way of theologizing, desires to be helpful in discovering the truth about black and white people, about our past and our present, about God's will for us in our common world."[25]

African theology is in the process of growth and development. The papers included in this book are a sign of that vitality.

ASIAN THEOLOGY

The Asian continent is composed of sub-continents. Each has a history that includes events that have proved decisive for all humanity. Each country evokes time-honored cultures and religious traditions along with new political programs and varying degrees of modernization. India, Vietnam, China, Japan, Iran, the Philippines, and the other Asian nations form a complex but fascinating mosaic.

The group of Asian theologians had a great impact on the Conference, which unfortunately cannot be reproduced in any book. However, it is important to point out some elements that would help our readers in understanding the Asian section of this volume.

Dialogue with the Traditional Religions

J. R. Chandran's paper, "Development of Christian Theology in India: A Critical Survey," provides a good synthesis of what has been accomplished in India from a stage of antagonism to one of dialogue between Hinduism and Christianity.[26] The presence of Prof. Lynn da Silva, director of the Study Centre for Religion and Society in Colombo, Sri Lanka, and author of several books on Buddhism,[27] helped the non-Asians in the Conference to enter into the non-Christian world. From the Catholic point of view, D. S. Amalorpavadass presented an excellent theological analysis of the various Oriental religions.[28]

Because of this Asian input, the Conference participants were reawakened to the need for a continuing dialogue with the different cultures and religions in Asia. In their final statement, the participants recognized "as part of the reality of the Third World the influence of religions and cultures and the need for Christianity to enter in humility into a dialogue with them. We believe that these religions and cultures have a place in God's universal plan and the Holy Spirit is actively at work among them."[29]

Nevertheless, the theology of the Third World does not focus mainly on these dialogues or on the reconceptualization of biblical revelation through symbols borrowed from other religions. Without denying the importance of either, the Asian theologians at the Conference were more concerned about looking for new ways of overcoming the ghetto-mentality of the Christian communities on their continent. This mentality, so deeply imbedded in their tradition, has been the result of their minority condition in the vast continent of Asia as well as the conservatism of the missionaries who brought their faith to them. The stress of a Third World theology and of an Asian theology is to discover the role of the Christian communities in their new situation brought about by the economic systems and technology.

Development, Liberation, and Theology

The Asian papers were written from the perspective of different cultures and backgrounds; nevertheless, they contained a common element: a true concern to adapt theology to the concrete situation in which they were living. They were aware of the values of their ancient cultures, yet it was not with the past that they wanted dialogue, but with the present, and, they hoped, with the future.

The prophetic role of theology is to discover the "signs of the times." Peter Lee describes this exigency in his paper, "Between the Old and the New." D. S. Amalorpavadass dedicated a major part of his article to the theme of development and liberation. J. R. Chandran concludes his paper with what he considers constitutive of Indian theology: "The main key to Indian theology is the discernment of the reality of Christ and his mission on frontiers of the church both with other faiths and with the struggle for justice."[30]

The Asian representatives cautioned against the ideological co-optation of the churches and theology when speaking of the contemplative attitude of the East and the resistance to the technological mentality of the West. They claimed that these attitudes were a way of legitimatizing the established order and maintaining the passivity of the masses.

LATIN AMERICAN THEOLOGY

Our book includes three papers by Latin American theologians. Prof. Enrique Dussel presents a brief history of the Catholic church in Latin America in the present century, including the major theological trends.[31] Beatriz Melano Couch writes of Protestantism and the development of Protestant theological thinking on the continent.[32] The Protestants are still a minority in Latin America; however, it has been an active minority in the churches that has affected the renewal and modernization of important groups and in recent years has contributed significantly to the development of liberation theology. The work of Gustavo Gutiérrez makes a clear distinction between the theology of the Third World and the theology developed in the First World.[33]

The theologians of Africa and Asia were eager to have this dialogue with the Latin Americans. At the same time, a few of them felt some suspicion and apprehension and even some defensiveness. This produced a certain tension, which was perceptible during the initial days of the Conference, but was successfully overcome toward the end.

The exchange that followed led the group to discover "dependency" as a common condition of their Third World countries and to search for a theology that addresses this condition.

It was a new experience for the Latin Americans to enter into the world of African and Asian religions. The Spanish conquest of their countries in the sixteenth century tried to eliminate, or assimilate, the indigenous culture. Only in recent years has there been any serious acknowledgement of "popular religiosity" as a locus of theology.

Their contact with the Africans, with their experience of racism, helped the Latin American theologians to take cognizance once more of the forms of discrimination against the blacks and indigenous groups on their own continent. A few of the Latin Americans are keenly conscious of this reality but their reflections on it have not yet been articulated in their writings.

Another sensitive point was the participation of women in the church and in theology. Again, the Latin Americans, while recognizing the secondary and limited role accorded women, have for the most part not as yet included that concern in their books. The Latin American theologians admitted having gained greater familiarity with feminist theology in their encounter with U.S. women, who have advanced in this area more than their counterparts in other countries.

It is hoped that the women who will be participating in this effort as well as in the future conferences will lend their much-needed feminine perspective to perfect and complete the interpretation of liberation theology. However, this will not happen as long as the churches remain incognizant of their sexism, continue to entrust power and authority solely to men, and fail to open the necessary opportunities to women.

The Conference was an occasion to analyze the interrelationship among the different forms of oppression. However, due to pressure of time, this could not be covered in depth, nor were all the concerns brought up at the meeting. The Latin Americans felt this limitation and their own papers could not include all the issues facing their theology. Although this was touched in the discussions, two of the concerns not mentioned in their papers are the different trends within the theology of liberation itself, and the current attempts by powerful sectors to discredit this theology. Despite these deficiencies, the participants felt mutually enriched by the dialogue to which they attested in their final statement.

We hope that these preliminary words will prove helpful to the reader whom we now invite to participate in discovering the universality of our Christian vocation through this dialogical process. God calls all of us to faith, obedience, and conversion. We are all sinners. "If we say we are free of the guilt of sin, we deceive ourselves; the truth is not to be found in us" (I John 1:8). When the twenty-two theologians from poor countries spoke as a group, they felt no superiority or exemption from this condition of sin.

We then conclude this part of the Introduction with words taken from the final document: "We have spoken from the depths of our lived experience. We kindly request all to accept our statement as a sincere expression of our consensus from our knowledge of what our peoples have gone through over centuries. We hope it will be of some service in spreading genuine and frank understanding among the peoples of the world."[34]

Many persons and institutions have helped in making both the conference and the resulting book possible. There is no way of naming them all. Nevertheless, in justice some must be mentioned. Sister Virginia Fabella of Maryknoll, who co-edited this book, also played a valuable role in promoting this process of theological reflection and coordinating the preparations for the Conference from the New York office. The Maryknoll priests and sisters in New York recognized the relationship of this endeavor to their own missionary effort and have helped generously.

The members of the North American (U.S.A. and Canada) and European Support Committees also gave moral and financial assistance. Specific mention must be made of those whose support was indispensable in this connection: Dr. Eugene Stockwell of the Division of Overseas Ministries of NCCCUSA; Rev. Robert C. S. Powell of the Africa Committee of the same Division, and Emilio Castro and Julio de Santa Ana of the World Council of Churches. Rev. François Houtart not only worked for the financial support of the Conference but also, with SEUL (European Service for Latin American University Students, Brussels), contributed much to the initial stages of this ecumenical dialogue.

In Africa, many people in Tanzania and Kenya were involved in the Conference. Heading the list are President Julius Nyerere, who enthusiastically welcomed the idea of the dialogue and helped in various ways to effect it, and Canon Burgess Carr of the All Africa Conference of Churches, who gave his encouragement and sent a representative to the Conference. Kofi Appiah-Kubi, Lt. J.W. Butiku, Dr. A.J. Temu, and a number of Maryknoll and other missionaries were among those without whose help the Conference could not have gone on.

The authors of the articles included in this book come from different countries and represent the suffering as well as the hope of countless millions. Their commitment to the liberation of all people is edifying. I express my appreciation to all the members of the Ecumenical Association of Third World Theologians in the person of its president, Dr. J.R. Chandran.

Orbis Books cannot be left unacknowledged. It has played a leading role in promoting a special awareness of the theology, culture, and life of the churches in the Third World among its readers. I wish to express my gratitude to Rev. Miguel d'Escoto, M.M., Philip Scharper, and in particular to John Eagleson, whose competent advice was indispensable in editing this book.

It is a painful experience for me to be away from my own country. But I derive my strength from my faith in Jesus Christ and in my commitment to the church in service of the poor. I attribute this deep faith in Jesus and loyalty to his church to my mother, Mariana, in Chile, whose remembrance sustains me in my efforts.

May this present volume speak for the voiceless majority in the world who have been without hope.

SERGIO TORRES

NOTES

1. There are those who do not agree with the expression "Third World." I prefer to use it as it is now part of international vocabulary and readily understood.

2. See below, Document 1.

3. See below, Document 17.

4. Among the more recent books, see *Mission Trends No. 3: Third World Theologies*, Gerald H. Anderson and Thomas F. Stransky, C.S.P. (Paramus, N.J.: Paulist Press; Grand Rapids: Wm. B. Eerdmans Publishing Co., 1976).

5. See below, p. 269.

6. See below, Document 6.

7. See below, p. 118.

8. See below, pp. 82–83.

9. James Cone, *God of the Oppressed* (New York: Seabury Press, 1975).

10. Ibid., p. 84.

11. See below, Document 9.

12. Gustavo Gutiérrez, *A Theology of Liberation* (Maryknoll, N.Y.: Orbis Books, 1973).

13. Lamennais, Mohler, and Dollinger.

14. Loisy, Tyrrell, and Le Roy.

15. Buber, Marcel, Tillich, Bultmann.

16. Reinhold Niebuhr.

17. Metz and Moltmann.

18. Congar, Chenu, Rahner, de Lubac, Küng, Schillebeeckx.

19. See below, Document 2.

20. Both of their articles have been published in German: See *Theologie im Konfliktfeld Südafrika*, ed. Ilse Tödt (Stuttgart: Ernst Klett; Munich: Kösel, 1976).

21. See below, Document 7.

22. See his *Farewell to Innocence* (Maryknoll, N.Y.: Orbis Books, 1977).

23. Gayraud S. Wilmore, *Black Religion and Black Radicalism* (New York: Anchor Press/Doubleday, 1973).

24. See below, p. 82.

25. See below, pp. 89, 93.

26. See below, Document 13.

27. Among them, *Reincarnation in Buddhist and Christian Thought* (Colombo: Wesley Press, 1968) and *Why Believe in God?* (Colombo: Wesley Press, 1970).

28. See below, Document 12.

29. See below, p. 270.

30. See below, p. 169.

31. See below, Document 14.

32. See below, Document 15.

33. Although the main thoughts contained in the article were expressed in the Dar es Salaam Conference, what is published in this book is a translation and condensation of a longer work to be published in Italian by Queriniana.

34. See below, p. 271.

1

Opening Address

*Sergio Torres, Executive Secretary of
"Ecumenical Dialogue of Third World Theologians"*

History

The theological consultation that begins today is the fruit of a long preparation. For years, many have thought of having a meeting of theologians from the three continents of Africa, Asia, and Latin America. There have been many meetings and consultations initiated and sponsored by the World Council of Churches, by the Roman Catholic church, and by regional organizations that have tried to establish contact and share the experiences of Christians from the three continents.

But perhaps this is the first time that a group of theologians are meeting to reflect in a systematic way upon the context of theology in Third World countries. Catholics and Protestants of different countries have come today to meet and know one another, to tell their history, and to explain how they understand the meaning of revelation in the midst of poverty and underdevelopment.

This meeting is the result of two separate initiatives, which were worked out together to form one project.

In 1974, a group of theological students in Louvain at the European Center for Latin American Students. the Rev. François Houtart, and

1

Professor Enrique Dussel began an investigation of the possibility of a conference among theologians of the three continents. This research, however, was limited to Catholics.

At the same time, a group of Latin American theologians expressed a similar desire to meet with other theologians of the Third World.

In August 1975, a conference took place in Detroit, U.S.A., that brought together Latin American theologians and Christians of North America. At the end of the conference, the Latin Americans reiterated special interest in the dialogue with Africans and Asians and decided to support the project initiated in Louvain. They designated me to represent them in a meeting with the committee in Louvain.

A meeting was held in Louvain in November 1975, where it was agreed to expand the proposed consultation by making it ecumenical, that is, with Catholic and Protestant participation. The Assembly of the World Council of Churches in Nairobi was a perfect opportunity to contact theologians. On that occasion, a steering committee was formed consisting of the following: J. Russell Chandran, Ngindu Mushete, Manas Buthelezi, Enrique Dussel, José Míguez Bonino, D.S. Amalorpavadass, and myself.

The steering committee assumed the task of continuing the efforts initiated in Louvain, defining the objectives of the proposed dialogue, and determining the participants to be invited. The committee also contacted the official representatives of the World Council of Churches, the Theological Education Fund, the All Africa Conference of Churches, as well as the Christian Conference of Asia.

The Objectives

This ongoing process of theological reflection will help the indigenous people of the three continents to decide which conceptions of church and of theology are to have more meaning for them and are to be operative in their own lives. It will also assist the American and European missionaries who are trying to be faithful to the great commission given in Matthew 28:19.

The goals of this process are as follows:

1. To give an opportunity to the theologians of the three continents to

know each other, to share their concerns and their theological reflections.
2. To make an evaluation of the theologies of each continent, to see their relationship to western theology, and to examine the new approaches being made.
3. To help the Christian communities to an indigenous understanding of revelation, and to enable them to renew their service to the Lord according to the cultural, economic, and political situation of each community.
4. To facilitate a more permanent dialogue among the Christian communities of these three continents.
5. To study the new relationships of the indigenous churches with the missionaries.

A Process of Theological Reflection

We do not want to have mere conferences. People are tired of attending conferences without follow-up. We want to start a process; the conferences have to have a time of preparation as well as some follow-up period.

We have developed a four-year plan of study, dialogue, and conferences. The stages are as follows:

1. *August 1976*, Conference at Dar Es Salaam, Tanzania, of leading theologians from Africa, Asia, and Latin America. After a day of sharing with one another the factors that have led each to his or her present theological position, there will be a day each on Africa, on Asia, and on Latin America with two parts to each day: first, the economic, political, social, and cultural context, and, second, an evaluation of the presence of the churches. Subsequent days will treat of these themes from the perspectives of each continent's religious experience: evaluation of the presence of western theology; outline of emerging theological models; toward a theology of the Third World.
2. *December 1977*, Conference at Accra, Ghana, to go into greater depth about the African reality and what the factors of an emerging African Christian theology are, particularly its relations to tribal

religions. This and the next two stages will include a broader representation of participants.

3. *1978*, Conference in Asia to go into greater depth about the Asian reality and what the factors of an emerging Asian theology are, particularly the presence and influence of the traditional Asian religions.

4. *1979*, Conference in Latin America, to go into greater depth about the Latin American reality, the emergent theology of liberation and the relation of churches to the political world.

We hope that in the process not only theologians will be involved, but also representatives of Christian communities, pastors and ministers, men and women, especially those who are struggling for justice, social change, and liberation. Our intention is to have grassroots people as well as professional theologians in the succeeding stages of this process.

Pluralism in Theology

The presence of theologians from three continents speaks eloquently for itself. For a long time now, Christian communities on these three continents have discovered that the universal discourse of theology does not interpret their reality. The local and regional character of the discourse demands a theological reflection proper to each of these vast and distinct geographical and cultural areas.

We have witnessed a change in the geographic location of theology, a movement away from Europe. The vast new areas present challenges to the gospel and demand new answers in each of the different contexts.

Furthermore, there exists an epistemological break. To understand revelation means to understand the new existential reality of millions of men and women struggling against hunger and misery.

This demands new categories of knowledge. The message of Jesus Christ has to be rethought, starting from the new ideological trends and the people's struggle for liberation, which are changing the world.

Pluralism in theology, therefore, will not become a mere intellectual game among homogeneous thinkers; rather there will be profound differences; these should not threaten unity, but render it more creative and fruitful.

The Gap Between the Poor and the Rich Countries

The context influences the perception of the content. There are many aspects that have to be taken into account when speaking of the context of theology.

We want to pay special attention to the most significant fact of our times: the gap between the developed and underdeveloped countries. This gap is being analyzed by political leaders all over the world; it has been the subject matter of the four UNCTAD sessions. It then becomes indispensable for the churches and the theologians to dedicate their effort and research to the study of this reality, which has a profound relationship to the will of God for this world.

Dialogue with Other Religions

Another important issue in this consultation is the relationship of Christianity with other religions of the world, especially in Asia and Africa. After centuries of misunderstandings and confrontations, we have come to understand better the values of these religions and we have discovered that those values represent seeds of the same revelation of the Lord of history.

The Relationship with Europe, U.S.A., and Canada

This present consultation is inscribed within a process of ecumenical dialogue between the established churches of the First World and the young churches of the Third World.

There exists a healthy reaction against the theological imperialism of the West. We believe that we should face this challenge in a spirit of faith and solidarity—but with truth and honesty. This assumes dialogue and, at times, confrontation.

The differences in theology reflect social and cultural differences. It behooves Christians of the Third World and those of the North Atlantic countries to work together for a new International Economic Order as well as for a new theological formulation.

We are grateful for the support and understanding we have found in the United States, Canada, and Europe, for the moral and the financial support individuals and groups have given this project.

Tanzania, Venue of the Consultation

We have come from distant places; we belong to different cultural traditions; we have seen a variety of political regimes. However, there is something that unites us deeply on this occasion. It is our profound admiration for this country and its president, Julius K. Nyerere, and this admiration we wish to proclaim with warmth and great joy.

Our presence serves as a salute to the heroic task of socio-economic development this country is undertaking, which is profoundly human and at the same time faithful to the best African traditions.

I ask for the inspiration of the Holy Spirit during our week of work. The poor and the oppressed in our countries are waiting for a word of hope from us.

AFRICA

2

Neocolonialism and Revolution in Africa

Patrick Masanja (Tanzania)

A discussion of the economic, political, and cultural context of Africa cannot avoid the discussion of such factors as imperialism, neocolonialism, multinational corporations, national liberation, the post-independent state, and the local bourgeoisie, for these have shaped and moulded contemporary Africa and continue to do so. A discussion on the above issues is also necessary in order to ensure that one is using the same language as one's interlocutors. But in a short paper of this kind we cannot exhaustively discuss these issues. We shall therefore content ourselves to give an overall view, bringing out those features that we consider as some of the basic characteristics of contemporary Africa. These features are intimately connected with the international situation of the second half of the twentieth century.

CHARACTERISTIC FEATURES OF AFRICA

Neocolonialism

One of the characteristic features of contemporary Africa is the fact that Africa is made up of countries enmeshed in a world economic, political, and ideological system that continuously subjects these countries to imperialist domination and exploitation. This domination and exploitation is not the same as that of the early twentieth century. "Imperialism has entered a new phase" (S. Amin). In Africa since the early sixties imperialism has discarded the outmoded formula of "direct occupation and colonization." But imperialist countries have resorted to the neocolonial formula whereby countries have all the outward manifestations of independence ("flag independence"), but the economic and political systems of these countries are tied to and dominated by the imperialist countries.

This system takes various forms from country to country. It has been established, however, that foreign capital is very dominant in most countries. For example, the mining sector is generally foreign owned and controlled. The multinational companies have invested in mining and are reaping great benefits from their operations. In the agricultural sector the large plantations are foreign-owned or foreign domination is through commerce and transport, monopolized by western countries, as well as through the pricing system, which is largely determined by the western countries. So-called foreign aid, foreign investments, and loans, through which capital inflow is always exceeded by profit outflow, are examples of another form of foreign domination. There are other more subtle forms of exploitation by multinational corporations in joint "partnership" with local private capital or even state investments. Studies show that, in fact, multinational corporations sometimes welcome the state participation in joint "partnership" with them, as this guarantees them monopoly control of the market as well as control of the labor force. All these are various forms of foreign domination of the economies of most countries in Africa, without any direct colonization or occupation of the countries concerned.

There is a fundamentally uniform pattern since foreign domination and oppression is by foreign imperialist powers, but there is diversity since this takes different forms in different countries and/or regions.

Struggle for Liberation

Neocolonialism, however, has its opposite. This can be aptly summarized in the famous phrase: "Countries want their independence, nations want their liberation, and peoples want their revolution." This is also one of the glaring features of contemporary Africa: the struggle for real liberation and real independence. These struggles are taking place not only in Africa, but throughout the world. The victorious struggles of the Vietnamese and Cambodian people against imperialism exemplify forces that have profoundly weakened imperialism. The struggles of the Third World countries for better prices for agricultural and mineral products also contribute to real liberation. The recent defeat of the imperialist coalition in Angola represents the defeat not only of western imperialist powers but also of their local collaborators. What is particular in Africa is the fact that the struggle for real independence is intensifying every day, especially in the countries under minority, apartheid regimes.

Thus imperialism has suffered defeats at the hands of various peoples in the world, as shown by economic difficulties and problems faced by imperialist countries today. This does not mean that it has been vanquished. On the contrary, in Africa, for example, a new international division of labor has developed with an international specialization and a worldwide distribution of functions (S. Amin) within an integrated system of economic, political, and cultural domination. In Africa the struggle for a "place in the sun" did not end with the formal independencies. The western imperialist countries are still fighting to preserve their places in Africa, to preserve their sources of cheap raw agricultural and mineral products as well as labor and markets for manufactured products. Independence in fact means breaking the monopoly position that each colonizing power had with regard to its colonies and opening up of those colonies to multilateral capital.

The Historical Development of Imperialism

There is another dimension to the contemporary situation in African countries that one might tend to forget. Imperialism is not in its early stages of dominating these countries. This is a historical process that has taken place for almost a century on our continent. In other words, an economic, political, and ideological system has planted itself and taken roots in these countries, which have become part and parcel of this global system. The internal situation of these countries is marked by the presence of economic, political, and ideological groups whose position is such that they benefit from the neocolonial "flag independencies" in most African countries.

Thus imperialism has two dimensions. It is a system originating and having its motive force in the metropolitan countries, a system of foreign oppression and exploitation. But it is at the same time internal exploitation, for the system has come to dominate and orient in a particular direction the economic and social structures of these countries. They have thus been fashioned not only to suit the interests of metropolitan countries but they have been fashioned to "the image of the masters."

Capitalism has developed internally, but this development does not come out of the internal evolution of the societies alone. It is also and fundamentally determined from the outside; the form of capitalism is dependent or, better, dominated capitalism. The end result is therefore determined by three factors: the way capitalism implanted itself in the precolonial societies, the type of precolonial societies existing then, and the conflicts and struggles which followed the imposition of this new mode of production.

Thus, for example, in some parts of Africa, notably in South Africa, Zimbabwe, parts of Kenya, and Algeria, the penetration of capitalism went hand in hand with European colonial settlements. The presence of rich mineral resources attracted foreign capital in the mining sphere—capital which needed cheap labor. In this case, labor was provided by the black people. Capitalist exploitation and colonization went hand in hand with racial oppression. In other parts of Africa, such as West Africa, capitalist penetration took the form of foreign capitalist monopoly of the import-export sector and the gradual drawing in of the peasantry to commodity production, the price of which is controlled externally. In the former social formation there is a proletariat and a local bourgeoisie of considerable autonomy. In the latter social formations the proletariat is a minority (numerically though not economically or politically) and the local bourgeoisie is petty and very much dependent.

A TYPOLOGY OF THE AFRICAN COUNTRIES

It is the position of this paper that the contemporary African situation is marked by the struggle between imperialism (neocolonialism) and national liberation. This struggle is not evenly developed in all the countries of Africa. There are varieties and differences—a diversity dependent on the concrete historical circumstances of each country, i.e., on the way capitalism was introduced in the different countries and the responses aroused. Using the criteria of unity and diversity in the struggle one could divide the countries in Africa into three broad categories. In the first category, which is itself not homogeneous, are all the countries that attained independence in the late fifties and early sixties. In the second category we place the former Portuguese colonies: Mozambique, Guinea-Bissau, Angola. The third group would include the countries of southern Africa (South Africa, Zimbabwe, Namibia).

Countries Attaining Independence in the Fifties and Sixties

Formal political independence came after the years of struggle for national independence, which became very much pronounced in the 1950s—a struggle against colonial domination and oppression. The nature and leadership of the struggle for independence had a great impact on what followed later. The colonial system had antagonized and alienated various groups within the colonized country. The majority of the inhabitants of the colonized countries were peasants and had their grievances.

In Kenya, for example, the alienation of land from the indigenous people was a source of constant grievance among the impoverished and the displaced Kikuyu. In Tanganyika, unpopular agricultural policies like tie-ridging or destocking were a source of conflict with the colonial state. The workers in the harbors, mines, or plantations were being subjected to very difficult working and living conditions and they were natural allies with peasants. Further, colonialism had introduced formal education, designed to facilitate the export of goods from these countries and train low-ranking officers to serve in the colonial state machinery. These elite, who had grievances in the discriminatory colonial system, joined hands with the other social groups against the colonial state. They became the natural leaders of this protest, for they were more "educated" and articulate than the other groups. The national liberation movements of the 1950s were anticolonial and anti-imperialist; the main cry was independence, but there was no clear consideration or formulation of what kind of society would emerge after political independence.

Many believed that with the attainment of independence under

Africans the economic and social problems would be solved. This proved disappointing to the peasants and workers in many African countries. Political independence meant only flag independence: the composition of a national anthem and the creation of missions abroad. The countries, however, remained tied to foreign domination and exploitation. Industry, agriculture, commerce, banking, and trade were still dominated by foreign companies. In fact, many African countries were under constant diplomatic pressure from the western countries to follow western policies in exchange for economic aid programs. The countries continued to be sources of raw materials for western industries as well as markets for the manufactured goods of Europe, the United States, and Japan. With independence there was increased competition by multinational companies to gain strongholds in these countries, manifesting itself in the numerous offers to establish "import substitution industries." This responded to the need of independent Africa to have consumer goods industries. But these industries show the characteristic features of dependency on the metropolitan countries for management techniques and technical know-how—the sum total of which is all in favor of metropolitan countries. Foreign domination of the economy therefore continued.

Government by Africans, however, was to introduce a new element. While formerly the government was foreign, now it was manned by nationals who, due partly to the colonial legacy and partly to the invitation of foreign companies, continued the economic exploitation of these countries through "foreign aid for development." This was to serve as a source of confusion in many spheres. Protest would be seen as a protest against indigenous government, thus blurring the struggle for the liberation of the masses of peasants and workers. Later some "progressive" governments were to stem this tide of neocolonialism. For the majority of cases, the exploitation and oppression of the peasants and workers by imperialism was to continue, paradoxically through the collusion and collaboration of African governments who became agents of foreign capital in their own countries. They received military protection from these powers in return for ensuring that labor and the peasantry were controlled, sometimes by physical force, more often by ideological weapons. Nationalism, which had been a rallying force during the independence struggles, was now playing a different role. In some countries concrete historical experiences brought home the need for transforming the societies and therefore the need for the struggle for economic independence through the liquidation of capitalism in all its manifestations. Once the problem had been clearly defined, real solutions could be sought through the construction of socialism and the strengthening of those social forces that could achieve this.

While during the pre-independence period all the inhabitants of a given country were called upon to unite against foreign domination, the struggle for real economic and political independence will rely on the forces favorable to socialism. This implies the recognition of the existence, internally, of social forces and groups who benefit from a neocolonial situation and who would therefore not desire any revolution. The contemporary economic and political situation in most African countries is characterized by the underlying struggle between imperialism in its neocolonial form and real economic and political independence, i.e., socialism. It is the struggle between, on the one hand, foreign multinationals allied to local dominant classes who want to continue the exploitation of the natural resources and wealth of these countries, and, on the other, the workers and peasants who would favor social transformation and real economic independence. This struggle develops unevenly depending on the concrete situation in each country, but overall one can say that it is becoming more and more difficult to prevent people from seeing the glaring inequalities of income, the corruption or outright theft of public funds, and the differences in the standards of living, education, and health between the workers and peasants on the one hand and those who are working for the common good or for the interests of the nation on the other. This phase of imperialism is indeed very complex. The struggle calls for the weakening of the imperialist powers who exploit and dominate the Third World countries, but the struggle also must weaken those forces in the Third World that favor this exploitative system.

Angola, Guinea-Bissau, Mozambique

Within the former Portuguese colonies in Africa, now the independent countries of Mozambique, Angola, and Guinea-Bissau, one is faced by a qualitatively different phenomenon. These countries have only recently attained their independence through armed struggle.

While most countries in east, central, north, and west Africa were gaining their flag independencies, the peoples of Mozambique, Angola, and Guinea-Bissau were struggling for their liberation from the Portuguese fascist regime. They were to gain their independence more than a decade after the others. They thus had the opportunity to learn the lessons from their concrete historical experiences, i.e., what neocolonialism actually means. The long years of protracted struggles were also decisive, for over the years many revolutionary elements were formed while pseudo-revolutionaries were weeded out. This gave the militants and their leadership political and ideological maturity as well as clarity. Capitalism penetrated these countries with colonialism, but there was some variation.

In the outward appearance and in the juridical sense of the word, these were Portuguese colonies, i.e., under the oppression and exploitation of Portugal. This tended to veil the real essence of the oppression of these countries, for in fact the Portuguese fascist regime was acting as a guarantor of western capitalist interests that were reaping great profits through investments in these countries. This does not mean that the Portuguese bourgeoisie was not reaping benefits, but only that these countries were not being dominated by Portugal alone, but by an international system whose dynamism was in Western Europe, especially England, and in the United States. This fundamental characteristic of western domination was to be unveiled in the course of the struggles for national liberation. Portugal, a backward country, had massive economic and military support from the western powers in its futile attempts to retain control of the countries and to stem the tide of national liberation which was gaining momentum during the 1960s. FRELIMO (Mozambique Liberation Front), PAIGC (African Party for the Independence of Guinea and Cape Verde), and MPLA (People's Movement for the Liberation of Angola) were aware that they were fighting not only Portuguese fascist colonialism as their enemy, but also the international capitalist system at the service of western imperialist powers.

The defeat of Portuguese fascism in April 1974, therefore, was an important step but only a preliminary step toward national liberation. From 1974 one sees frantic efforts by the Portuguese bourgeoisie to create a neocolonial situation, for example, plans by de Spinola for a Lusitanian Commonwealth dominated by Portugal. This was rejected by the liberation movements, for the "entire" enemy had not been vanquished. The correctness of this analysis was clearly revealed in the Angolan war of national liberation against imperialist aggression by the western powers in collaboration with Angolan puppets, the apartheid South African regime, and at least one African regime. The seizing of independence from Portugal was not the end of the struggle. Imperialist interests were strong in Angola, and they wanted to continue this domination and exploitation under a neocolonial government of Angolan puppets whom they tried to prop up politically, diplomatically, and militarily. When this failed under the vigilance of the MPLA, direct imperialist intervention was adopted (South African troops, mercenaries, etc.). The collaboration of at least one African regime is not surprising, for its interests are the same as those of imperialist countries.

The liberation movements in these countries were different from each other. Let us take the example of Guinea-Bissau. Right from its inception the PAIGC put great stress on the importance of theory and the scientific method of analyzing society. Hitherto the scientific method in Africa was only discussed. With the founding of the PAIGC, a new epoch had begun in Africa. Here were people who were applying a scientific method of analysis as a guide for action, as a guide to their emancipation and the liberation of their country, a liberation which was to come true in practice. Amilcar Cabral stressed the importance of revolutionary theory and the necessity of knowing the "historical reality" that the national liberation movement wanted to transform. This is an important precondition in the struggle against imperialism. The careful analysis of the historical reality, the assessment of class forces within the country both in the urban and rural sphere, would provide practical approaches and guidelines for action. A thorough scientific analysis of the social structure in Guinea-Bissau was made by Cabral himself. As he writes: "In outline the methodological approach we have used has been as follows. First, the position of each group must be defined: To what extent and in what way does each group depend on the colonial regime? Next what position do they adopt toward the national liberation struggle? Then we have to study their nationalist capacity and, lastly, envisaging the post-independence period, their revolutionary capacity" (A. Cabral in a seminar held in the Frantz Franon Center in Treviglio, Milan, May 1964).

In this way, the PAIGC was able to determine the major contradiction. "For us the main contradiction was that between, on the one hand, the Portuguese and international bourgeoisie which was exploiting our people and, on the other hand, the interests of our people." The nature of the struggle was clearly defined: "However, to free themselves from foreign domination is not the only desire of our peoples. They have learned by experience under colonial oppression that the exploitation of man by man is the biggest obstacle in the way of the development and progress of a people beyond national liberation." In other words, it was not only a question of getting rid of foreign domination of the political and economic structure and the manning of the same structure by indigenous people who continued the exploitation. It meant setting up different political and economic structures that would ensure effective (not formal) popular control and the creation of an economy that leaves no room for exploitation.

Over the years of armed struggle, especially in Guinea-Bissau and Mozambique, the liberation of the rural areas from foreign instruments of oppression went hand in hand with the setting up of new forms of economic and political life in the liberated zones. Cooperatives, popular assemblies, and cooperative economic ventures were promoted and social services were set up. The main focus was the setting up of new types of schools or medical facilities, oriented toward the needs of the masses and not to a small section of the population. This difficult task went hand in hand with the setting up of new political, administrative, and legal structures that would reflect the changing situation. This was a difficult time: The collapse of Portuguese colonialism unleashed the struggle between internal forces of reaction and the progressive forces. The former opt for the inheritance of the colonial structures and system by local people. The latter want to eliminate foreign domination and develop the new embryonic structures that were set up in the liberated zones. The future of these countries greatly depends on which of these forces will be triumphant. The key difference, however, from most other African countries discussed above is that the united front of progressive forces is in the dominant position. It is progressively asserting this political dominance, whereas in most other African countries, this would seem to be the opposite.

Southern Africa

Namibia, Zimbabwe, and South Africa are in a period of struggle for national independence. The struggle has greatly increased with the independence of the Portuguese colonies. The presence of settler regimes who have a racist ideology has tended to veil the nature of the struggle, but with time it is becoming clearer, in spite of the fact that it is depicted as a struggle only for majority rule. The immediate enemy is not the white population, but the Smith regime, and the core enemy is the international bourgeoisie. The southern part of Africa is marked by the presence of regimes that have marked themselves as champions of racial oppression and segregation. Here capitalism took the form of direct European settlement, using all the known forms of imperialism (including plunder, murder, rape, burning, etc.) to dominate the indigenous people. It alienated the land from them and threw them into reserves where they could be called if needed to be lowly paid labor for the mines, plantations, and factories of the settlers. The resistance of these indigenous people has enabled them to escape the fate of the Indians in the Americas under the ruthless and criminal onslaught of settlers from Western Europe.

Here the struggle is on three levels: racial emancipation, national liberation, and social transformation. In southern Africa we are faced with a situation whereby the three are united into one. For the same regime that practices racial oppression and exploitation is at the service of the multinational companies that impede national independence. And this same fascist state defends and protects the capitalist system in South Africa, Namibia, and Zimbabwe.

In this part of our continent imperialism is attempting to adjust itself to the fast changing situation, for example, by attempting to set up independent Bantustans in South Africa, by supporting regimes in Namibia, and by establishing an acceptable majority rule in Zimbabwe.

Two imperialist countries on the side of the regimes want to play the "impartial arbitrator" (Kissinger) to ensure a solution acceptable to their interests.

THE CULTURAL CONTEXT OF AFRICA

We have to place the ideological and cultural sphere of contemporary Africa in its global social context. The realm of ideology and ideas is a reality in all societies. Ideology is a whole system of ideas and social representations—different ways of viewing the world and of situating human beings in this world. These ideas are not objective representations of the world but their existence is real. In societies divided into classes, the oppressors have a sense of being and self-perception that their position and role is natural and can be justified. The oppressed have a sense of being and security that their condition is normal or can hardly be otherwise. The ideological sphere forms their consciences, their attitudes and their behavior, making them adapt to their tasks and to their conditions to support and accept their oppression.

All dominant classes have had recourse to ideological instruments, and the struggles of people to overcome their oppressors have also had to overcome the ideology and culture of their oppressors, changing their consciousness and perception and therefore their behavior. The bourgeois struggle and revolution was waged in the ideological sphere as well as on the economic and political level.

As regards contemporary Africa, we have to recognize that imperialist powers used not only physical force when they occupied these countries; ideological instruments were used as well in different forms—racial superiority, liberalism, etc.—all justifying in different ways the domination of these countries. The struggle for real independence of the Third World in general and of Africa in particular will have to be waged in the ideological sphere to overcome the ideological hegemony of the bourgeoisie.

This brings us to the role of religious institutions in contemporary Africa, institutions that are part of the ideological and cultural sphere. What role can the church as an institution play in the struggle for national liberation and social transformation in Africa? That this is a conference of Third World theologians is indicative that there are attempts at defining a new role for the church. But before going on to define the new role of the church one has to analyze historically and concretely what the church's role has been in Africa. When and why did the church come to Africa and what role has it played in the *historical* process that has moulded and shaped the African continent? Since the church is a cultural and ideological institution, the question that arises is: Will the church be among the forces of neocolonialism or among the forces of social transformation? How much does an African hierarchy or an 'African" liturgy contribute to the struggle? These are some of the questions that call for an answer.

3

The Presence of the
Church in Africa

P. A. Kalilombe (Malawi)

In trying to determine what the theologian's role in the Third World is to be, we are forced to deal first with preliminary questions of great importance, because our final answer will depend very much on the findings obtained from such a preliminary inquiry. One such question is to assess the role that the churches have played, and are still playing, in the making of our Third World countries.

I have been asked to propose some reflections on the presence of the church in Africa as seen from the Catholic side. But this is a tall order. Africa is such a vast and variegated continent. There can be no one simple church history description that could account for the richness and complexity of the church's experience in the different countries of the continent. So what I should rather do is merely to offer a number of remarks concerning my own country, Malawi, a country that I know a bit better and have been interested in. But I assume that what can be said about the churches in Malawi will yield some constants which, with modifications, are valid for other African countries. After all, what we are looking for here is a sort of working "model" serving as a point of departure for discussing typical patterns of the churches' presence in Africa.

The Churches in Malawi

Compared with some parts of Africa (like Zaire, Angola, Mozambique, northern Africa, and the coastal areas), Malawi was rather late in becoming a field for Christian evangelization.[1] It was only after Dr. David Livingstone had "discovered" Lake Nyasa in 1856 and had drawn the attention of the world to the horrors of the slave trade in the surrounding areas that missionaries from England and Scotland began work in what was to become Nyasaland, and eventually Malawi. The first group to attempt this work were members of the Universities' Mission to Central Africa (UMCA), a missionary organization sponsored by the Anglican church and drawing its members from the English universities which had been aroused to action by Livingstone's missionary appeal. After initial efforts in the early 1860s, they withdrew for some time in the face of disasters due to climate and inexperience. They were to return a bit later, but meanwhile the Church of Scotland had also organized their missionary expedition. They started work in 1875, and were joined in 1889 by fellow Presbyterians, the Dutch Reformed church of South Africa. There was soon a veritable missionary "scramble for Nyasaland" as other smaller Protestant missionary bodies arrived on the scene, coming especially from America (Baptists, Methodists, Seventh-Day Adventists, etc.). The Catholic missionaries were the latecomers, although a small group had arrived in the very midst of the colonial struggle between Portugal and Britain, which was to end with Nyasaland being declared a British Protectorate in 1896. Real work could start only in 1901 with the arrival of the White Fathers and their fellow Catholic missionaries, the Montfort Marist Fathers.

It is to be noted that missionary work in Malawi was well ahead of colonization. Nearly twenty years of missionary presence and activity preceded the formal declaration. in 1896, of the British Protectorate. In actual fact, the protectorate was declared with the justificatory aim of protecting the numerous citizens of Britain who had already started to settle as missionaries, traders, or planters. But for the missionaries, this protection was to prove a mixed blessing. It soon became clear that the objectives and methods of the colonial administration went counter, in many important points, to those of the missionaries. This was especially the case as far as the natives were concerned. Much of the early history of the Christian missions in Malawi concerns struggles and misunderstandings between the colonial administration and the missionaries. In general it can be said that the churches stood for the long-range interests of the local population.

1976 is the centenary of mission work in Malawi. The statistics show that this work has been a big success. In a total population of nearly five million people (according to the latest population estimates), more than two million are Christians, fairly equally divided between Catholics on one side and Protestants and Anglicans on the other. There is also a sizable Moslem community, though its number is relatively small. The remaining inhabitants are followers of traditional religion, though most of them will tend to claim connection with one or the other Christian body when asked to declare their religion. The making of modern Malawi (the new name that replaced the one of Nyasaland when the country became an independent republic in 1964) is certainly the work of those who have been influenced by the presence of the Christian missionaries.

Nineteenth-Century Catholicism and Its Influence on the Missions

The early missionaries who started work in 1901, and those who followed them in the next decades, were products of a particular stage of the Catholic church which is sometimes called, for the sake of convenience, nineteenth-century Catholicism. The church they planted and watered with their sweat and blood struck roots in this special terrain. Its theology and outlook has been deeply marked thereby, just as a person is basically determined for life by family background and early life and experience.

Nineteenth-century Catholicism bore clear traces of a long post-Reformation experience. The traumatic events of the Protestant Reformation in the sixteenth century had provoked a Catholic Counter Reformation. This was a period of struggles against the dissident churches in which the mother church strove to refute the heresies and errors of its protesting opponents. The theology of this period is consequently a defensive, apologetical, and combative one. The theology manuals of the period are usually a series of theses or topics of controversy, in which the need to fight back and to attack prevents a serene, balanced, and objective exposition of the Christian message in its totality. It tends to give undue importance to the areas of controversy while neglecting other aspects which may be of greater significance in the total experience of the church.

On the other hand these struggles helped to create a siege mentality within the church itself. The church tended to close in on itself and to keep in check forces of possible internal dissensions and weakening. The powers of the hierarchy over the laity were increased; administration became more rigid and centralized both on the universal church level (Roman Curia) and the local levels (dioceses and parishes). In all aspects of church life more importance was put on obedience and conformity to regimentation and authority from above than on principles of participation, dialogue, or freedom of expression. In fact there was a growing fear of deviations and pluralism.

This tendency was reinforced as a result of the dangers created by the Enlightenment and the growing tendencies toward free scientific research and rationalism. We see it at its height during the anti-modernistic period at the turn of the century when a veritable anti-deviation psychosis seemed to reign. Many enactments of the First Vatican Council, which was cut short in the political turmoil of 1870, and subsequent papal pronouncements and directives from the Roman Curia, give the impression of a heroic effort to contain growing disruptive forces and to maintain the monolithic structure of the church. This church acts as though it were destined to continue to exist calmly in a stable and static world: a homogeneously structured church, strongly hierarchical and disciplined; bishops, priests, and religious giving direction and inspiration to a mass of laity whose striving is toward compliance with what they are taught and told. Here is a feeling of security; there is pride in belonging to such a world-wide communion kept together by a clear system of belief, discipline, and practice.

And yet meanwhile, ever since the end of the Middle Ages, profound changes had been taking place in the world affecting the structures of society, economic systems, and political situations. The discoveries of the New World in the fifteenth and sixteenth centuries had widened people's vision of the earth and its human geography and history. The formation of new nations in Europe and America not only modified boundaries of former empires and kingdoms but also induced new patterns of social and political relationships. The ideas of liberty, fraternity, and equality preached by the French and American Revolutions were not empty slogans. They heralded the death of an old order of things and canalized a dynamic process whereby a new world was being born. The industrial and scientific revolutions gave other finishing touches to this new world.

It was no more the same world of old in which the supernatural was intrinsically tied up with the everyday preoccupations and interests of people. Secularization had already set in. No longer was there that artificial alliance characteristic of a theistic society in which temporal realities (the state) related to the spiritual ones (the church) as two perfect societies needing each other and playing the game of "who uses whom" for selfish interests. In the new situation there was clear separation (not mere distinction) of the two spheres. If anything, the secular claimed its autonomy and kept moving toward a totalitarianism which would render the church superfluous and irrelevant.

The nineteenth-century church had difficulty in finding its balance in the midst of such changes. It found it hard to see in the new situation anything but a threat to the very existence of faith and religion. By a kind of instinct of survival it took a reactionary attitude. We find, for example, large sections of traditionally Catholic areas of France clinging to royalist hopes and taking refuge in anti-republican activities. And when the pope lost the "papal states" to revolutionary Italy many Catholics all over the world saw it as a religious disaster. It was as if they believed the church's existence to be dependent on the old forms of social and political structures.

The early missionaries were products of this age. To understand their vision of realities and their missionary objectives and methods one has to remember that their theology and formation were situated in what Gutiérrez calls a "Christendom mentality":

In the Christendom mentality, and in the point of view which prolongs it, temporal realities lack autonomy. They are not regarded by the Church as having an authentic existence. It therefore uses them for its own ends. This is a sequel of the so-called "Political Augustinianism." The plan for the Kingdom of God has no room for a profane, historical plan.

The Church is regarded substantially as the exclusive depository of salvation: "Outside the Church there is no salvation." Because of this exclusiveness, notwithstanding certain qualifications which do not change the overall picture, the Church feels justified in considering itself as the center of the economy of salvation and therefore presenting itself as a powerful force in relation to the world. This power will spontaneously and inevitably seek to express itself in the political arena. Under these circumstances, participation in temporal tasks has a very precise meaning for the Christian: to work for the direct and immediate benefit of the Church.[2]

Tensions, Problems, and Hopes for the Local Church

Such was the church in the world at large when the missionaries started their work in Malawi. But seventy-five years have passed since the first missionaries arrived. Whatever reflections one may wish to make about the weaknesses of that nineteenth-century church and its theology, it is only fair to grant that the work of the Catholic missionaries has been a great success. It has borne fruit beyond expectations. Today the Catholic church in Malawi has seven dioceses serving a community of some million members. Of the seven bishops at the head of these dioceses, four are local Africans. A growing number of local priests and religious are taking over slowly from the expatriate missionaries. This is indeed a promising young church. Like other such churches in Africa today, it has great hopes for the future, but it also has tensions and fears.

In one way the tensions that face this young church are basically the same as those facing the whole Catholic church. They are the result of the tremendous changes which have taken place in the church in recent years, and are continuing to take place. The defensive attitude of the nineteenth century could not go on forever. Sooner or later the church had to accept dialogue with the changing world and accept the consequences. The Second Vatican Council (1962–1965) has become the symbolic reference point for all these dramatic changes: It only made an official inventory of what had changed in the years that preceded this Council, and opened the way to new changes.

For the young churches in the missions this wind of change and renewal is a source of special tensions, among which is the problem of "credibility gap." Perhaps this is an imprecise term for the kind of feeling I am talking about. It is the feeling of having been "taken for a ride" by the church. The Catholic faithful in Malawi remember the church as having been telling everybody over the years that it was the true church of Christ: one, holy, catholic, and apostolic. It was a monolithic and indivisible church, infallible, always right, and basically irreformable. This was a big claim. But with heroic efforts, and God's grace, people accepted this church on those terms. They thought they had found the "precious pearl" and so they had sold all they possessed in order to buy this field. And now comes Vatican II, and with it a new language: "Oh no, the church needs renewal, change, and reform. Your ancestral religion and practices should be adapted for use in the church. The non-Catholics are not enemies, but brethren of the same family. Latin is not the official language of the church. Celibacy of priests is open to discussion, etc. etc. . . . " People are confused. In desperation they ask: "When the first missionaries came they told us that all they taught us was pure truth. Now members of the same church come and want us to accept contrary things. How come that now we have to change? Was it then not true that our church is founded on a Rock? Did the first missionaries deceive us? . . . But if those who came first deceived us, who tells us that you who are talking to us now are not likewise deceiving us?"

Such feelings explain why the majority of Malawian Catholics are not particularly excited about all these new ideas and changes pouring in from Europe and America. They prefer an attitude of "Let us wait and see," and in the meantime cling to what was given them first. This is the case not only of the simple lay folk. Many African bishops, priests, and religious share similar feelings. Outsiders sometimes interpret this attitude as "conservatism," resistance to change, fear of the unknown, and what have you. I think this is to miss the point. In reality what that "conservatism" is trying to say is this: "We may indeed have to change and adopt new ways. But from now on, it will be on our own terms. We will not be dictated to anymore like small ignorant children. We refuse to jump onto the bandwagon of the older churches." This is an important message.

Curiously enough, the problems that the church is facing today are the consequences of the very success of missionary work. When one looks at the Catholic church today one has the impression that it is a strong, powerful church. In fact it is not. It is basically a weak and brittle church. Its weakness consists in that it is really a dependent church. Its strength comes from the continual help it receives from the overseas older churches. These are the ones that every year, directly or through Rome, offer assistance in personnel and in money. Our church is so dependent on this overseas aid that if some day it dried up, we would not have the church we have today. This is a sobering thought.

What has to be pointed out, however, is that the dependence in personnel and finances is a sign of a more basic dependence. Our church depends on the overseas church for its very shape and form. It is an imitation of the way the church exists and operates in the circumstances of Europe and America. It is a transplanted church, a carbon-copy of the older churches. We are not sure that all the organizational, practical, and material needs for which we need this continual outside help are really called for by the local situation and problems. If the church were to become incarnated in our country, would we need so much outside help to keep it going? Would it have those strange problems which can be solved only by making appeal to charities from overseas?

But there is a final level of "dependence" in our church which needs careful examination because here we are dealing with the basic understanding of church itself. The shape of church that we have inherited is an elitist church. Specifically it is a clergy-ridden and clergy-dominated church. If you were to ask people what the church is, there is much chance they would mention the priests and the religious. They might probably include also the catechists and similar auxiliaries who are simply an extension of the clergy. And they would be right. As things are, the running of the church, its internal life, and its witnessing to the world are totally dependent on this group. They organize and execute the main functions that keep the church going: preaching of the Word and the feeding of the flock through sacraments, sacramentals and prayer, and leadership and guidance.

And yet the church of Christ is the whole Body: all the faithful, with their specific charisms and roles. The clergy and their associates are just a minute percentage when compared with this whole Body. There is something basically wrong when 99 percent of the church is at the mercy of just 1 percent of it, when a small group holds all the power of decision and the majority has simply to follow. It all ends up with this minority imposing on the majority its own views, its way of looking at realities, its interests and problems. The church has suffered for a long time from this type of domination.

The young churches today would like to change the system. We need a new set-up whereby the laity will be fully part of the life and work of the church. Probably the hope of new vigor and progress depends on such an overhauling of the system. In Malawi, as in the neighboring countries of Eastern Africa, the conviction is growing that we need to build smaller Christian communities to replace the big artifical "parishes." In such small basic communities, all the members of the church will be able to take an active part in the life and work of their community within the concrete context of their daily life. And this will give a new lease of life for the church.

NOTES

1. For most of the historical details in these first pages I have used Ian Linden, *Catholics, Peasants & Chewa Resistance in Nyasaland* (Berkeley and Los Angeles: University of California Press, 1974).

2. Gustavo Gutiérrez, *A Theology of Liberation* (Maryknoll, New York: Orbis Books, 1973), pp. 53–54.

4

Approaches to African Theology

Charles Nyamiti (Tanzania)

The modern socio-political changes that have taken place on our continent have inevitably led to a new vision hardly suspected a few decades ago. With the advent of these changes Africans have clearly realized that social and political independence goes hand in hand with new tasks and responsibilities. This state of affairs has awakened among African political leaders and citizens a strong awareness of self-reliance, co-responsibility, cultural adaptation, and the great value of the African cultures.

The church, being not of this world but in it, has also been deeply influenced by this movement. Accordingly, the African churches have been led to a similar self-reliance in ecclesiastical affairs, co-responsibility and cooperation among the local churches, adaptation in all spheres of Christian life, and awareness of the great value and relevance of the African cultures for this task of adaptation.

Naturally, one of the important fields of Christian adaptation is theology, and endeavors of theological adaptation are now a common feature of our churches. It is perhaps still too soon to predict the future of this theological renewal in Africa. But, judging from the writings or discussions on what is called African theology, one can, roughly speaking, already distinguish at least three such types (I deliberately make exception of the African Oriental schools, e.g., in

Egypt or Ethiopa): (1) That which—for want of better terminology —could be called the *speculative school,* characterized by a marked tendency toward systematization and philosophizing. This school roughly corresponds to the French-speaking and Catholic theologians' school. (2) The *social and biblical school,* distinguished by a pragmatic and biblical approach. Being relatively strong in ethnological and social questions, this school seems to attach little importance to speculation. One may roughly identify it with the English-speaking and Protestant theologians' school. (3) The *militant school,* found especially in South Africa. Its main emphasis is on the need for an indigenous theology of liberation from white oppressors—an attitude it shares in common with that of the supporters of the so-called black theology in America.

Of course, being at their initial stage, these schools are not yet as clearly defined as it might appear; they even overlap in some cases. But there are already clear indications to show the shape they are gradually taking. One significant feature is that their characteristics are determined by western influence rather than by African cultures.

This fact is normal at the elementary stage in which the African church at present finds itself, where it is naturally bound up with other shortcomings in its efforts toward indigenous theology. This leads me to a short exposition of some methodological considerations on African theology. It should be added that I am here concerned chiefly with the adaptation of systematic theology to black sub-Saharan Africa, although I do not consider systematic theology as the only theological branch relevant to theological adaptation in Africa. Most of the ideas given here will be found more amply developed in my previous papers on the same subject.[1]

Obviously, it is impossible to cover the whole scope of African theology, even from the methodological standpoint alone, in the limits of this essay. I shall confine myself to a short exposition of some considerations that seem to me of vital importance and likely to promote the subject further.

Theological adaptation in Africa can be said to be as old as the African churches themselves, and in this sense African theology is, to a certain extent at least, as old as Christianity in our continent. For if African theology implies the expression and presentation of Christian doctrine according to the needs and mentality of African peoples, it is clear that missionaries, native priests, and catechists have regularly, in one form or another, endeavored to adapt the Christian teaching to the requirements and dispositions of their hearers. It is also natural that African converts have, up to a certain degree, always understood and lived their Christian faith as Africans, i.e., according to their cultural make-up. One may rightly presume, therefore, that a careful investigation will reveal an old, latent form of African theology among the African communities. But the conscious systematic efforts to build up such theology are of recent origin. The first *ex professo* discussions on the subject occur, as far as I know, not earlier than the 1960s.

The evolution of this movement can be roughly divided into two main stages: first, that of the *introductory subjects*, involving the awareness of and discussion on the need and possibility of an African theology. This naturally led to, and was often accompanied by, discussions on the nature, problems, and methods of the subject. The next main stage is *adaptation*, i.e., the application of the general principles of theological renewal to concrete cases, either by an effort to solve particular African problems (e.g., polygamy, ancestral cult) with Christian principles, or by attempting to adopt African elements into Christian theology.

Of course, the chronological evolution of the subject does not always correspond to this sketch; some of the items last mentioned are at times found in those previously indicated, and vice versa. But the division may be said to correspond to the general sequence of events.

In the following paragraphs evaluation will be made with regard to the various items contained in the above schematic division.

Contextualization of African Theology

It is no longer necessary to emphasize the need or possibility of an African theology. The time for such discussions is now passed; we are actually at a higher stage of the question. Essays confined to such topics are at present justly considered out of date. Failure to see such need or possibility may now be rightly judged as unjustified conservatism. Those who are still not convinced of this should remember that, in accordance with the prescriptions of Vatican II, theological adaptation to various cultures is growing rapidly all over the world. In fact, in this matter Africa is lagging behind not only the West, but even the countries of Asia and Latin America.

But a different judgment is required with regard to the nature, problems, and method of the subject. This question is essentially bound up with the creation of African theology and will practically always remain as long as that theology will have to be made. Even among westerns scholars the situation is not different. The discussions concerning the validity of the views of Rahner, Bultmann, Metz, or Lonergan are in fact debates on the nature, problems, and methods of modern western theology.

In my opinion, the difficulties regarding the right appreciation of this subject are due mainly to narrowness of approach to the factors involved, i.e., the African situation and Christian theology. Thus it often comes about that one fails to see that it is the entire African situation in all its historical dimensions (past, present, and future) that has to be taken into account. Either one limits attention exclusively to the past as the "ideal" moment of African culture, or one rejects the past as outmoded and confines interest to the present and future. And among the elements concerned attention is sometimes limited only to *some* of the items (e.g., African traditional religions, African Independent churches, liberation movements) instead of extending the scope of investigation to each and every cultural and historical phenomenon. The term which can be used as a guide to the right approach to this problem is the one proposed recently by P. E. Hoffman, namely, "contextuality" (or "contextualization"). This term "includes and goes beyond 'indigenization,' which tends to be used in the sense of responding to the Gospel in terms of a traditional culture. Contextualization is more dynamic and open to the modern evolution of the Third World. It does not mean mere conformity to the past and present situations but critical and prophetical confrontation with the movement of history."[2]

To those who conceive it as the mere confrontation of revelation with scientific philosophy, African theology can be had only after building up an African metaphysics capable of being used afterward to expound Christian doctrine. Others, however, believe that African philosophy exists already and consists in African world views expressed in mythopoeic or symbolic language. According to this view

African theology should evolve through the expression and presentation of revelation by means of this mythopoeic philosophy characteristic of the African way of thinking. This opinion ignores the use of philosophy and attempts to build up a theology directly by confronting Christianity with social and political problems of the African communities.

None of the above views is wholly satisfactory, since the subject of African theology is so vast and complex that no single science or approach can cope with it. Nor could sociology, ethnology, or psychology compensate for the lack of philosophical understanding of the African cultural phenomena. It is also incorrect and even dangerous to confine oneself to a mythopoeic way of thinking under the pretext that this is the manner of approach proper to Africa. In spite of the prevalence of its traditional mode of life, Africa already belongs to the technological and scientific age. Now, as Congar rightly remarks, the coming of science and technology inevitably leads to "naturalism, desacralization of the world, rationality, passage from a world of symbols to the world of realities. . . ."[3] Hence, the right solution consists in the dialogue between the African symbolic mentality and the modern rationalistic way of thinking; a purely mythopoeic theology is unfit for the modern African elite and can hardly cope with the problems of modern Africa.

Finally, it is wrong to pretend that African theology can only be had after African scientific philosophy has been made. Not only is such philosophy not absolutely indispensable for it, but also the two could develop simultaneously, as was the case with traditional Christian philosophy and theology. Indeed, as will be shown later, the employment of African elements in theology will demand a systematic and critical reflection on them. This will contribute at the same time to the building up of African scientific philosophy.

Pastoral Adaptation

Fortunately, the evolution toward African theology has progressed further than the mere discussion of "introductory subjects." African scholars have already been attempting to apply the general principles of theological adaptation to particular cases in the African milieu, either by striving to solve specific pastoral problems in the light of the gospel or by endeavoring to adopt African cultural elements into Christian theology.

The first kind of adaptation can be seen in writings dealing with problems such as polygamy, marriage, initiation, divination, ancestral cult, and communal solidarity. The general treatment of such subjects consists usually in an analytical description of the African theme in question and its evaluation in the light of ecclesiastical doctrine. The exposition often ends with general practical conclusions and suggestions.

Although these essays cannot as such be said to contain genuine African theology, they are nonetheless its true beginnings, and not its mere preparations. This is partly due to the African themes chosen to confront Christian teaching. We are here in the realm of creating African theology. Hence, to a certain extent these essays, taken together, determine the level which has been reached and the direction toward which it is evolving. As such, then, research work regarding the evolution of the subject cannot rightly ignore them. It remains true, however, that in order to have a complete theology other factors have to be taken into account and included in these writings. As a rule, university dissertations are among the best essays of this type. Unfortunately, these essays are usually in the possession of a few individuals or some university archive. Would it not be possible to find means whereby such works could be available to all African institutes?

Treatment of African Themes

It seems that relatively better results are obtained by adopting African elements into Christian theology. Several steps can be distinguished in this method. First, the authors choose from the African situation themes which can serve this purpose. This is done by seeking in African cultures (especially traditional religions) typical themes, and, afterward, their Christian parallels, e.g., ancestral cult and cult of saints, communal solidarity and Mystical Body, and so forth. The authors look also for the emphasized or frequently occurring religious motives in African communities such as Independent or historic churches, or in the sermons of African preachers. Among the typical cultural themes frequently mentioned are the spiritual view of life, the sense of family, communal solidarity and participation, cult of ancestors, initiation rites, fecundity, time, vital and dynamic approach to reality, theism and belief in other spirits, African anthropocentrism. Some of the emphasized Christian elements frequently mentioned are the Holy Spirit, communion of saints, Mystical Body, sacraments of initiation (baptism, confirmation, Eucharist), and sacramentals.

The second step is to introduce African values into theology. Usually, one does this by pointing out the erroneous elements to be rejected and the positive values compatible with Christian teaching. The "adoption" of these positive values is generally done by emphasizing the African themes and their Christian parallels, and by giving some practical pastoral suggestions that further research be made in the direction indicated by the African and Christian themes. Let us now examine critically each of these procedures.

As far as this first step is concerned, this is a legitimate and even indispensable undertaking. Each theology has its particular themes of preference; and these normally coincide with the values or problems prominent in the community for whom the particular theology is intended. It seems to me, however, that research in this matter reveals several deficiencies.

Instead of extending their field of research for such themes to the whole of the African situation, some of the writers limit their attention to only a part of it, e.g., African religions, instead of the total African culture, or to African traditional cultures, instead of including modern societies. Some of the lists containing such themes exclude such typical modern elements as African socialism, nationalism, personalism, tribalism, and liberation, to mention but a few.

The authors generally confine their interest to the *positive* themes compatible with Christianity and neglect the negative factors like magic, polygamy, superstition, poverty, disease, and ignorance. This omission is a serious pastoral deficiency, because the themes mentioned by the authors are meant to be proposed as deserving particular attention. Obviously, the theologians' task is not limited to the confrontation of the positive values of their culture with revelation. Among their chief duties is to combat the shortcomings and errors in their communities. Indeed, negative themes can also serve to determine the specificity of a theology and even contribute to its development. History shows that the flourishing of the doctrines of the Trinity, Christology, grace, sacraments, the church, and other mysteries is owed partly to the combat against the errors opposed to those teachings.

Finally, the attention of theologians seeking themes for African theology has so far been limited to the *typical* or *emphasized* African or Christian elements. Probably this is especially true because such elements are believed to determine the specific value or originality of African culture and theology. However, another very important factor for determining such originality is the integration or interconnection of cultural themes. A culture is not an inert lump of different parts without connection among themselves, but is a system resembling an organism in which most, but not necessarily all, of its parts are organized and interrelated through their functions and goals. Such interrelation differs from region to region in such a way that similar cultural ideas are often differently correlated in different contexts. As a consequence, the form of a cultural trait is largely determined by its context and not only by the qualities inherent in it.

In view of this, the number of factors contributing to originality in African theology increases greatly. First, not only the prominent or accentuated themes, but each cultural element appears with African originality, depending on the degree of its integration in the cultural ensemble. Second, viewed in the light of the African context, each Christian theme appears with African originality.

In fact the interrelation of the elements of a culture is even more important than accentuation of particular themes in determining the uniqueness of a given culture or theology. That is why the African originality of the emphasized themes appears more sharply when they are viewed in relation to their African context than in the mere fact of their being accentuated. Indeed, cultural or theological elements which are formally identical differ largely in the way they are concretely integrated in different cultural contexts. For want of space, let one example suffice to illustrate this.

Let us take the theme of "family." We know that this theme is prominent in African societies. But it is evident that the African originality of this theme does not consist in its being accentuated, since non-African societies accentuate it as well. It is only when it is considered in its cultural context that its African individuality appears. Thus, for instance, the theme is emphasized in both African and western communities, but the African family is, in addition, more extensive: It extends to the whole clan and sometimes even to the whole tribe. It includes all living members of these groups, besides being mystically connected to the ancestors and, through social pacts, to outsiders such as friends and others. Moreover, the relations between the members of an African family differ in many respects from those of the West. Think, for example, of the matriarchal or matrilineal societies, of the affinal relations, of the *patria potestas* which somehow connects the family to priestly functions. Besides, membership within the African family (clan or tribe) is usually brought about by special initiation rites showing thereby the sacredness of the family. In other words the category "family" in Africa evokes not only blood communal membership of a few living members, but also the themes of clan, tribe, affinity, maternity, *patria potestas*, priesthood, ancestors (thereby including the themes of mythical time, archetypes, heroes, founders), initiation and hence fecundity, life, power, sacrality, and so forth. To appreciate fully the African originality of the category "family," the themes it evokes should in their turn be examined in the light of the African context.

To put it rather technically, although the formal content of the category "family" is identical in Africa and in the West, the mode of its integration in its cultural contexts is different. And it is particularly in this concrete mode of integration, i.e., in the local coloring of the cultural themes, that the originality of the African themes has to be sought.

Now, what is the relevance of this factor to the subject of theological adaptation?

To answer this question, let us by way of example take again the theme of "family." Supposing that one is using this theme for the purpose of theology, it would not suffice, as is often done, to insist that that theme requires accentuation of the doctrine of the Mystical Body, or that grace should be presented not as an individual but a communal participation in the life of the church. Of course all this is true and has to be emphasized. But this kind of insistence will not of itself contribute much to originality, since all these elements are accentuated everywhere in modern theology. What is required is that after having determined the prominence of the theme in African communities, the theologian should further seek its African individuality. As we have seen, this can be done by investigating how the theme is integrated into the African cultures. We have also seen that when so considered, the category "family" evokes clan, tribe, ancestors, affinity, friendship, priesthood, initiation, etc.—all understood in an African sense. Now when these African ideas are transported into the corresponding Christian analogous themes, the statement "grace is familiar" (in the African sense) would imply not only that grace is communal and ecclesial, but also "ancestral," and as such Christian (Christ is the Ancestor par excellence), paradisical (suggested by mythical time), heroic (suggested by the idea of ancestral heroes), friendly, initiative, and therefore sacramental, paschal, pentecostal, pneumatic, eucharistic, dynamic, fecund, eschatological, etc.

In order to do full justice to the African originality of the category "family," all these theological themes should still be examined in the light of the African context. This will allow them to appear with further African connotations.

The principles behind this procedure are that African themes have to be understood in the light of their cultural context and as such to be expressed in terms of analogous Christian themes, and conversely the Christian mysteries have to be expressed in terms of the analogous African themes seen in the light of their cultural ensemble. This implies that the Christian mysteries have to be presented as perfecting and fulfilling the African cultural values—a fact which perfectly corresponds to the prescriptions of Vatican II.

It goes without saying that these theological interpretations should afterward be rigorously verified to see whether or not they are in full harmony with the data of revelation; otherwise one runs the risk of impoverishing or even falsifying the Christian teaching. It is, moreover, through such process of verification that "dormant themes" in revelation are awakened.

Adoption of African Values

Perhaps the most difficult and central problem in creating African theology consists in the effective adoption of African elements into sacred science. As we have seen, this is done mainly by showing first the errors in the African ideas and afterward by repeated emphasis upon African themes and the analogous Christian teachings, together with the indication of some general practical suggestions. But the results so far achieved in this domain are, on the whole, far from satisfactory. Essays of this type often give the impression of being compositions in comparative study of religions rather than vehicles of authentic African theology.

Among the reasons responsible for this deficiency are a lack of intrinsic employment of cultural themes and a narrowness of approach to the factors involved. By lack of intrinsic employment of cultural themes is meant that the African ideas are used as a mere propaedeutic providing exterior illustrations or subjective preparations, but do not enter internally into the theological elaboration of revelation so as to form an organic part of it. Thus by pointing out the errors and other non-Christian aspects in the African themes and by mere emphasizing of the Christian analogous truths one practically remains on the comparative level, which sets the African and Christian elements side by side without allowing them to coincide into a theological unity. An example of such intrinsic use would be the application of the African category of "ancestor" to Christ (*the* Ancestor) or to grace (e.g., grace is "ancestral"), not merely in a figurative or metaphorical sense, but according to the analogy of proportion so as to identify it formally with Christ and grace. Another example would be the use of the African dynamic and vitalistic approach, spiritual worldview, anthropocentrism, or sense of communal solidarity and participation for the purpose of demonstrating, explicating, or even defending revealed data.

Obviously, in order that African worldviews and categories may be properly used in this manner, it is imperative to criticize them vigorously, to correct and explicate them so as to bring them to the scientific level. For the purpose of theology, not only profane sciences will have to play the role of modifying or justifying such elements, but also, and in the first place, Christian revelation, to which the African ideas will always have to be subordinated, will have to play such a role. Such a process will sometimes lead to the modification of the verbal formulation of some of the African categories to correspond to the Christian mysteries they are intended to designate. It is highly recommended, and is even demanded by the nature of the subject itself, that in the argumentation an effort be made as far as possible to provide *African arguments,* namely those which conform to the African mentality, problems, and aspirations so as to meet Africans, as it were, on their own field.

Another reason for the meager results from the confrontation of African themes with revelation is the narrowness of approach to the elements involved. It often happens that themes are studied as isolated items having no connection with other phenomena, or that they are investigated from only one or two viewpoints. But the ideal requires an approach from as many different perspectives as possible. The reason is that any cultural element is multidimensional and has various relations to other realities. These relations connect and determine the related themes. The same applies to Christian mysteries; the various revealed data do not exist in an isolated fashion independent of one another, but are correlated among themselves to form an organic whole. Thus it is possible to clarify one or more Christian mysteries in the light of others.

This fact entails consequences of great practical importance for our subject. In virtue of the interconnection of mysteries it will be possible to acquire far better and more original results than those obtained by the method previously described. Thus, instead of simple repeated emphasis upon the Christian themes accentuated in African communities, one will have to use each of these themes as a leitmotiv for explicating even the whole of revelation. The same measures will have to be taken when dealing with a cultural theme. Not only will each cultural theme have to be studied in the light of its total cultural context and from as many scientific approaches as possible, but one will also have to inquire how such an element is related to each of the Christian mysteries, and how each of them could be expressed in terms of it.

Examples of this procedure are abundant in theology. To give but a few modern examples, one has only to recall how the categories of historicity, humanity, hope, or future permeate the theology of Metz, Moltmann, or Pannenberg. Likewise, the theme of salvation history determines the presentation and interpretation of the total Christian revelation in the unfinished volumes of *Mysterium Salutis.* In like manner black theologians in the United States and theologians in Latin America strive to rethink Christianity in terms of liberation.

It is from this perspective, though not exclusively, that South

African theologians are attempting to approach Christian doctrine. Confronted with the situation in their own land, they decry the racialism of their milieu and plead for a black theology of "liberation from," as they say, "slavery, contempt, and oppression by the white minority." As one of them puts it, such theology is intended to be "a theology of the oppressed, by the oppressed, and for the liberation of the oppressed."

It would certainly be wrong to ignore or condemn *en bloc* this movement as a political maneuver of "a bunch of way-out radicals." One cannot but admire the pastoral approach of the theologians concerned. Instead of attempting to build a theology from vain speculations they strive to do so by reflecting, in the light of the gospel, upon the concrete situation of their own countries. In itself this procedure is quite legitimate, and the theme of liberation chosen for this purpose will, if properly handled, inevitably lead to positive results. As such then, this movement essentially belongs to all African theology, and deserves respect, interest, and support not only on the part of African theologians, but of all those who are interested in human liberty and other rights.

However, several warnings and suggestions in this regard seem to be necessary. First, in all their endeavors the theologians should keep a serene attitude. One has to admit that in its general tone this movement is extremely militant. Although such an attitude is perfectly understandable, it is nonetheless liable to lead to lack of objectivity and to distortion of the facts. This would be detrimental not only to black theology, but to the liberation movement as well. One should, moreover, beware of reducing black theology to the theme of liberation from white segregation. Admittedly, this is a relevant topic; but African theology—as indeed any other—is an extremely vast and complex subject which cannot be reduced to one such theme alone without undue narrowing and impoverishment. Besides political or social liberation, South Africa has certainly other problems which deserve equal if not sometimes even more interest on the part of theologians. Finally, let us beware of undue provincialism. Just as each one of us is called to cooperate with South Africans in their struggles, so also are the latter called to participate in creating a theology adapted to other parts of our continent. "Union is strength" is a most useful device, especially when the participants are so few as

African theologians are. One should go even farther. In the world of today, the problems of adaptation cannot be properly dealt with unless one takes into account not only one's own total socio-cultural milieu, but also that of the universal church.

What Still Remains to Be Done?

It would certainly be incorrect to maintain that there is already a genuine scientific African theology. Those who are of the opinion that there can be no such theology often refer to this lack to confirm their view. However, a careful study of the process of adaptation in Africa will reveal a steady progress toward an indigenous theology whose shape can already be dimly perceived by the keen observer. From discussions of its mere possibility and necessity, one comes to a better appreciation of its nature and the intricacy of its problems as well as the variety of its methods. It is now commonly accepted that authentically African theology cannot be made by simple translation of western or other non-African theological writings into African languages, nor by replacing foreign categories and formulas with African equivalents. One has also to realize that theological adaptation implies more than mere indigenization of Christian teaching by traditional cultures; it involves, besides, the manipulation of all the cultural and historical themes in the African world—both the traditional cultures and the political and economic circumstances in the modern phase of Christianity's worldwide development. Various African and Christian themes which will typify such theology have already been discovered. African religions and cultures are being more and more compared to Christianity, and the parallelisms or divergencies between them are being more and more comprehended. An effort is being made at the same time to reflect upon African themes and problems in the light of the gospel and the modern situation as prescribed by Vatican II. The results of all these efforts obviously mean more preparatory work for African theology.

Yet it remains true that African theology is still in its early beginnings and up to the present moment the subject has mostly been dealt with in an elementary manner, without the breadth or profundity of a mature scientific discipline. This is normal for any beginning. But I believe the time is now ripe to shift our subject from its infancy to a more mature level. In this direction there is still a lot to be done. A broader conception of the subject has still to be acquired, and a more comprehensive and synthetic approach of the Christian and African elements has still to be made. There have not yet been experiments to use African ideas according to the various principles of analogy, or to expound revelation scientifically and philosophically by means of African themes. A regular and intrinsic use of African categories and worldviews is still waiting. Our theological feeling and general orientation are largely determined by western influence. We have not yet begun to use African arguments, nor do we possess any African theological manuals.

One more remark still remains to be made. The subject of African theology is inevitably bound up with the whole area of Christian life and, as such, cannot be approached in isolation—which means that theological adaptation demands renewal in other spheres of the African churches. Among these spheres three deserve special mention, i.e., theological institutes, liturgy, and canon law. Here again there is still much to be done. Our institutes are still fundamentally modeled on those of the West; liturgical adaptation consists chiefly in translation of Latin rites; and the African church is, even in its canonical code, still a "Latin church." It would be unfair to blame anyone for this state of affairs. But it is nonetheless true that the future well-being of the African church and the full flourishing of its theology demand a far more authentic and profound adaptation than that which has been so far realized. This is certainly the mind of the last ecumenical council addressed to each African Christian in particular, and to all people of good will.

NOTES

1. Charles Nyamiti, *African Theology: Its Nature, Problems and Methods* and *The Scope of African Theology*, published in Gaba Pastoral Papers nos. 19 (1971) and 30 (1973).

2. See L. Kaufmann, "Theological Education in the 1970s," in *African Ecclesiastical Review* (AFER), Kampala, Uganda, vol. 15, no. 3 (July 3, 1973), p. 251.

3. Y. Congar, *La foi et la théologie* (Paris, 1962), p. 231.

5

The African Theological Task

Kwesi A. Dickson (Ghana)

In the last few years there has been a marked interest in the need to restate Christian realities in order to reflect African thinking. It must be said at the outset that the discussions are at too early a stage to give indications of theological trends. The point, however, has been clearly made that for the Christian church in Africa to become truly the church of Christ in Africa it must not live on second-hand theology.

Issues for African Theology

The expression "African theology" needs to be explained. In a sense there can be only Christian theology, a propositional articulation of the Christian faith. However, inasmuch as such articulation is done by individuals in and through their cultural situations, theologizing can and must assume many different hues depending on where it is done. There can be no meaningful theologizing unless done through the presuppositions of the theologian; the alternative is to live on predigested theology, theology that has been handed down by the theological giants from generation to generation. One recalls how the old Tillich on a visit to Japan was bewildered by the cultural scene there, so much so that he wondered how he could rewrite his theology in order to make it more catholic. Tillich's theology has a validity, though this is best judged by those who stand within the

European cultural tradition; he had every right to theologize as he did. Similarly, Japanese theologians would theologize in distinctive terms, taking their background into consideration. Of course, it would be ideal to make Tillich's dream come true, i.e., to do truly catholic theology, but whether this is possible is another question.

The protagonists of African theology work on the basis of the assumption that knowing the accepted theological formulations that have been handed down these many centuries in the history of Christianity does not make one a theologian. Theologians are those who have thought through this theological deposit and the biblical faith in and through their own circumstances. The call for black theology (in the U.S. and South Africa) and a theology of revolution (South America) illustrates the need for theological thinking to be done in context to ensure that it remains vital and meaningful.

Several conferences and consultations have been called to discuss African theology, to examine what methodology might be adopted, and to assess what may have been achieved.

Three areas in particular need to be explored: the understanding of biblical teaching, the church's liturgy, and the restatement of Christian belief. All these areas need to be explored against the background of traditional African life and thought and the forces that today impinge upon it.

The foremost of these areas, as it is being increasingly recognized, is *biblical study*. The evidence is clear that biblical study, for various reasons, has not featured prominently in departments of religion in black African universities. Coupled with this is the realization that certain of the Independent churches approach the Bible (particularly the Old Testament) in a way that suggests an inadequate understanding of its nature and meaning. There is the need to make a serious study of the Bible, which, after all, is an indispensable source of theologizing since it reveals what God has done. This serious study should include relating biblical teaching to the circumstances of Africans. The aim of biblical study should be not only to understand the background of the Bible but also to discern its message for Africans in the particularities of their circumstances. Relevant biblical commentaries will have to be produced. In this connection it is noteworthy that the West African Association of Theological Institutions at a recent annual meeting voted to work toward the production of a biblical commentary, one that will not only take African students through a critical study of the Bible, but also relate its message to the circumstances of its readers.

With respect to *liturgy*, a certain amount of work has been started. The recognition of the unreal nature of the church's foreign type of worship has resulted in serious study, on the one hand, of African traditional liturgical patterns and, on the other, of the use to which African Christians sometimes put received liturgical forms. The latter is of considerable importance because liturgical forms, if they are vital, grow out of worshipping communities; so an ecclesiastical fiat that dictates liturgical patterns in detail may not necessarily evoke the right kind of response from those who are forced to use them. Pointers to what a liturgical pattern should entail should be seen in the spontaneous changes made in received music, the impromptu prayers made during worship, the unannounced singing that surges from the congregation during the preaching, etc.

The matter of *the formulation of Christian thought* to reflect original thinking is one that has not been explored with any seriousness, though there is some awareness of the need to undertake such an exercise. The history of doctrine shows that at various times distinctive positions have been taken on the basis of prevailing cultural and other circumstances. Thus, starting from the patristic age, theories of atonement were put forward that fitted neatly into prevailing modes of life and thought, ranging from the ransom theory in an age of brigandage and general unrest to the forensic theory in a period replete with ideas of law and jurisprudence. Thus an important prerequisite for the restating of Christian doctrine is judging what the word of God is for a particular people in their circumstances. Now the circumstances, as far as Africa is concerned, may differ from area to area. Thus the political situation in southern Africa is different from the west African situation. This is already being reflected in South African black theology, which is closer to the U.S. black theology than to what is likely to issue from the west African situation. The important thing is to let God speak in and through relevant situations.

The Format of African Theology

A related matter is format. Traditionally Christian doctrine has been divided into various doctrines—of man, atonement, the work of

Christ, etc. The categories may not be worked out in the same detail by every writer, but a certain amount of uniformity exists. Christian doctrine, as the present writer recently observed, is often "the result of biblical truth being interpreted in a western way, which interpretation may obscure some aspect of the faith or indeed omit reference to matters which are taken account of in the Scriptures, but which are not part of the active, living experience of western theologians." This may be illustrated by looking at traditional Christian theological understanding of the death of Christ. Christ's death tends to be seen as an event whose true meaning lies in the resurrection; in other words, Christ's death is a prelude—and a regrettable one at that—to the resurrection. Our reading of the biblical evidence suggests that this was not the understanding that prevailed among Christ's followers from the inception of the church, or Paul would not have set himself the goal of preaching Christ and him crucified (1 Cor. 2:2). In African life and thought the biblical evidence of the meaningfulness of Christ's death would be readily appreciated; for in Africa the celebration of death makes it clear that death is not conceived as putting an end to natural human self-expression. More than that, the rites surrounding death have the effect of cementing relationships: the drumming and dancing, the steady stream of visitors, and the sharing of chores with the bereaved all point to the emphasis put on the positive aspect of death.

African Christians wanting to restate Christian teaching for themselves and their people should not work from the assumption that the traditional categories of doctrinal statement are immutable. To accept these categories without question might very well mean being constrained to do theology "in terms of areas of thought defined in the West"; originality would no doubt suffer.

The concerns stated here necessitate adopting certain measures with regard to ministerial training. By and large seminary systems in Africa hew closely to systems found in the West, with the result that African ministers of religion are better suited to operate in conditions that are closer to the western than to the African type. They are seldom in a position to discuss the concerns brought up here. It is essential, as a matter of urgency, that training for the ministry should be re-examined in order to give greater impetus to the development of ideas and the rooting of commitment such as the quest for an African theology would thrive on.

6

Unity of Faith and Pluralism in Theology

Ngindu Mushete (Zaire)

For some, the existence of pluralism in theology is self-evident and poses no problem; it is even integral to Catholicism, a normal and permanent task of the church. For others, the question of such pluralism elicits mistrust and reservation. It appears to threaten the unity and harmony of revelation.

This is a serious question but it is not a new one. As I see it, the confrontation between unity and plurality has been present from the very beginning of Christianity, which was first expressed in Aramaic and then in Greek, a language profoundly different from Aramaic. What is quite new is the possibility of applying plurality on a far wider scale, enlarging its scope to a worldwide basis.

The argument against plurality comes, in large degree, from too sharp a contrast between the concepts of unity and plurality. This contrast seems to me to be superficial and accidental. It springs from the fact that the relationship between the two concepts has not been adequately stated nor clearly defined.

Let us be specific. All theology is a reflection on the content of faith. Theological knowledge is very complex. On the one hand, it presupposes a divine manifestation through revelation, and, on the other, the use of rational power.

I agree with Studer that faith using reason as a handmaid directs theological reflection toward a universal and objective synthesis.[1] Relying on the integrity of revelation as given in the person of Christ, and also on the universality of the principles of human reason, the task of theology is to grasp the profound meaning of the divine mystery, the purity of revealed truth. According to St. Paul:

May the Father bestow on you gifts, may he strengthen you inwardly through the working of his Spirit. May Christ dwell in your hearts through faith, and may charity be the root and foundation of your life. Thus you will be able to grasp fully, with all the holy ones, the breadth and length, and height and depth of Christ's love, and experience this love which surpasses all knowledge, so that you may attain to the fulness of God himself (Eph. 3:16–19).

Unity—which the church never ceases to insist upon and which all theological reflection should strengthen—is based on revealed truth as such, on the transcendental character of Christian revelation.

However, divine revelation, totally given in Christ, has been defined and transmitted in diverse teaching, as can be seen in the history of theology. Daniélou has emphasized differences in languages and in philosophical systems, differences which necessarily affect every theological construct.[2]

Far from being in opposition, unity and pluralism complete and complement one another in a kind of reciprocal causality: communion of faith, diversified teaching.[3] Too often an inexact and incomplete idea is developed by considering diversity as if it is always and everywhere characterized by the same intensity and rigorous exclusivity—even though at times, unfortunately, arguments considered original degenerate into theological opposition and even schism.

What exists in fact are slight differences in accent, insufficient to shake the community of faith on any particular revealed dogma. But expressed at the level of thought or translated into the external forms of Christian life (worship, apostolate, institution) with marked differences, they give each particular church a noticeably different appearance. Not to be ignored, however, are the difficulties brought by the integration of Christianity with the new forms of thought. The words of Pius XII are still true: In the midst of all cultures Christianity is like the mighty oak in the midst of brushwood. His statement calls us to humility in theological research. Christianity is a transcendent mystery and, according to Antoine, a *"signum levatum"* to all nations, a challenge to all cultures.

The divine message is for the whole world. It can be spoken in every language, as it was in Greek, Latin, French, German, and Russian. As long as the faith is safeguarded, theology can be authentically expressed in Arab, Chinese, Bantu. "God," writes Medzo, "is no longer communicating with a chosen race of people, but with the whole of humanity." This dialogue, which embraces faith in the Christ who saves, cannot continue unless Christianity makes use of every culture.[4]

This is an accepted task for the church, a requirement of catholicity. The church is catholic, says de Montcheuil, not only because it brings truth to all people, in all eras, but also because it requires the collaboration of every civilization, the contribution of all people to bring to light the riches entrusted to it in order to build the eternal city of God.[5]

The magisterium of the church, intransigent about unity of faith, has never rejected diversity. Vatican Council II accepted the value of human culture. The church has pointed out the place in the divine plan for diversity in nations and culture: The church is not a monolithic society; rather, it is the people of God, made up of series of local churches that contribute to the riches of the universal church.

The seed which is the Word of God sprouts from the good ground watered by divine dew. From this ground the seed draws nourishing elements which it transforms and assimilates into itself. Finally it bears much fruit. Thus, in imitation of the plan of the Incarnation, the young Churches, rooted in Christ and built up on the foundation of the apostles, take to themselves in a wonderful exchange all the riches of the nations which were given to Christ as an inheritance (cf. Ps. 2:8). From the customs and traditions of their people, from their wisdom and their learning, from their arts and sciences, these Churches borrow all those things which can contribute to the glory of their Creator, the revelation of the Savior's grace, or the proper arrangement of Christian life.[6]

To successfully achieve this goal every socio-cultural entity must undertake a theological reflection that takes into account the philosophy and wisdom of its people.

If this goal is to be achieved, theological investigation must necessarily be stirred up in each major socio-cultural area, as it is called. In this way, under the light of the tradition of the universal Church, a fresh scrutiny will be brought to bear on the deeds and words which God has made known, which have been consigned to sacred Scripture, and which have been unfolded by the Church Fathers and the teaching authority of the Church.

Thus it will be more clearly seen in what ways faith can seek for understanding in the philosophy and wisdom of these peoples. A better view will be gained of how their customs, outlook on life, and social order can be reconciled with the manner of living taught by divine revelation. As a result, avenues will be opened for a more profound adaptation in the whole area of Christian life. Thanks to such a procedure, every appearance of syncretism and of false particularism can be excluded, and Christian life can be accommodated to the genius and the dispositions of each culture.

Particular traditions, together with the individual patrimony of each family of nations, can be illumined by the light of the gospel, and then be taken up into Catholic unity. Finally, the individual young Churches, adorned with their own traditions, will have their own place in the ecclesiastical communion, without prejudice to the primacy of Peter's See, which presides over the entire assembly of charity.[7]

To foster the development of such theological reflection the church requires that young clerics be sensitized early in their formation to problems posed by the universality of the church and the diversity of nations.[8]

One last remark. The era of individual civilizations, cultivated within closed boundaries, is over. Humanity is growing toward a cosmic civilization made up of all people with common values. But this "universalization" is not "uniformization." There will always be room in this cultural unification for a certain diversity. Tsibangu writes that we are moving toward a universalization of thought. But universal civilization will not rise on the ruins of individual originalities.[9]

What is true of all thinking in general is also true of theological reflection in particular. As Etienne Borne points out, pluralism in Christian thought and pluralism in human thinking both represent the same fact and the same problem.[10] Like human thought, theological reflection must be enriched by all resources gained from individual cultures. Of course, this will have to be done according to its own methods and nature with great care both for doctrinal purity—that is to say, expression of revealed truth as such—and for incarnation —that is to say, an insertion into the living thought of all people and all times. In other words, theology must become more philosophical while maintaining a clear distinction between "revealed truth" and "human truth."

The concrete application of these principles raises particular questions that cannot be resolved without a close study of the attempts, failures, and successes that have been recorded. However, correctly understood, the perspective of plurality in theological reflection points to an orientation and opens a way that calls for the attention of theologians and promises important progress in a better understanding of revelation.

NOTES

1. B. Studer, "Encore la théologie africaine," *Revue du Clergé Africain* 16 (1961):110–11.

2. "We should understand revealed truth as it is given in revelation, at different levels and in different modes. We try to understand it by using every human resource. This cannot be achieved unless revealed truths are inserted and integrated into our more or less conscious worldview" (T. Tshibangu, *Théologie positive et théologie spéculative* [Louvain, 1965], p. 373). In the same way, Daniélou views as perfectly legitimate the attempt to make use of all that is best in philosophy for theology.

3. Grelot writes: "Unanimity of witness, participation in the same faith, agreement in understanding the mystery of Christ do not signify uniformity. Divine revelation, wholly given in Christ, is now adequately formulated only in diversified teaching which illuminates its content under the guidance of the Holy Spirit. To attain the fulness of truth, it will be necessary to listen to all the witnesses, because they complement each other. The variety of their viewpoints enrich the Gospel they serve" (P. Grelot, *Bible, Parole de Dieu* [Paris, 1965], p. 17). There is a particularly enlightening statement on this point in Daniélou: "Knowledge is one. There are not several world systems. But the human mind advances in spite of obstacles toward a more complete understanding of the cosmos. Philosophy is one. Every philosophy, worthy of the name, seeks a universally valid interpretation. If this is denied, it is because of loss of faith in intelligence and in truth. Thus theology is primarily one. Normally, theology progresses in the understanding of revelation. But to achieve unity, it must make use of all human resources. . . . There will be plurality to the degree that one theologian accents one insight, or opens up a new perspective. But plurality exists within a common search. It is like the growth of a tree of which the branches continue to grow but which draws the same sap at the roots, receives it through the same trunk, and grows in the same sunlight" (J. Daniélou, S. J., "Unité et pluralité de la théologie," in *Semaine des Intellectuels Catholiques* [Paris, 1961] p. 129).

4. J. Medzo, "Le christianisme est-il une culture universelle?" *Tam Tam*, April-May, 1962, p. 16.

5. Y. de Montcheuil, *Problème de la vie spirituelle* (Paris, 1947), pp. 84–85.

6. "Decree on the Church's Missionary Activity," no. 22, in Walter M. Abbott, S.J., ed., *The Documents of Vatican II* (New York: Herder and Herder, 1966).

7. Ibid. See also "Decree on Ecumenism" no. 14: "However, the heritage handed down by the apostles was received in different forms and ways, so that from the very beginnings of the Church it has had a varied development in various places, thanks to a similar variety of natural gifts and conditions of life. Added to external causes, and to mutual failures in understanding and charity, all these circumstances set the stage for separations." And again in no. 17: "What has already been said about legitimate variety we are pleased to apply to differences in theological expressions of doctrine. In the investigation of revealed truth, East and West have used different methods and approaches in understanding and proclaiming divine things. It is hardly surprising, then, if sometimes one tradition has come nearer than the other to an apt appreciation of certain aspects of a revealed mystery, or has expressed them in a clearer manner. As a result, these various theological formulations are often to be considered as complementary rather than conflicting."

8. "From the very beginning, their doctrinal training should be so planned that it takes into account both the universality of the Church and the diversity of the world's nations. This requirement holds for all the studies by which they are prepared for the exercise of the ministry, as also for the other branches of learning which it would be useful for them to master. They will thereby gain a general knowledge of peoples, cultures, and religions, a knowledge that looks not only to the past, but to the present as well. For anyone who is going to encounter another people should have a great esteem for their patrimony and their language and their customs.

"It is above all necessary for the future missionary to devote himself to missiological studies: that is, to know the teachings and norms of the Church concerning missionary activity, the roads which the heralds of the gospel have traversed in the course of the centuries, the present condition of the missions, and the methods now considered especially effective"("Decree on Missionary Activity," no. 26).

9. T. Tshibangu, "Débat sur la théologie africaine," *Revue du Clergé Africain* 15 (1960), p. 346.

10. E. Borne, "Pluralité des philosophies." *Catholicisme, un et divers*, Semaine des Intellectuels Catholiques (Paris, 1962), p. 1_1.

7

Toward Indigenous Theology in South Africa

Manas Buthelezi (South Africa)

"ETHNOGRAPHICAL" APPROACH[1]

Missionaries' Quest for Indigenous Theology

The church, which is a creation of the gospel message addressed to the whole world, does not consequently lose its solidarity with the world. One word that perhaps sums up the salient features of this solidarity is "indigenous." The indigeneity of the church is the presupposition of its mission in the world.

The church as a "communion of saints" does not exist in airy abstraction isolated from the concrete affairs of people and has not become a semi-angelic fellowship. The phenomenological aspect of the reality of this communion pertains to its faith and life. It listens to the Word of God preached in words and phrases coined according to the rules of grammar, syntax, and diction. It enunciates the essence of its faith in theological categories informed by human logic and epistemology. It sings praises to God in songs that are a product of human poetical imagination and musical composition. It expresses the genius of its discipleship in, with, and under the given cultural and social structures.

In the milieu of churches in Africa and Asia, the focus has been on the urgency of indigenous church structures and theology. This arose from the feeling that there is a "hermeneutical gap" between the existing functional western moulds and preaching and teaching the Christian faith in these countries and the respective traditional thought patterns.

John V. Taylor has summed up this problem as follows:

Christ has been presented as the answer to the questions a white man would ask, the solution to the needs that Western man would feel, the Saviour of the world of the European worldview, the object of the adoration and prayer of historic Christendom. But if Christ were to appear as the answer to the questions that Africans are asking, what would he look like? If he came into the world of African cosmology to redeem Man as Africans understand him, would he be recognizable to the rest of the Church Universal? And if Africa offered him the praises and petitions of her total, uninhibited humanity would they be acceptable? [2]

One of the basic presuppositions has been that of thinking that the phenomenon of the "hermeneutical gap" of current Christianity in Africa arises from epistemological factors. Already in the last century Duff Macdonald illustrated this with rather a touch of humor.

One cause of error is that we mix up what the African tells us with our own ideas, which are European. As a consequence of this, we put questions to him that he cannot understand. Many of our questions strike the African exactly as a question like the following would strike a European, "If seventy miles of the sea were burned, who would be the losers, the Insurance Companies? or the Harbour Administration? or ———?" If an African put this question to a European, the European would laugh at him; but if the European put it to an African, the latter would be more polite. and would think that the European was very ingenious in finding out a supposition that would have never occurred to himself. [3]

Along the same vein, Junod attached much importance to the study of the "African soul" as well as of its fears and longings. He is of the opinion that, in failing to study African institutions and customs, the missionary betrays his Master. In another context, he gave the missionaries an edge over the secular representatives of western civilization on the basis of the opportunity they have to understand the "African soul." He maintained that nobody will have a lasting influence on the Bantu people without understanding that the greatest thing in them is their soul. [4]

John V. Taylor, to whom we have already referred, has sympathetically argued the case for the validity of the categories of thought found in the African worldview. He has illustrated his case from his concrete experiences in Africa. One of the presuppositions of his case is that the African worldview, which is at the same time inherent in and independent of the traditional religion, "stands in the world as a living faith, whether in the residual paganism of millions, or in the tacit assumptions of very many African Christians, or the neo-African culture of the intellectual leaders."[5] Taylor feels that the African insights can enrich and supplement the heritage of the universal church.

In his discussion of "indigenous theology," Bengt Sundkler sees the possibilities for a "Christian theology in Africa" in the usage of certain traditional insights. He writes:

Theology, in essence, is to understand the fact of Christ; theology in Africa has to interpret this Christ in terms that are relevant and essential to African existence. Here the background in the myths of African religion is important, for it provides certain broad patterns of which theology in Africa must take account.[6]

African theologians must use as their point of departure the "fundamental facts" in terms of which the African interprets existence, according to Sundkler. To demonstrate his case, Sundkler refers to what he calls "the two foci of the theological encounter in Africa," namely, the concept of the "beginning" and the notions of the "community of the living and the dead." Like Taylor, Sundkler's presupposition is that there is a store of traditional ideas that should be used as a frame of conceptual reference for African theology. He sums it up as follows:

Traditional African thinking was mythical. It was bound up with the Beginning of Things, with Creation and the Primeval Age; the Myths of the Origin of the First Man and Mankind are fundamental to this conception of life and the world. They constitute an "original revelation," which is re-enacted in annually recurrent festivals, in a rhythm which forms the cosmic framework of space and time. The myths span the whole of existence, from heaven to the hut and the heart of the individual; in fact, from cosmos to clan. Macrocosm and microcosm are tuned to each other and are included in an all-embracing order.[7]

Writing from another angle, in his work on Bantu philosophy, Placide Tempels also presupposes what he calls "the presence of a corpus of logically coordinated intellectual concepts, a 'Lore.' "[8] He therefore refutes the assumption of those who are of the opinion that "primitive people possess no system of thought."[9] "To declare *a priori* that primitive peoples have no ontology and that they are completely lacking in logic, is simply to turn one's back on reality."[10] The presence of this corpus of traditional intellectual concepts is a vital phenomenon not only among the un-westernized Africans but also among the "évolués" and the "déracinés."

Need we, then, be surprised that beneath the veneer of "civilization" the "Negro" remains always ready to break through? We are astonished to find one who has spent years among whites readapt himself easily by the end of a few months to the community life of his place of origin and soon becomes reabsorbed in it. He has no need to readjust himself because the roots of his thought are unchanged. Nothing and nobody made him conscious of any inadequacy in his philosophy.[11]

At the same time, Tempels feels that the Bantu are not capable of articulating that which is latent in them by way of formulating a philosophical treatise which is complete with an adequate vocabulary. Hence "it is our job," says Tempels, "to proceed to such systematic development. It is we who will be able to tell them, in precise terms, what their inmost concept of being is. They will recognize themselves in our words and will acquiesce, saying, 'You understand us, you now know us completely, you "know" in the way we "know." ' "[12]

One of the elements in this approach to the quest for indigenous theology in Africa is the belief that, by analyzing and characterizing cultural factors with regard to their historical development in the African church milieu, it becomes possible by means of the "sifting" medium of the gospel to root out "un-Christian" practices and "baptize" those that are consonant with the gospel. Furthermore, by discovering those cultural factors and understanding them in the light of the totality of their respective worldview, it is possible to arrive at a hermeneutical principle by means of which one can translate the "Christian gospel" into a form congenial to the "African mind."

Since this theological method uses as a point of departure elements of the traditional African "worldview," which, from the literary point of view, exists as an ethnographical reconstruction, we shall refer to it as an "ethnographic approach."

Kroeber, in defining ethnography, has remarked that "by usage rather than definition, ethnography deals with the cultures of the non-literate peoples." Unlike history, which deals with written documents, ethnography "does not find its documents; it makes them, by direct experience of living or by interview, question, and record. It aims to grasp and portray sociocultural conditions: merely summarized at first, and often moralized."[13]

Shortcomings of the Approach

Over a long time heated discussions on "indigenous theology" have left some with a feeling that the whole thing is virtually an occupational pet-project of missionaries who have suddenly become aware of the fact that they have to change the content of their leadership role during the passing of the "missionary era," if they are to have a place in the post-colonial dispensation at all. It is against this background that one has to understand Taylor's pointed remark: "Yet in all this a warning light flickers from the fact that the enthusiasts are mainly non-Africans. This can partly be explained by the conservatism of African clergy. The real reason is that the white 'indigenizers' are too superficial, and Africans know it."[14]

In one of the letters written to the editor of *Isithunywa*, a church periodical, E. Sibisi queries, as a matter of principle, what he reckons to be the unwarranted leading role played by missionaries in making suggestions about the specific ingredients of an "indigenized church." The case in point is an attempt to popularize traditional tunes in liturgical music. Sibisi says: "In my opinion it is a waste of money and time that Africans should be taught the traditional Zulu way of singing, and that, of all people, the ones who have to teach that kind of singing should be foreigners. Furthermore, why should the matter of singing according to traditional chants not be initiated spontaneously by Africans themselves, rather than be imposed upon us."[15]

There is, of course, a strong possibility that the objection of Sibisi may be countered by means of an equally valid argument, namely, that it is salutary for a church, especially during our ecumenical era, to open itself toward theological insight and suggestions from outside. Should the facilities and experiences of the European churches not be regarded as an ecumenical asset for the African churches, which on the whole do not have such facilities and wealth of centuries-old experience? Does indigenization mean self-sufficiency and programmed isolationism? We know, of course, that ecumenical ties may be a good catalyst in the struggle of African churches to be themselves. It was under the impulse of this spirit that, in one of the sectional reports during the All-Africa Lutheran Conference, it was recommended:

that the churches [in Africa] avail themselves of the existing programs of the various Lutheran World Federation commissions and that we encourage exchange programs involving experts in the fields of stewardship, education, parish life, etc., and that we further recommend that assistance, including adequate materials, be given in the conducting of courses of training with experts coming from the African churches, Lutheran World Federation, and other national and international organizations such as the National Christian Councils, the World Council of Christian Education and Sunday Schools, etc.[16]

These considerations, sound as they are, cannot be used to disprove Sibisi's basic theses. They are parallel, rather than incompatible with the thrust of Sibisi's argument. It is very easy to confuse the question of "indigenous theology" with that of salutary exchange programs among churches. The confusion occurs as soon as people think of indigenization in programmatic terms. If indigenization is thus conceived, it becomes a mechanical program in which objectively identifiable motifs of the African worldview are used to indigenize an already existing church which is un-indigenized. In other words, we have before us two known objective entities: our task of indigenization simply consists in relating them. It is like a jig-saw puzzle in which you have, on the one hand, the design, and on the other the pieces that have to be fitted together in such a way that they image the design.

When we talk about the problem of indigenous theology in Africa, are we really dealing with such self-evident tangibles on the basis of which we can introduce indigenization in the church as a crash program? If questions like the handing over of church leadership to indigenous personnel seem to tempt us to think that it is possible to program "indigenization" in Africa, it is because these are external matters of administration and outward organization which make sense only when they are studied against the background of colonialism and European imperialism. But, if, by indigenization, we have in mind theology as a reflection on the Christian faith, we are then dealing with an internal matter of African genius that defies programming. We shall return to this point later. We should only mention for the present that, when we talk about indigenous theology in Africa, the temerity to have on hand the self-evident objective ingredients for its creation may lead to disappointing results. Sibisi has called our attention to this fact. In his letter, he asks: "By the way, is there still a past to which it is said we must return? Where is it? Who still live according to its precepts?"

Even though Sibisi does not spell it out himself, there is more in these questions than first appears on the surface. One may, for instance, jump to the conclusion that Sibisi does not do justice to empirical facts. To be sure, it is possible to demonstrate empirically that there are many Africans who still live according to the precepts of that "past." Taylor may be proved right at this point. Yet we feel that Sibisi's questions have an import which is worth taking seriously.

There is a difference between psychologically "living in the past" in order to compensate for the virtually existential emptiness of the present, thereby trying to mitigate the conscious awareness of the horror of its oppressive destitution, and "living in the past" because it is able to offer something substantial within the framework of the concrete realities of the present, as much as it used to. Who can blame those who have the feeling that the missionaries, with their right hands, are diverting our attention to our glorious past so that we may not see what their left hands, as well as those of their fellow whites, are doing in the dehumanization of our lives in the present? Who can blame a person who sees no wisdom in "writing theological poetry" about a past era while our human dignity is being systematically taken from our lives every day in the present?

There is danger that the "African past" may be romanticized and conceived in isolation from the realities of the present. Yet this "past" seen as a worldview is nothing more than a historical abstraction of "what once was." Rightly or wrongly, one cannot help but sense something panicky about the mood which has set the tenor and tempo of the current concerns about "indigenous theology." The context of Sibisi's critical observation is a case in point.

The missionary seems to be having a guilty conscience. Looming above the horizon of the sunset of the missionary era is the horrifying specter of the question history seems to be posing to the missionary: How can a church which fidgets under trappings and paraphernalia of a past colonial era survive in a post-colonial and revolutionary Africa? This question does not rise merely as a presentiment that is without concrete roots. If we think of the current spate of the Africanization of political, social, and economic life in many states in Africa, one cannot help wondering whether Christianity will not in the course of the process be dismissed as an irrelevant life proposition. Statements have been made to the effect that Christianity is merely a spiritual arm of European imperialism in Africa. Can the "arm" hope to outlive the "body" of imperialism? This is a nagging question whether or not we believe that Christianity was a batallion in the force of imperialism.

There is a sense in which one can say that when the missionaries seem to be presumptuous in suggesting "indigenous theology" to the African, they are strictly speaking looking for a solution to problems that stem from their own psychological "hang-ups." The missionaries have therefore to play a leading role in the formulation of indigenous theology in order to make sure that it solves their own problems as well. The suggestion here is that when the Africans seem to be encouraged to produce indigenous theology, they are just being used—as they have always been—to solve the psychological problems of the missionaries.

Hoekendijk has observed that the breakdown of Christendom as a solid, well integrated cultural complex dominated by the church in Europe has, among other factors, stimulated a romantic urge among many missionaries to go to Africa and Asia in order to rebuild and relive the life of the "good old days" of Christian Europe. In his words: "These are some of the undisclosed motives. In fact, the word 'evangelize' often means a biblical camouflage of what should rightly be called the reconquest of ecclesiastical influence. Hence this undue respect for statistics and this insatiable hunger for ever more areas of life."[17]

Furthermore when the missionaries came back to Europe on furlough, they were shocked by some of the radical theological accents that grew out of the new secularist Europe. Their theological "home base" from which they had drawn spiritual resources as they faced heathen "beliefs and superstitions" had all of a sudden been undermined by "liberal theology" proponents. The missionaries suddenly discovered that they were culturally and spiritually strangers in their own home. It is no wonder that the old traditional African rural culture seemed to fit the pattern of their dream about good old Europe. While they realized they could do nothing to stem the tide of cultural developments in Europe—especially if their training qualified them only to serve as missionaries abroad—they could realize emotional and spiritual compensation in Africa where their intellectual and theological expertise was relatively speaking not yet challenged. The task of the formation of African indigenous theology would then provide a convenient setting for the realization of the romantic ideal. The missionaries passionately wanted to "marry" Africa after Europe had proved "unfaithful in her love." African indigenous theology would be the theme of the new "love poetry" which would hopefully prove itself more superior and satisfying than the new "adulterous love poetry" of new Europe.[18] So much for the metaphor.

The point is that it is not necessarily bad if missionaries seek cultural and theological shelter in Africa, but that it is bad if they at the same time dictate what kind of a shelter we should make for them. The case in point is an overemphasis on the old traditional world as the point of departure in the evolution of indigenous theology.

Without actually saying it, the implicit suggestion they seem to be making is that the old traditional insights represent more what is truly African than the insights of the modern Africans. The "true African" is the one who is described in the books of the ethnographers rather than the one whom we see in Johannesburg, Durban, and Cape Town trying to make ends meet in the framework of Influx-Control legislation. Just as modern Europe is a conglomerate of cultural and spiritual aberrations, the modern African is a cultural caricature of the "true African" who is the African of the "good old days."

The difficulty with an ethnographically reconstructed African worldview is not so much that it is necessarily inaccurate and not true to the original, as that this reconstruction as such can be readily regarded as a valid postulate for African theology. It is too presumptuous to claim to know how much of their past the Africans will allow to shape their future, once they are given the chance to participate in the wholeness of life that the contemporary world offers.

Second, allowance should be made for the fact that, even if Europe had not impinged upon Africa, Africa could still have undergone a metamorphosis on its own under the impulse of the changing needs of its people. Such internal changes could obviously not leave the worldview unaffected. It is, of course, understandable if people speak of the African past as having been something static, especially if one remembers that, for many centuries, African history has been nothing but an extension of European history, the history of its discovery and settlement by European peoples. Hence, the concept of progress in Africa has been identical with that of the Europeanization of Africa. Before Europe came to Africa, Africa was standing still! In acculturation studies, very often, the aborigines emerge from the process as bottom-level members of the society and culture of the one who makes the study. One of the intriguing things becomes the mystery of their backwardness, that is, why in the first place they did not acquire on their own the level that the new culture regards as the norm of progressing peoples.

The essence of the weakness of the "ethnographical approach" is its tendency toward cultural objectivism. Too much focus is placed upon "the African worldview," as if it were an isolated and independent entity, of value in itself apart from African people as they exist today. What we miss is the person, the *causa efficiens* of the African worldview. The worldview takes precedence over its creator, the African person. That is why we remain incarnated within the orbits of a past African worldview and in the process miss present-day Africans and their existential situation.

"ANTHROPOLOGICAL" APPROACH

Essence of the Approach

The thesis here is that the point of departure for indigenous theology is not an ethnographically reconstructed worldview, but African people themselves. When we speak of an "anthropological" approach we are thinking of the person, not as an object of study—the theme of anthropology as a discipline—but as God's creature who was entrusted with "dominion" over the rest of creation. We are thinking, not of the "colonial person" who is the object of "dominion" by other people, a "black problem" to the white politicians, but a "post-colonial person" who has been liberated by Christ from all that dehumanizes.

We are thinking of persons not as "third person" entities: persons who are talked about and discussed and whose "minds" are analyzed and systematized, who become important simply because their problems provide fruitful material for specialists; we are rather thinking of the "first person"—the Ego.

In his discussion about the selfhood of the church, D. T. Niles has used an illuminating illustration that sheds light on the statements we have made above:

> Thinking about the discovery of the self, my mind went back to my two boys when they were babies. They would say: "Baby wants ball," or I would say, "Does baby want milk?" Baby was the object that could be pointed out. On behalf of this object a request could be made. I would say, "Show baby," and my son would point to himself. Then suddenly, because it was sudden, Baby spoke and he said, "I want sweets," and my wife said, "You must eat your rice now." The self was the same but it had ceased to be an object to itself. It was no more the self to which relationships were established, rather it established its own relationships. "Baby" had become "I," "It" had become "You." Most of the churches founded by missionary societies found their self-hood in very much the same way. For many decades they were objects. They spoke about themselves and were spoken to in the third person. They were dots on a map of the mission field. Then suddenly church spoke to church. The forms of address became "I" and "You." The churches had become themselves.[19]

If we set out with the aim of defining the possibilities and postulates for indigenous theology in Africa, we must from the very onset be cognizant of the fact that we are dealing with a subject that belongs to the realm of human creativity. There is a sense in which we can speak of scientific theology as an art form and the theologian as an artist. This belongs to the aesthetic character of theology.

As soon as we predicate "indigenous" to theology, we imply that this particular theology is an artistic projection of the *causa efficiens* whom we know to be an indigene in relation to a particular milieu. Indigenous theology, therefore, means more than just a theology that treats as its object "indigenous" problems and issues, that is, *res indigenae*. The focus of current discussions and suggestions about indigenous theology seems to be on *res indigenae* like polygamy, *confessio Africana*, African liturgical forms, etc.

One is then left with the impression that the matter of the selection and the definition of the indigenous theological problems has been settled; all that remains is the emergence of someone who has the ingenuity of finding the solution to these already known problems; the assignment is cut and dried. The reason for this tendency is not hard to find. Currently the people most knowledgeable and articulate about the problem of indigenous theology in Africa are those who are either associated with missionary circles or have themselves personally experienced the problem of "missionary encounter" as missionaries. It is these problems of "missionary encounter" that are to be the subject matter of indigenous theology.

Therefore, what seems to be in the forefront of the task of indigenous theology is the discovery of the solution to these problems that could not be solved during the "missionary era." To pretend as if these problems are not important in the practical life of the church would, of course, be unrealistic. Yet, at the same time, we have to recognize that there are problems which, as phenomena in any community, may be only symptoms of a real and basic problem. There may be "problems" which, in the final analysis, may turn out to be no problems at all: They may be a byproduct of a gross misunderstanding of the situation.

The virtually exclusive concern with *res indigenae* tends to locate the problems that indigenous theology has to resolve at the point of the conflict between two worldviews: the European and the African. The human factor recedes to the background, if recognized at all. It then becomes a problem of epistemological entities, of fixed impersonal data—things "out there," the body of categories for interpreting the universe. These categories are static entities which form something that can be located, studied, and defined—thanks to ethnography. Hence, Tempels can confidently say: "It is we [Europeans] who will be able to tell them [Africans], in precise terms, what their inmost concept of being is. They will recognize themselves in our words and will acquiesce saying, 'You understand us, you know us completely, you "know" in the way we "know." ' "

This statement of Tempels reveals the element of truth involved in the statement that the missionaries who urge the production of "indigenous theology" are really seeking a solution to their own problems: The Africans are only a means to an end. At worst, the Africans have to bow to opinions and ideas of those whom they have been conditioned to associate with authority and enlightenment. At best, they have only to choose between alternatives that are offered to them. The consequence of this is that their minds have become channels, rather than fountains of ideas.[20] Even when it comes to those things associated with the African "worldview," one gets the impression that these are in effect objective entities that lie outside the Africans. Some curious student can study these and then go back to the African and ask: "Is this not the way you think?" Then the African will courteously echo the expected answer: "You understand us: you know us completely. . . . "

This objectification and impersonalization of the "African mind" explains why it is then found necessary to teach the Africans to be interested in their *res indigenae*. By implication these *res indigenae* now exist outside their consciousness, and it has become necessary that someone must pedagogically familiarize the Africans with them and arouse their interest in them. If this is a logical absurdity, it at least points to a psychological reality.

Historical factors have caused the Africans to develop a masochistic complex, that is, the realization of personal fulfilment in unconscious self-hatred and the despising and loathing of everything with which their egos are identified in social and cultural life. The degree to which one is ready to go through this psychic mortification virtually becomes the criterion for ascertaining the level which one has reached in the course of the realization of the image of a "civilized and Christian man." The sublimated center of ego-existence becomes the outside human image of the missionary or Westerner. It is very easy to confuse this psychological inversion and depersonalization with conversion and sanctification. The social counterpart of this inversion has been the bourgeois socio-cultural church life pattern around the mission station.[21]

It is our contention that the point of departure for the evolution of indigenous theology is not the manipulation of objectivized *res indigenae*, but the Africans' initiative in the context of their present existential situation. The first step is that the Africans should have both the material and spiritual means to be themselves. To be a person means to have power to be truly a person; it means power for liberation to be a person. Indigenous theology without freedom of thought is a contradiction in terms; freedom of thought without access to the material means of participating in the wholeness of life is like capacity without content.

No one can deny that, in principle, African churches do have the formal freedom to be themselves and to produce their own theology. The discussions about indigenous theology presuppose the existence of this freedom. Yet even apart from the fact that the principle has not yet been subjected to any rigorous test, there are obvious factors that seem to preclude its practical application.

Tshongwe has said that "when our seminaries can produce heretics, not through ignorance but conviction, then I would say the African is beginning to think." Let us pursue what is at stake in this statement.

Etymologically, the word "heresy" means an "act of choosing." Thus in classical antiquity it had a connotation of choosing to follow a distinctive *bios*. In Sextus Empiricus this meaning is expressed:

The word "believe" has different meanings: It means not to resist but simply to follow without any strong impulse or inclination, as the boy is said to believe his tutor; but sometimes it means to assent to a thing of *deliberate choice (hairesis)* and with a kind of sympathy due to strong desire.

As the above reference suggests, there was an inseparable relationship between the "act of choosing" and the "content" or "nature" of the thing chosen. Thus the "heresy" (choice) of a philosopher was always related to the "heresy" or "dogmata" of a particular "heresy" (school) of philosophy. It is interesting to note that Josephus refers to the Pharisees, Sadducees, and Essenes as philosophical partisans or *hairetistai*. The Christian concept of "heresy" issued from the new situation created by the historical introduction of the "Christian church." *Ekklesia* and *hairesis* become opposites (Galatians 5:20). Yet *hairesis* did not have the technical meaning it later acquired, especially at the time of the crystallization of ecclesiastical dogma. It is worthy of note that by implication 2 Peter 2:1 discriminates between salutary and destructive "heresies." Hence *hairesis* is qualifed by *apoleias*.

As a matter of fact, historical ecclesiastical dogma has been a fruit of theological freedom, even though it has very often seen that freedom as a threat to it. Yet in essence—if you allow me some semantic indulgence—ecclesiastical dogma is nothing but a corporate "heresy" made from pre-existing sets of *theologoumena*.

Theology in Africa must reflect the throbbings of the life situation in which people find themselves. A theology of tranquility and dogmatic polish in times of restlessness due to people's alienation from the wholeness of contemporary life can only be the product of theological dishonesty. What we need is a theology of restlessness. By this we mean a theology that does not take itself seriously as the last word since it is the product of people who are indigenes of a world in process of formation. A theology that tries to find its point of departure by making "platonic" flights to an imagined past, where there was still an ordered system of ideas and indigenous concepts, may in fact be paying the heavy price of abandoning an important theological reality, namely, present-day people in creation under God.

To say that theology must get its cue for indigeneity from the existing human situation does not make the whole problem of indigenous theology any easier, especially when it comes to the question of freedom of thought. Alongside the clamor for indigenous theology, one also hears expressions like "our Christian heritage" and "the faith of our fathers." These expressions are used either in a broad ecumenical or narrow confessional sense. What seems to be self-evident in their usage is not only their meaning but also the implicit suggestion that the ecclesiastical kinship group which has that heritage has a commitment not only to keep the heritage alive, but also to pass it on intact to the next generations. Such a heritage may, for instance, be a historical creed and confession or a specific traditional system of theology.

Under the theme "The Faith of our Fathers" the Second All-Africa Lutheran Conference at Ansirabé made the following resolution, among others: "That the Lutheran confessions as expressed in the Book of Concord are still valid and relevant and the best doctrinal foundation for the Lutheran Church."[22]

At stake in this statement is more than just the old academic distinction between the fundamental and non-fundamental articles of faith, or the confession of faith and its theological elaboration. Regardless of whatever hermeneutical principle we may choose in making this distinction, it is immediately obvious that the Book of Concord, with regard to its content, represents more than just a statement of "first principles" or fundamentals of faith in its primordial forms. Rather, it represents a systematic theological tradition; a confluence of religious, cultural, social, and political ideas, as well as a type of a thetical summary of the Greco-Roman tradition of the intellectual history of the church up to the sixteenth century.

Hence to speak of the "relevance" and "validity" of the Lutheran confessional corpus is more problematic than self-evident, especially as, at the same time, we have to express concern for the evolution of indigenous theology in Africa. It is one thing to speak of the Lutheran Confessions as historical documents that have a historical value, but it is another thing to make a confessional resolution out of an attempt of promoting their present relevance and validity.

In the organization of indigenous churches in Africa, it has sometimes been necessary to merge several mission synods that have been working in the same geographical territory side by side. Some Lutheran Synods have insisted on the recognition of the Book of Concord as expressing the doctrinal basis of the new church. It has to be remembered that in most, if not all, newly organized African churches the theologically sophisticated elite has been composed solely of missionaries. Therefore all the theological battles at the time of the merger discussions and the organization of the new church were merely a replay of the theological tensions and fights "back home" in Europe or America. The Africans had only to play the sorry part of purporting to grasp and feel what the whole theological hullabaloo was about. Very often they played their part remarkably well, to the great delight of their theological mentors.

Wherever it exists, worldwide confessional kinship solidarity is something salutary, not only because it has been a catalyst for the ecumenical movement, but also because it has helped positively in the growth of the so-called "younger churches" through the special attention they have received from their respective confessional kinship groups. Lutheran churches, in varying degrees, have been among the most insistent on the confessional basis of church fellowship. This is a multi-dimensional problem and we do not intend to take it up here. But we do want to raise the question whether, in the course of its emphasis on the doctrinal basis of Christian fellowship, Lutheranism, for instance, has not sacrificed the "human" for the "ideological."

In common parlance, "our Christian heritage" or "the faith of our fathers" includes a common holding of a definite attitude toward the question of human life and destiny. In the doctrinal or confessional contexts, this involves a mandatory historical understanding of the essential details of that which constitutes the characteristic outlook of the ecclesiastical kinship group, as an outward manifestation of its esprit de corps.

Ecumenical theology, in the sense of the catholic tradition of theology, is strictly speaking another name for the broad theological concepts that have survived as minimal points of agreement in the historical disputes among the theological schools of thought and have emerged from the Greco-Roman cultural background. It is these broad concepts that have served as a point of departure in the modern ecumenical dialogues, and they have been introduced to the churches in Africa and Asia as an unbroken traditional package from the European churches. We use the phrase "unbroken package" analogously to what Bonhoeffer means in his criticism of what he calls "positivist doctrine of revelation," when he says: " 'Like it or lump it': virgin birth, Trinity, or anything else; each is equally significant and a necessary part of the whole, which must simply be swallowed as a whole or not at all."[23]

If some aspects of the historical definitions of the Christian faith are already posing epistemological problems in the West, one begins to wonder whether African and European churches should not seek for another way of expressing kinship solidarity, rather than through the form of an uncritical profession of allegiance to a body of ideas about the faith. This should not be construed as a disparagement of the significance of doctrine in the life of the church. On the other hand, we want to raise the question whether the ideological basis of ecclesiastical kinship solidarity is adequate, even if it were not for its attendant epistemological problems. This leads us to the crucial point.

In our opinion, the category of the "human" has been neglected as a theological motif for understanding the expression of ecumenical solidarity in the interest of the ideological, namely, confessions and doctrines. Recent theological developments, as illustrated by the studies of the World Conference on Church and Society in Geneva 1966, can only be welcomed with cautious optimism. The same is true of the theological accents of the Lutheran World Federation Assembly which met at Evian in 1970.

People in the "Third World" have learned that subscribing to certain confessions and doctrinal definitions is no guarantee that they are accepted on the basis of their integrity as human beings by those who happen to subscribe to the same doctrinal formulae. The confessional and doctrinal ecclesiastical umbrella has proved itself a poor shelter against the rain of racism. Very often solidarity on the basis of the profession of allegiance to the common "faith of our fathers" serves as a smokescreen for diverting attention from the patterns of socially and even ecclesiastically entrenched alienation on the human level. Yet genuine oneness in Christ manifests itself best on the level of "naked humanity," where the masks of "common faith" and "common confessions" as the basis of fellowship are very often removed.

The shift from the "ideological" to the "human" expressions of ecclesiastical kinship solidarity will serve as a freeing factor for indigenous theology. Considerations of a confessional esprit de corps will no longer be a haunting specter for theological freedom in Africa, since there will be another way of expressing this kinship solidarity.

In other words, this will leave African churches free to make their own theological options (heresies). Yet, at the same time, by focusing on the human, it will be possible for us to realize that material destitution, like ignorance, is no healthy atmosphere for the production of indigenous theology. In order to be an indigenous theologian, you must undergo rigorous educational discipline; in order to get education, you must have money, you must, as a human being, have access to the economic facilities of life; in short, you must have access to the wholeness of life.

The point I have been arguing here is in essence that the problem of indigenous theology in Africa primarily consists not so much in what the content of that theology must be (ethnographical approach) as in its *causa efficiens*, the Africans themselves (anthropological approach). The problem is not primarily that the Africans are finding it difficult to do theology or that they are failing to find the content for their theology—as suggested by the "ethnographical approach." It is simply that the life they find themselves in denies them the resources and tools for even making a beginning. We should pay more attention to the problem of and factors that account for the present lack of trained indigenous theologians, than to the question of what the content of African theology should be. The latter will be the life-task of African theologians as soon as they exist. Let us give promising young people as much theological educational exposure and discipline as possible, and leave the rest to them.

In order to illustrate the "anthropological approach" we shall single out the case of "blackness" as one of the reference points in our method of theologizing.

Case Study of the Concept of Blackness

The last two years have been characterized by the evolution of the phenomenon of black consciousness in South Africa. This in turn called for the need to relate the Christian faith to the experience of black people. This is what it means to be black in South Africa.

Blackness is an anthropological reality that embraces the totality of my daily existence: It daily determines where I live, with whom I can associate and share my daily experience of life. Life, as it were, unfolds itself to me daily within the limits and range of black situational possibilities. The word of God addresses me within the reality of the situation of my blackness. I can only go to black churches and the only pastor who normally can minister to me is a black like myself.

If I am a pastor, I can understand my ministry only within the context of a black flock. Christian brotherhood? Well, the only brothers with whom I can share daily the experience of Christ are black people like myself: Only with these can I listen to the word and receive the sacraments.

This situation is neither a dream nor a mere fantasy: It is spiritual reality as it daily unfolds to me. Therefore I have to take this seriously and try to understand the redemption in Christ within the context of my black experience.

As far as the question of redemption is concerned, traditional Christian theology has not addressed itself to my situation. It has left me with the impression that my blackness is a negative rather than a positive quality. Liturgically, blackness is associated with death and mourning, while whiteness is a symbol of joy and victory. According to the author of the book of Revelation (3:5 and more often), the victorious and resurrected saints are portrayed as dressed in white.

One can, of course, go on and on; but this should suffice to illustrate what I mean when I speak of theologically taking seriously the present situation of black people. For lack of a better term, I would label this method of theologizing "black theology." Therefore, for me, "black theology" is nothing but a methodological technique of theologizing. It is one case of what I called an "anthropological approach."

NOTES

1. Cf. B. Moore, ed., *Black Theology: The South African Voice* (London: Hurst, 1973), pp. 43–46.

2. J.V. Taylor, *The Primal Vision: Christian Presence and African Religion* (London: SCM Press, 1963), p. 16.

3. Duff MacDonald, *Africana, or The Heart of Heathen Africa* (London: Dawsons of Pall Mall, 1969; first published 1882), 1:3.

4. See H.A. Junod, *The Life of a South African Tribe*, 2 vols. (New York: University Books, 1962; first edition, 1912). See for example 2:361–64.

5. Taylor, *Primal Vision*, p. 21.

6. B.G.M. Sundkler, *The Christian Ministry in Africa* (London: SCM Press, 1962), p. 99.

7. Ibid., p. 100.

8. P. Placide Tempels, *Bantu Philosophy*, p. 9. The English version is a 1959 rendition of the 1959 French version *(La philosophie Bantoe)*. The original Dutch work was published in 1946 and translated into German in 1956.

9. Ibid., p. 10.

10. Ibid., p. 11.

11. Ibid., p. 12.

12. Ibid., p. 15.

13. A.L. Kroeber, *An Anthropologist Looks at History* (Berkeley and Los Angeles: University of California Press, 1963), pp. 131–32.

14. Taylor, *Primal Vision*, p. 15.

15. Zulu language edition of the Monthly Parish Bulletin of the Evangelical Lutheran Church in South Africa, Southeastern Region, Durban, Lutheran Publishing House.

16. Third All-Africa Lutheran Church Conference, Addis Ababa, 1965.

17. Hans Hoekendijk, *Die Zukunft der Kirche und die Kirche der Zukunft* (Stuttgart: Kreuz-Verlag, 1964), p. 85.

18. See M. Buthelezi, "African Theology and Black Theology: A Search for Theological Method," in H J. Becken, ed., *Relevant Theology for Africa*, Report on a Consultation of the Missiological Institute at Lutheran Theological College, Mapumulo, September 12–21, 1972 (Durban: Lutheran Publishing House, 1973), pp. 20f.

19. D.T. Niles, *Upon the Earth: The Mission of God and the Missionary Enterprise of the Churches* (New York: McGraw-Hill, 1962), pp. 140–41.

20. See Moore, *Black Theology: The South African Voice*, p. 119.

21. On masochism see also ibid.

22. "Der Glaube unserer Vater," Report of Section II of the Second AALC, 1960, published in J. Althausen, ed., *Christen Afrikas auf dem Wege zur Freiheit 1955–69* (Berlin: Union Verlag, 1971), p. 74f.

23. D. Bonhoeffer, *Widerstand und Ergebung*, rev. ed. (Munich: Kaiser, 1970), p. 312; Eng. trans., *Letters and Papers From Prison*, enl ed. (New York: Macmillan, 1971), p. 286.

8

Coming in out of the Wilderness

Allan Boesak (South Africa)

Black theology is a theology of liberation. Black theology believes that liberation is not only "part of" the gospel, or "consistent with" the gospel; it *is* the gospel of Jesus Christ. Born in the community of the black oppressed, it takes seriously the black experience, the black situation. Black theology grapples with black suffering and oppression; it is a "cry unto God" for the sake of the people. It believes that in Jesus Christ the total liberation of all people has come. It refuses to believe that the gospel of Jesus Christ is the narrow, racist ideology white Christians have made of it. Black Christians cannot believe that the last word about Christianity is that it is a "white man's religion," a "slave religion" designed for the oppression of the poor.

The development of a *black consciousness* in the last decade brought with it a black "Christian consciousness." It has become impossible for black Christians to escape the pressing questions of history: How can one be black *and* Christian? What has faith in Jesus Christ as Lord to do with the struggle for black liberation? What was (and still is) the role of the Christian church in the oppression and liberation of blacks?

When trying to answer these questions, it becomes abundantly clear that white questions or white answers can no longer suffice. Our theological reflection must take seriously precisely what Christian theology has ignored and has thereby been so white: the black situation. Black theology is thus the critical reflection of black Christians on their involvement in the black liberation struggle, always keeping in mind that the oppressor cannot be liberated unless the oppressed are liberated. In its focus on the poor and the oppressed, the theology of liberation is not a new theology; it is rather the proclamation of the age-old gospel now being taken out of the deadly hold of the mighty and the powerful and made relevant to the situation of the oppressed, poor blacks. It represents a new way of theologizing, a different way of believing. It places the gospel in its authentic perspective, that of liberation, and seeks to proclaim the gospel according to its original intention: as the gospel of the poor (Luke 4:18f.).[1]

In this involvement black theology seeks the God of the Bible, who is totally and completely different from the God whites have for so long preached to us. The God of the Bible is the God of liberation rather than of oppression; a God of justice rather than injustice; a God of freedom rather than enslavement and subservience; a God of love, righteousness, and community rather than of hatred, self-interest, and exploitation. Black theology knows that it is not only people who need to be liberated; the gospel too, so abused and exploited, needs to be liberated. In this liberation movement through history black Christians are joyfully engaging themselves. Black theology, as Manas Buthelezi has correctly observed, is one of the most meaningful (albeit one of the most misunderstood) events of our time.[2] For blacks, it is the discovery of the unique meaning of Jesus Christ in our lives; it is learning to say: You're a Soul Brother, Jesus.

Black theology is not new. Although the term stems from 1966, the content is as old as the attempts of white Christians to bring the gospel to blacks. There has always been a distinct black understanding of Christianity and the message of the Bible. It is therefore wrong to suggest that black theology is the product of the "theology of revolution"; some claim that this "theology of revolution," conceived in 1966 by the "white" World Council of Churches, in turn was translated into a black theology in the United States and then exported to South Africa by a white man.[3] Not only has there been a black theology as long as white Christians have been preaching to blacks, but there have always been strong links between blacks in South Africa and the United States. The very strong ties between some churches in South Africa and the United States confirm this.

But we return to our thesis: This definite black understanding of the gospel has always been very clear. Gayraud Wilmore in an excellent historical study on black religion confirms this:

Blacks have used Christianity not as it was delivered to them by segregated white churches, but as its truth was authenticated to them in the experience of suffering, to reinforce an ingrained religious temperament and to produce an indigenous religion oriented to freedom and human welfare.[4]

By the "ingrained religious temperament" Wilmore means the African religious temperament, which in a certain sense formed the basis on which blacks were trying to understand the gospel. This "black" understanding of the gospel meant not only that blacks believed that the gospel and Jesus Christ were all about liberation; they also refused to believe that the biblical message could be anything else than that.

Black Christians have always known the central message of the gospel, and if they could not find it in the preaching of the white missionaries, they looked for it in their own way:

They were fully aware that the God who demanded their devotion and the Spirit that infused their secret meetings and possessed their souls and bodies in the ecstasy of worship, was not the God of the slavemaster with his whip and gun, nor the God of the plantation preacher with his segregated services and unctuous injunctions to humility and obedience.[5]

White theology could never give answers to the urgent questions of black people, simply because in that sphere that whites created, blacks could never ask these existential questions. But even so, the efforts of white people to bar blacks from religious teaching, in spite of religion being so effectively used as opiate for blacks, made blacks suspect that whites knew that there was something so dynamic, a truth so explosive and liberating in the gospel message, that it was worth embracing and making one's own. This conviction was voiced again and again through black history. In the United States, Frederick Douglass said in 1846:

I love the religion of our blessed Savior. I love that religion which comes from above, in the wisdom of God which is first pure, then peaceable, gentle, . . . without partiality and hypocrisy. . . . I love that religion that makes it the duty of its disciples to visit the fatherless and the widow in their affliction. I love that religion that is based upon the glorious principle of love to God and love to man, which makes its followers do unto others as they themselves would be done by. If you demand liberty to yourself, it says, grant it to your neighbors. . . . It is because I love this religion that I hate the slaveholding, the mind-darkening, the soul-destroying religion that exists in America. Loving the one I must hate the other; holding to one I must reject the other.[6]

In South Africa, it was said of Isaiah Shembe's preaching at the end of the previous century

You, my people, were once told of a God who has neither arms nor legs, who cannot see, who has neither love nor pity. But Isaiah Shembe showed you a God who walks on feet and who heals with his hands, and who can be known by men—a God who loves and has compassion.[7]

This is black theology. Henry McNeal Turner, saying "God is a Negro" in 1894, made a profound black theological statement.[8] The breakaways of blacks from the white dominated, segregated churches, were also theological statements. The leaders, when they made the exodus-event central to their preaching, were preaching a black theology. The idea of the Black Christ, rampant throughout Africa and America in the nineteenth century and earlier, was black theology. Theodore Weld, already speaking of the "God of the oppressed" in 1842, was a black theologian.[9] Black Christians have always known that the gospel of the poor is not a "white religion," and that spark of knowledge is now kindled into a flame. This knowledge has sustained black people all along: There is a God of freedom, and we, his people, shall be liberated. This is what has made black people sing through all those incredible centuries:

O Freedom, O Freedom! O Freedom over me.
And before I'll be a slave
I'll be buried in my grave
And go home to my Lord and be free!

BLACK THEOLOGY IN SOUTH AFRICA

One of the most important differences between black theology in South Africa and that in the United States is one of background: In contrast to the U.S. blacks, South Africans have almost no historical documents from the hands of blacks themselves with regard to black history and black theology. White (church) historians have given their views and interpretations of historical events, but there is a remarkable vacuum with regard to sermons and historical documents written by blacks themselves out of which black thinking, theologically and otherwise, can be reconstructed.

This means that documentation of black interpretation of historical events in church and politics may be considered fairly new; and such interpretation must be done within the framework of a government policy which restricts, censors, and bans anything that the government considers undermining to the present system. Black Americans have never really had such restrictions, bannings, house arrests, publications "that come on the list," etc. This also says something about the political situation in which blacks in South Africa have to do their theology. We have no constitution which at least makes the pretension of protection of human rights. On the other hand, in South Africa blacks are the majority and the political issues are much more clear than in the United States.

Black Consciousness

The growth of black consciousness is, because of this particular political and ecclesiastical situation in South Africa, of a special significance. What does this mean for the black South African? In the first place, it means a black solidarity that encompasses not only the Africans, but all the different groups in the black community. It means that blacks no more speak of "coloured" (what does it mean anyway?) or of any particular group designated as "non-white" by the white government. We are black people, and we share the solidarity of the oppressed. Black theology in South Africa seeks a black community that cuts across all the artificial barriers of separateness, apartheid, of being-closer-to-white-peopleness that up till now have divided us. It seeks a community of blackness, a community in which reconciliation with our black selves and with our black brothers and sisters is of prime importance.

Blackness does not in the first place designate skin color. It is a discovery, a state of mind, a conversion, an affirmation of being (which is power). It is an insight that has to do with wisdom. The grave responsibility for blackness belongs to blacks who must make South Africa a country where both black and white may live in peace: "We have seen enough of white racism," says Adam Small. "We have suffered enough from its meaning; we cannot want to be racist in our blackness." This is an awesome responsibility and a task black people can take upon themselves only in the name of the Lord, for in doing this we shall have to have the power to love white people (Baartmann). In this we shall try not to make them understand us, but to understand ourselves and hopefully to make white people see what they really are. This can be done only by the "real black people":

The real black people are those who embrace the positive description "black" as opposed to "non-white," which is a definition in terms of others, not in terms of yourself. . . . This forces white people to recognize their whiteness and all its consequences.[10]

This is a profound statement of power. In a country where blackness is non-beingness, where people have no rights, no dignity, no respect; where an extremely refined system of racial laws shouts inferiority at the black person on every level—in such a situation blacks say with Small (and I shall quote him at length):

Our insight is this: we will live without apology, or as if apologizing. . . . Whites have goaded and do goad us to humiliations which all add up to our believing that we live by their grace. Now we are rejecting that idea. . . . This has been the biggest impertinence on the part of whites, this idea that they hold life for us in their hands. Our movement towards our blackness means the realization, clear realization, that no one at all, no man, holds life in their hands for us. We are not beggars for life. . . . Protest will therefore play a role in our future actions but we will realize that protest is a kind of begging; but again, we cannot beg. Protest will be a secondary form of expression altogether. . . . The primary form of expression for us will be the manifestation of our blackness time and time again and again; whether whites will understand this or not will not be the point at all. *We are not there for whites, we are there.*[11]

It must be clear that black theology is not out to deproblematize the situation. We do not look to "integration" as the "solution" to our problems; neither are we out to declare God "colorless"—not after what the white god has done.

Black Consciousness and Black Theology

This takes us from black consciousness to black theology. Almost at
once we meet the call for a "re-examination of Christianity." There is
strong resentment that the African religious heritage was constantly
discarded as "barbarism" and "heathenism," while Christianity and
western culture were indissolubly linked to one another under one
divine cloak. The role of missionaries and missions is being looked at
critically and re-evaluated in the light of the black experience. Missionaries did much more than "just preaching the Word": "Their
arrogance and their monopoly on truth, beauty, and moral judgment
taught them to despise native customs and traditions and to seek to
infuse into these societies their own values" (Buthelezi).

Black theology seeks a gospel that is relevant for the black situation. It seeks a God who will not rest until all his children are liberated
and who will not accept that a lie exist unchallenged. Blacks detest the
way western theology has departmentalized life and brought into our
thinking the western dualistic pattern of thought—which is completely foreign to the biblical mentality and to African traditional
thought.[12] Therefore black theology proclaims the totality of God's
liberation and in the total liberation seeks the realization of what
Buthelezi calls the "wholeness of life."

It must be abundantly clear by now that black theology cannot be
easily divorced from African theology. In calling for the actualization
of the gospel for the black situation, at the same time it is also an
essential correction on traditional western theological thinking.
Pityana phrases it thus:

Christianity is rooted in an explosive system that is basically selfish. . . . The
church must go back to the roots of broken African civilization. It must
examine the traditional African forms of worship, forms of marriage, sacrifice
and why these things were meaningful and wholesome to the traditional
African community.[13]

Responding to the gospel in terms of traditional culture and responding to the gospel within the context of a given situation do not
necessarily have to be contradictory. Yet, a contextual theology, like
black theology, clearly is, must be authentic. It must not yield to
uncritical accommodation, becoming a "cultural theology" or a "reli-

gion of culture." An authentic situational theology is prophetic, critical, not merely excavating corpses of tradition, but taking critically those traditions from the past that can play a humanizing and revolutionizing role in our contemporary society. It is taking from the past that which is positively good, thereby offering a critique of the present and opening perspectives for the future. This is a process always arising out of genuine encounter with the Word of God and the world, challenging and changing the situation. It is dynamic, always "giving account of the hope that is within us" in a given situation, always committed to the central message of the Bible: liberation.

Black theology in South Africa has taken upon itself "to speak a word of hope to people without power. And this word of hope cannot contain any promise that one day they will have power over others, even those others who oppress them now. It must be a hope that one day we will live together without masters or slaves" (Motlhabi).[14] Black theology, according to Bishop Zulu, must "lead black people to see that white people, when white people treat them as less than human, when they exploit black men, are being unfaithful to the revelation of God in Christ." But to Pityana black theology must also be "a call upon black people to affirm the words of Eldridge Cleaver: We shall have our manhood or the earth shall be levelled by our efforts to gain it. . . . " No wonder Zulu has difficulty "with some exponents of black theology who give the impression that theology should be the handmaid of the black revolution and that this revolution necessarily should be violent." Black theologians, he warns, must guard against equating God being on the side of the oppressed with the oppressed being on the side of God.[15]

FOCUS ON POWER

Power is the most conspicuous point on which black theologians in South Africa and the United Sates seem to differ. But the division is not as easy as all that.

We have already quoted the words of Pityana, who also says that "black consciousness is black theology . . . and [black consciousness] implies the awareness by black people of the power they wield as a group economically and politically."[16] Even clearer is Simon

Maimela, who believes that black theology must stress that black people are meant to be free—spiritually and politically—and that black theology must keep this thought alive in the hearts of those who are engaged in the struggle for liberation. This liberation is God's concrete situational work for blacks. Whatever is demanded by the struggle is just, for it is a means through which God effects liberation. Blacks may join the struggle without any reservation knowing they are doing the will of God: liberating God's people.

Black consciousness is the human responsibility—given to people by God—to affirm themselves (Gen. 1:28) and to make decisions about their future. Blacks shall not be oppressed as a people but shall rule the earth: This is what black theology should bring home to black people.

What is of concern to blacks, then, is not so much a hunger to hear more and more about God and his being but to find out what God has to say about their suffering and oppression. They would like to know what he is doing and what significance he has for their own struggle on behalf of black solidarity and power.[17]

Directly the opposite seems the dictum of Manas Buthelezi, who outrightly rejects an interpretation that links black theology to black power. He regards this an "indiscriminate alignment of Christian black awareness with an emotionally charged political concept."

To interpret the quest for a black theology purely in terms of the awakening of black nationalism or the consolidation of black power forces us to trifle with one of the most fundamental issues in modern Christianity.[18]

Ernest Baartmann, another South African, has this to say:

Black consciousness is not absolutely synonymous with black power. In my opinion, black power includes the use of force. . . . One must begin with what gives the black person inner power: the love of God and the power that the gift of this love itself is; love for myself, which enables me to love my neighbor.[19]

This does not mean, however, that blacks will not use violence under any circumstances. Black consciousness is a search for power for blacks, but, Baartmann concludes, the real power is the power of love. Let us look at these statements more closely.

In the same year that Buthelezi made his dictum, he held a series of lectures at the University of Heidelberg. Here he argued that as people are created in the image of God, they have received a "delegated authority" over creation. They have a "special status" which goes along with the wielding of power. In contrast to this, Buthelezi continues, the blacks' experience of life is that of powerlessness. He argues that the power God has given people is essential to humanness. Being denied the sharing of power, therefore, means to be brought down to the level of subhumanity. "Any discussion about the humanization of life which excludes the dynamics of power is a fruitless theoretical exercise," Buthelezi says. In this sense, he goes on to speak of the black person's humanity as a "colonized humanity." To be truly human is to have some form of power, to have "dominion" over one's created self; otherwise the created self becomes a caricature. To destroy the caricature and search for true and authentic humanity is human liberation. "How," Buthelezi asks, "can I have the power to be, that is, dominion over my black self?"

How must we understand this in the light of what we cited above? It is my contention that Buthelezi cannot be "used against" the concept of power, as we have seen. He not only speaks of power, but of power within a theological context. I understand black power as the "power to be " (Tillich)—the courage to affirm, in spite of everything else, one's human dignity. I agree completely with Buthelezi that power is essential to humanity. Primarily, black power is the inner reality of the affirmation of one's blackness, which is one's true humanity. Seen thus, black power can be described as the power of truth, the truth that unveils the real self as a person with dignity and responsibility, created by God to share with God the power of dominion over creation, including dominion over the "created black self." Once this is discovered, the basis for new relationships is created. The certainty of one's infinite worth before God gives one the courage to be, to affirm oneself. To have power is to be able to live according to God's plan, in accordance with one's God-given humanity. This also means that blacks must be able to realize this responsibility in the social-historical world. Human responsibility presupposes freedom which, as Cicero has already observed, is power shared. Black power is thus the ability to be, resulting in the freedom to create the possibilities for the realization of full humanity.[20]

If Buthelezi intends his stance as a warning that black power must not be equated with violence as such (as held for example, by James Cone and Joseph Washington), he is doubtlessly correct. It is, however, not possible for him to foster a theological argumentation like that in his Heidelberg lectures and still reject black power as he did.

Baartmann is no less interesting. Let us begin by establishing that he does indeed speak about power. Again, we must conclude that the understanding of black power as purely a force of violence and destruction, or as the black counterpart of the white nationalism which has left such terrible scars in the history of the world, is also Baartmann's difficulty. But Baartmann must take black power seriously. What is the difference between "power for blacks" (that black consciousness strives for) and "black power"? Interesting also is his statement that the power of love must convince whites to share power with blacks.[21] What kind of power can whites in South Africa share with blacks if not economic and political power; is this not what blacks want as *black* power? Furthermore, what form will the "power of love" take in the South African situation? Baartmann has already answered these questions. We can now safely conclude that black theologians, when they speak about authentic power, cannot but speak of black power and its alignment with black theology. Black theology, in its concern for true humanity, is shattering the myth that black power is evil *because* it is black. Black power is the legitimate expression of our humanness; it is black people at last resuming their responsibility as whole human beings.

Finally, one of the most important aspects of black theology in South Africa is its continuous dialogue with African theology, not as two separate theologies, but as two aspects of the same theology, two dimensions of the same existential and theological experience. Buthelezi's dealing with white theologians' views on African theology, his critique of their "ethnographical approach" over against his "anthropological approach," is therefore invaluable.[22] Buthelezi offers an indigenous theology that is essentially different from the traditional "white African theology"; it is a contextual theology that opens perspectives for authentic black theological thinking. In Buthelezi's terms: Black theology is indeed indigenous; it presupposes a freedom of thought and participation in the wholeness of life; it is a "theology of restlessness," committed to ultimate liberation.[23]

TOWARD AN ETHIC OF LIBERATION

As complementary to Buthelezi's "Toward an Indigenous Theology" let me endeavor to propose some perspectives toward an ethic of liberation for black theology.

A Situational Ethic

Black theology is a situational (contextual) theology, the situation being that of our blackness. We have warned earlier on that an authentic situational theology remains critical and prophetic as regards the situational experience, because it is critical reflection on the liberation praxis *under the Word of God*. This means that all reflection and all action is finally judged in the light of the liberating gospel of Jesus Christ. As a theology of liberation it is not merely "God-talk," not merely theoretical reasoning, a *logos* about the *Theos*. It proclaims the Word which has always been a liberating deed; it is joining the liberating activity of Yahweh who has revealed himself in Jesus the Messiah. Thus theology becomes a liberating activity with an openness to the world and to the future; it becomes a prophetic word, but also a prophetic manifestation of the Word. As critical reflection under the Word of God it is "subversive with regard to ideologies which rationalize and justify a given social and ecclesiastical order, . . . preserving the [Christian community] from fetishism and idolatry, as well as from a pernicious and belittling narcissism."[24] Liberation theology is the fruit of a believing community sharing and experiencing history with God.

The danger that such a theology succumb to absolutistic claims is very real. In this respect James Cone's theology is particularly vulnerable. Cone claims God *solely* for the black experience.[25] I submit that to make black as such the symbol for oppression in the world is to absolutize one's own situation. Black theology, says C. Eric Lincoln in a critique on Cone,

is bound to the situation in this sense, that God's confrontation with white racism is but *one* aspect of God's action in a multi-dimensional complex of interaction between man and man, and God and man.[26]

Cone's mistake is that he has taken black theology out of the framework of liberation theology, thereby making his own situation (being black in America) and his own movement (liberation from white racism) the ultimate criterion for *all* theology. By doing this Cone makes of a contextual theology a regional theology, which is not the same thing at all. Cone is right in claiming that the *only* Christian expression of theology in the United States (and also in South Africa) is black theology, inasmuch as the gospel is a gospel of liberation and theology therefore is a theology of liberation—in our case *black liberation* to begin with. But in making this the criterion for all liberation theology, is Cone not wide open for an ideological takeover? Moreover, if black is simply determinative for oppression and liberation everywhere, if the only legitimate expression for liberation has to be black, does not Cone close the door to other theological expressions of liberation? Can the Latin American theologian concede that the *only* way to recognize God working in history is through the "most radical deeds of black power"? Can, for instance, the American Indian liberation theology (God is Red!) share in this absolute claim for blackness?

Black theology is a theology of liberation in the situation of blackness. For blacks, it is the only legitimate way of theologizing, *but only within the framework of the theology of liberation.* Black theology therefore finds itself in intention and method not only alongside African theology but also alongside the Latin American theology of liberation, and it is in this expression of Christian theology that western theology will ultimately find its salvation.

We have already alluded to the fact that black theology speaks of "total liberation" in the same way that Buthelezi speaks of the "wholeness of life." It focuses on the dependency of the oppressed and their liberation from this dependency on several levels: psychological, cultural, political, economic, and theological. It follows that the ethic of this theology is an ethic of liberation. Its character is situational, social, and eschatological. It does not, however, arise *out of* the situation, but *in* the situation. The situation is never an entity in itself that autonomously determines the ethic of liberation; it has a history and the results of the action within a given situation will have some bearing on the future.

Jan Milic Lochman names the primary concerns of a Christian

social ethic: Objectively, the aim is to change inhuman conditions; subjectively, it is solidarity with the oppressed.[27] We would like to change the sequence and add another dimension: The first objective of a social ethic must be the identification of inhuman conditions, which has to do with the (re-) education of the people and the discovery of one's own negative involvement leading to positive engagement; the second objective must be solidarity with the oppressed; the third must be the changing of oppressive and inhuman structures.

Black theology knows that the biblical message of God's liberation has historical as well as eschatological dimensions. It does not only rest upon the historical event of the exodus, but it also points to the future: the future of God which is the future of his people. This eschatological dimension must not lead to a theological paralysis, as has so often been the case with western theology—a waiting-patiently-upon-the-Lord kind of attitude—nor must it lead to a theological escapism, which for so long has been a favorite way out for blacks. Black theology realizes that New Testament eschatology is a call to arms, a summons not to be content with the existing situation of oppression, but to take sides with the oppressed and the poor and subsequently for the new humanity and the new world (Rom. 6:4; 12:2). Black theology agrees fully with Rasker on this point: "In other words, an eschatologically oriented ethics will cease to be an ethics of rules and regulations and will tend to become an ethics of change and transformations."[28]

Love, Justice, and Liberation

Following the direction pointed out to us by Martin Luther King, Jr., black theology takes Christian love very seriously, opting for agape, which stands at the very center of God's liberating actions for his people. For this very reason we despise any attempt to make of Christian love an ineffective sentimentality. We contend with King and James Cone that it is impossible to speak of love without speaking of justice, righteousness, and power. In speaking of righteousness we do not mean the forensic, metaphysical righteousness in the Pauline sense of the word, but the kingly justice and righteousness whereof Jesus speaks. When Jesus speaks of the "poor" or the "poor in spirit" and of righteousness that shall be given them, he speaks of those who represent the socially oppressed, those who suffer from the power of injustice and are harrassed by those who consider only their own advantage and influence. As regards the term "righteousness," Ridderbos has conclusively shown that Jesus meant the kingly righteousness in the sense of the Old Testament. He says:

The poor . . . look forward to God's redemption of his people from the power of oppression and injustice. . . . And it is this longing for liberation that is called "hunger and thirst after righteousness," in the beatitudes of Matthew. . . . It must not be understood in the Pauline sense of imputed forensic righteousness, but as the kingly justice that will be brought to light one day for the salvation of the oppressed and the outcasts. . . . It is to *this* justice that the "poor" and the "meek" look forward in the Sermon on the Mount.[29]

Speaking of God's love without God's righteousness thus betrays an oppression-mindedness that black theology cannot tolerate. Cone is correct when he asserts that righteousness is that side of God's love that expresses itself through black liberation. We cannot accept, however, Cone's contention that "to love is to make a decision against white people."[30] We accept rather King's line of argument, which discriminates between hate for an unjust system and hate for the perpetrators of that system—which is to say that white people are the enemy as long as they are the oppressors. In reading Cone, one cannot help but feel that Zulu was right to warn against the danger of equating God's love with our own human expression of love and against the simple identification of "God being on the side of the oppressed with the oppressed being on the side of God."

Liberation theology reclaims the Christian heritage and reinterprets the gospel to place it within its authentic perspective, namely, liberation. In so doing, it questions the historical role of the Christian church, the alliances of the church with the "powers that be," and insists on a true church, i.e., a church that takes the liberating gospel seriously. In other words, as Cone says: One cannot speak of a Christian church and a segregated church at the same time. Liberation theology seeks a church that ministers to the poor, not merely with a sense of compassion but with a sense of justice. This means that the church ought to discover that the state of poverty and oppression is ugly, bad, and unnecessary; that the condition is not metaphysical but structural, a coin of which the other side is affluence and wealth; that poor, oppressed people are not merely loose individuals but a class. A theology and an ethic thus engaged accepts theology not merely in terms of what it says but in terms of what it does (for the oppressed). It presses for active engagement of the church in socio-political affairs in its search for the truth that shall make us free. This truth is not a description of reality but an involvement in reality, just as faith is active engagement in obedience to God, "the action of love within history" (Hugo Assmann). The ethic of black theology, so we have seen, is an ethic of liberation. As such it is an ethic of change and not merely an ethic of survival. Challenging the external as well as the internal dependency of oppressed people, the change it calls for is qualitative.

It is our contention that black theologians have not yet taken this aspect seriously. J. Deotis Roberts's goal for blacks is to share in "the good life"; Major J. Jones and Joseph R. Washington want "equality," Jones through "rapid change," Washington through "revolution"—violent or nonviolent.

Fundamental to this, it seems to us, is the reasoning that racism is the *only* demon. While absolutely not minimizing racism (who, coming from South Africa, can?), we must ask: Is this indeed the only issue? It seems to us that there is a far deeper malady in the United States and South African societies that manifests itself in the form of racism. Was the deepest motivation of the Portuguese in Southern Africa racism? Or of the United States and the multinationals in Latin America? In this, black theologians fail to see what Malcolm X and Martin Luther King have already pointed out: the relation between racism and capitalism. Let us for the moment focus on Cone:

We will not let whitey cool this one with his pious love-ethic but will seek to enhance our hostility, bringing it to its full manifestation. Black survival is at stake here, and we black people must define and assert the conditions. . . . [31]

This may sound fine, but what does Cone have in mind? We contend that it is not enough only to speak of survival, which in a deep sense seems to suggest a certain hopelessness—just "making it," just "getting by." Black theology is a theology of survival, says Cone; we suggest it should be more than that. Cone knows that all is not well—not even when blacks have economic and intellectual power.[32] His answer to this problem is "revolution."

In black-white terms, Cone's revolution means a refusal to accept white definitions, white values, white limitations. This forms the process of liberation for blacks, "by any means necessary." If this liberation is, as Cone says, not only *from*, but also liberation *to*, what end has he in mind? We get a clue when he admits that "reconciliation is only possible between equals." Equality is what Cone wants, but he lacks, it seems to us, a sound social critique, an *Ideologiekritik*, and hence he lacks the sensitivity to define precisely and constructively this "equality." In the same issue of *Evangelische Theologie*, Frederick Herzog puts this cogent question to Cone: "What is the meaning of 'equality' in this society?"[33] Indeed, that is the ultimate question. Reconciliation requires a new image of humanity, and that new humanity requires new structures in society. New wine in new skins! How new are the black people who move out of their old lives of poverty and dejection into the unchanged structures of an oppressive and exploitative system? In defining and analyzing the black situation Cone is doubtlessly brilliant. But if he cannot go beyond that, his analysis will become nothing more than an emotional catharsis for blacks and a spiritual masochistic experience for whites—nothing new in our traditional relationship.

Herzog asks something else of Cone: Can Cone guarantee that his theology will not become a justification for a black bourgeoisie, indeed, servant to it; and can black theology offer an alternative for the present U.S. system, i.e., can black theology prepare the way for a U.S. socialism?[34]

When Cone endeavors to answer Herzog, he does not answer him at all. The question remains: not whether blacks want to be equal to whites, but whether we want to be equals in *this particular* society. To our mind that would mean becoming equals, partners in exploitation and destruction. Surely we must see that "getting into" the main-stream of U.S. society would not solve the problem at all. U.S. exploitation and oppression do not begin and end with black people only! The dependency of black people would not be broken. In the final analysis the liberation from dependency for black theology *must* mean a totally new social order. Black theologians should not be discouraged by those who deem this "utopian," for all through black history, black people have lived through their strong belief in that "land beyond Jordan," in that reality which is there, beyond the whip and the slavemaster, beyond the poverty and the humiliation, leaving black children a legacy of hope. In the words of Rubem Alves:

This "utopianism" is not a belief in the possibility of a perfect society, but rather a belief in the non-necessity of this imperfect order. Christian utopianism is based on the vision that all social systems are under God's historical judgment.[35]

In breaking away from the old, oppressive structures of our society, seeking new possibilities, creating room for the realization of our God-given authenticity, black theology seeks the true purpose of life for blacks as well as whites. We want to share our dreams and hopes for a new future with whites, a future where it must not be necessary to make a Christian theology an ideology or a part of a cultural imperialism. Black theology, by offering a new way of theologizing, desires to be helpful in discovering the truth about black and white people, about our past and present, about God's will for us in our common world.

Black theology believes that it is possible to recapture what was sacred in the African community long before white people came: solidarity, respect for life and for humanity, community. This will surely not be easy and we have a long way to go. True community lies beyond much struggle and despair, beyond the reconciliation that will not come to us without conflict. It will come only through faith and courage. For us, this is the courage to be black. But again, this is no otherworldly dream; it is as real as Africa itself. *Motho ke motho ka batho ba bang* is an age-old Sotho proverb, the equivalent of which can be found in almost all African languages: One is only human because of others, with others, for others. This is what we mean. It is authentic, it is worthwhile, it is in the most profound sense of the word gospel truth.

NOTES

1. See G. Gutierrez, *A Theology of Liberation*, Eng. trans. (Maryknoll, New York: Orbis Books, 1973), chap. 13. Both Gutierrez and Buthelezi see poverty as bound up with a material situation that causes alienation and makes a truly human lifestyle impossible. Buthelezi says that because of it blacks "are not able to receive the gifts of God."

2. M. Motlhabi, ed., *Essays on Black Theology* (Johannesburg: University Christian Movement, 1972), p. 3; reprinted in B. Moore, ed., *Black Theology: The South African Voice* (London: Hurst, 1973).

3. This apocryphal account of its origin was zealously repeated and diffused by whites in South Africa. See the *Nederduits Gereformeerde Teologiese Tydskrif*, no. 4, 1972; also the now infamous Le Grange Commission Report on the Christian Institute and the University Christian Movement, which makes this the official view of the South African government.

4. G. Wilmore, *Black Religion and Black Radicalism* (Garden City, New York: Doubleday, 1972), p. 5.

5. Ibid., p. 14.

6. In P.S. Foner, *Selections from the Writings of Frederick Douglass* (New York, 1964), p. 55. Frederick Douglass (1817–95) escaped from slavery in 1838, became a vigorous advocate of the abolitionist movement, and served in a variety of posts and enterprises. For seventeen years he was the editor of the *North Star*, which he founded.

7. Isaiah Shembe (1870–1935) was the founder of a strong Independent African church. Around 1937 his son's preaching was heard by Sundkler. See B.G.M. Sundkler, *Bantu Prophets in South Africa* (London: Oxford University Press, 1962).

8. Henry McNeal Turner (1834–1915) was bishop of the African Methodist Episcopal church in the United States. His famous remark is part of his discourse to the state legislature of which he was a member when it decided to exclude black members. Turner went on to say that the heathens in Africa believe that they are created in the image of God. See James Cone, *Black Theology and Black Power* (New York: Seabury Press, 1969).

9. Theodore Dwight Weld (1803–95) was a famous U.S. abolitionist. His speeches and writings helped to stimulate Harriet Beecher Stowe to write *Uncle Tom's Cabin*.

10. Adam Small in Motlhabi, ed., *Essays on Black Theology;* see also Moore, ed., *Black Theology: The South African Voice*.

11. Ibid.

12. See Gutierrez, *A Theology of Liberation*.

13. See Moore, ed., *Black Theology: The South African Voice*, pp. 78–79.

14. See Motlhabi, ed., *Essays on Black Theology;* also Moore, ed. *Black Theology: The South African Voice*.

15. A. Zulu, "Whither Black Theology?" in *Pro Veritate* 11 (March 1973), pp. 11–13.

16. Pityana in Motlhabi, ed., *Essays on Black Theology*, p. 39; also in Moore, ed., *Black Theology: The South African Voice*.

17. See Maimela in T. Sundermeier, ed., *Christus, der schwarze Befreier*, Essays on Black Consciousness and Black Theology in South Africa (Erlangen: Verlag der Evangelisch-Lutherischen Mission, 1973), pp. 109, 119.

18. Buthelezi in Motlhabi, ed., *Essays on Black Theology*, p. 3; also in Moore, ed., *Black Theology: The South African Voice.*

19. Baartmann in Sundermeier, ed., *Christus, der schwarze Befreier*, p. 88.

20. The whole problem of power, black theology, and black power is discussed in detail in Boesak, *Farewell to Innocence: A Socio-Ethical Study on Black Theology and Black Power* (Maryknoll, New York: Orbis Books, 1977).

21. Baartmann in Sundermeier, ed., *Christus*, p. 88.

22. U.S. blacks do not talk in terms of these two viewpoints. But they, too, accuse whites of not respecting blacks as *persons* with a right *to be* in U.S. society: Blacks have been the subjects of study. Most reports on blacks have not managed to really grasp their situations as human beings.

23. See Buthelezi's article in this volume.

24. See Gutierrez, *A Theology of Liberation*, p. 12.

25. James Cone, *A Black Theology of Liberation* (Philadelphia: Lippincott, 1970), pp. 23, 76.

26. See J. Cone, "Schwarze Theologie im Blick auf Revolution, Gewaltanwendung und Versöhnung," in *Evangelische Theologie*, 34 (January 1974), pp. 4–16; 80–95. C. Eric Lincoln's comments and criticisms are in the same issue.

27. See J.M. Lochmann, "The Just Revolution," in *Christianity and Crisis*, July 10, 1972.

28. A.J. Rasker, "Theologie und Revolution," in *Evangelische Zeitsimmen* (Hamburg, 1969), p. 11. See also his contribution to the Eighth Ecumenical Gathering on Pentecost held by the Arnoldsha n Evangelical Academy: "Theologische Erwagungen zur Revolution," in *Entwicklungspolitik und Gesellschaftsordnung*, vol. 88 in the series published by the Evangelical Academies of Hessen and Nassau (Frankfurt: Verlag Evangelischer Presseverband, 1970), pp. 8–29, especially pp. 16f.

29. H.N. Ridderbos, *De Komst van het Koninkrijk* (Kampen: Kok, 1972), p. 171; emphasis added.

30. Cone, *A Black Theology of Liberation*, p. 138.

31. Ibid., p. 37.

32. Ibid., p. 41.

33. *Evangelische Theologie*, January 1974, p. 78.

34. Ibid.

35. R. Alves "Christian Realism, Ideology of the Establishment," in *Christianity and Crisis*, September 17, 1973.

ASIA

9

The Context of Theology

Orlando P. Carvajal (Philippines)

POSING THE PROBLEM

In this paper, we shall define theology very simply as an understanding of our belief in God and its bearing on our contemporary life-experience. Defined in this manner, we take theology out of the exclusive domain of the professional theologian. And rightly so. For, one way or the other, we all engage in theological reflection. We all possess a theology. In some, this is conscious, systematic, and explicit. In most others, it is unconscious, spontaneous, and implicit. Throughout most of the paper we will be dealing with theology as implied in our lifestyle.

As Christians who are alive within a specifically Filipino social reality and who participate in a specifically Filipino experience, we integrate our theistic belief with contemporary social reality through three different systems of theological thought. The first uses God and religion as a tool for the perpetuation of the law and order of what is believed to be a divinely willed social reality. The second invokes God and religion to effectively and qualitatively change the present social reality, which is seen to be not divinely willed but the fruit of a historically conditioned system of oppression. In between, a third defends a position of neutrality vis-à-vis the social reality, which is considered to have nothing to do with religion.

Curiously, all three faith-life stances are claimed by their respective proponents to stem from sound Christian theology. The political, economic, and cultural values of each of the above patterns are all equally claimed to be genuine Christian values. The simple and incontrovertible fact, however, is that they are antagonistically contradictory modes of relating theistic belief with contemporary Filipino experience.

What explains the difference? Where lies the root of such a contradiction? The core object of theological reflection is constant, i.e., belief in God and its relation to one's subjective experience. All three systems ask the same theological question: What is the relevance of my belief in God to all aspects of life on earth? Nevertheless, the same question is approached differently. We are all supposedly Christian, but we in fact come up with antagonistically contradicting answers.

A preliminary hypothesis is to put the blame on a possibly wrong assumption. Because we call ourselves Christians, we presume that we are using the categories of a Christian theology in our analysis of reality. Because we think we are Christian, we take it for granted that we look at life through a Christian theological microscope and integrate life's experience through one and the same set of Christian thought patterns. If that were the case, then we should have arrived at the same answer to one and the same question which we passed through one and the same Christian filter. The fact that we do not arrive at the same answer but find ourselves defending contradictory positions can only mean that it is not primarily our Christianity that determines how we look at things. Our contradicting position can only mean that it is not a uniform set of Christian categories that we use to integrate our belief in God with our contemporary experience. Our heretofore unquestioned assumption is therefore wrong. Some other prior category determines our total reality outlook, including our supposedly Christian posture vis-à-vis our belief in God. This category is different for different groups of people. Hence, the different answers.

The burden of this paper is to show that the variable determinant factor is the historical condition of our material life, in the context of which we pose our theological questions. Different material-historical conditions give rise to different worldviews, which become the framework for theological reflection thus significantly determining the method and content of this reflection. Christian theology is only one aspect of a prior and more fundamental worldview that is materially and historically determined. Instead, therefore, of Christian theology determining our worldview, the opposite is true. Our materially based worldviews determine our theology. We differ in worldview because we labor under different material-historical conditions. This is at the root of our radically contrasting modes of integrating belief in God with our total social reality.

THE THREE WORLDVIEWS

The quality of human consciousness is generally of three different types, marked off from each other by the predominance of a particular worldview within the framework of which people integrate their subjective experience into meaningful patterns. We are able to distinguish three distinct worldviews, which we shall call the monistic, the dualistic, and the dynamic. Each of these grows out of the material conditions of different types of social systems. The monistic grows out of the material conditions of primitive-communal, slave, and clannic societies. The dualistic has its roots in the material conditions of feudal and capitalist societies. The dynamic is slowly gaining ground with the decline of world capitalism and the corresponding advance of socialism. This is true for all of humankind in general. For individuals, however, the three worldviews do not simply correspond to historical types of societies, but are found in individuals as three aspects of their total outlook on contemporary reality. Except for a few of us who are able consistently to integrate our historical experience within the exclusive framework of one worldview, most of us can be said to belong to a particular worldview only in the sense that one is more predominant than the others in our total approach to reality. This is especially true for us Filipinos because of the fundamentally semi-feudal and semi-colonial character of the conditions of our social life.

The Monistic Worldview

The monistic worldview is characteristic of a primitive-communal society. It has its roots in the primitive conditions of material life, a situation that is determined by the primitive character of the productive forces of society. Tools for survival, the material instruments to control the forces of nature are so rudimentary, so inadequate to make the individual self-reliant, that the possibility of an individualist approach to life is precluded. Consequently, everything is owned communally. Communal property ownership as an economic structure is born from the material-historical exigency of very primitive productive forces.

Communal ownership, however, only helps people to mitigate the rigors of primitive existence, in short, to survive. The primitive productive forces that give rise to the necessity of communal ownership do not afford people the scientific knowledge to explain nor the technical skill to master the forces of nature. They are still in near total ignorance and helplessness vis-à-vis the forces of nature, an ignorance and helplessness that are equally shared by all. Something still is needed to explain nature and place it within people's power to control.

Thus, belief in deities comes to the fore of primitive people's consciousness. The existence of supernatural beings endowed with superhuman powers is posited; and primitive people begin to have a deity for just about anything that is beyond their primitive condition to explain and control. Negative phenomena like a typhoon or defeat in war or disease are blamed on the displeasure and anger of the deities. Positive phenomena, on the other hand, signify their pleasure. Primitive religion is a simple matter of pleasing the deities or appeasing their anger once provoked; and the fundamental religious activities are the observance of tribal taboos to please the deities and the performance of ritual offerings to appease them.

An integrated system of looking at reality starts to evolve out of and around the materially caused and historically conditioned primitive consciousness of the existence of deities. According to this system, the universe is a single house with two stories. Hence, the word monistic, from the Greek word *monos*, meaning "one," to describe this worldview. Earth, the lower story, is occupied by mortals. The heavens above, the second story, are the realm of the immortal gods.

These control the world and its people with their superhuman powers. Human beings, therefore, relate to them in fear and awe of their mysterious powers. The mortals below can only see themselves as the helpless objects of the deities' pleasure or displeasure. They, therefore, relate to themselves accordingly, almost as playthings of the gods, completely at the latter's mercy. Nature is also looked on with fear, for it is through nature that the deities unleash their awesome powers. Since the mortals are equally poor, ignorant, and helpless, disasters and calamities seldom attain less than community-wide proportions. Consequently, a strong community responsibility develops toward the observance of taboos and the performance of rituals. One person's breaking of a taboo can bring disaster on the whole tribe, and so any infraction is severely dealt with by the community.

Everything, finally, is seen as unchanging. People can never tell how the gods would react if they changed things. Besides, primitive people go through their brief lives without seeing any marked change in their environment. This one world is made static and stable by the gods. Human beings dare not tamper with it for fear of incurring their divine ire.

The Dualistic Worldview

History moves on and people's tools for production improve. Metal tools take the place of the crude stone tools of a preceding age. Animals are domesticated and pasturage frees people from the wretchedness of hunters. Tillage and handicrafts also appear on the scene. These different types of productive activity brought about by better tools and a slightly improved understanding of nature's forces result in a division of labor and the free exchange of their varied fruits. In the process of this free exchange a few accumulate more wealth than others and soon after gain the corresponding power to own not only things but also people. These are the slaves, people who are left behind with nothing in the scramble for possession of the improved instruments of production. Private ownership replaces the communal system. The common and free labor of all the members of a tribe gives way to the labor of slaves. The human community is now divided into two classes of people, the masters and the slaves.

Another type of society comes about when further refinements in the tools of production require that workers become owners of a share of the fruits of their labor in order that they have some initiative and take more productive interest in their work. Because of this material exigency it is inevitable that the slaves succeed in their struggle for freedom. They become serfs and enjoy a material condition that is better, if only slightly, than what the preceding slave system afforded them. Now they are able to own a few things and to enjoy a few basic freedoms. Their new masters, the feudal lords, no longer own them, at least not absolutely as in the slave system. Still, although not as helpless as the slaves who don't even own their own lives, the serfs remain poor and ignorant because they don't own the basic means of production, i.e., land, but only a small share of its fruits. Land and the bigger share of its fruits belong exclusively to the feudal lord. The division of the human community into two classes continues to be the determinant fact of social life.

The contradictions inherent in such a dualist society are incarnated in a struggle between the serfs and feudal lords that ends in the liberation of the serfs from the bonds of serfdom. They gain access to the means of production and a historical stage of capitalist appropriation begins. The profit incentives of private ownership push forward the growth of the productive forces. The machine is born which, above all, is an instrument to reduce the cost of production and augment the surplus value of labor for the benefit of the owner. Thus a new class emerges—the industrial bourgeoisie—and the outlines of a new system—capitalism—start to be etched out. In the individualistic and free scramble for capitalist appropriation, many are left behind to become the hired workers to operate the new instruments of production. They own only their labor, which they sell for a price (wages) to the capitalist. The class of the proletariat comes into being. Society remains divided and classist in the new capitalist social system.

The slave, the feudal, and the capitalist types of societies are all distinguished by one common social reality; the division of the human community into two classes of people, slave and master in the first, serf and lord of the manor in the second, worker and employer in the third. They are all dualistic societies. The dualistic worldview evolves out of the conditions of material life of this divided community. Unlike the monistic worldview, which is shared by all in a primitive-communal society, the dualistic worldview is fundamentally a class outlook. It grows within the framework of the material conditions of the owning class and takes on the nature of a philosophical and theological justification of their privileged position in a dualist society. Since the slave, the serf, and the industrial worker are doomed to continued poverty and relative ignorance by the three socio-economic systems, they either continue to hang on to their monistic worldview (this is logical considering that the material basis for this worldview remains in their life as a class) or accept the dualistic worldview that is imposed on them by the systems through the schools, the churches, and the other superstructures of a dualist society.

With the leisurely pace of life afforded them by their ownership of the instruments of production, the owning class is now in a position to progress culturally. Unlike the non-owners, who were tied down to the business of survival through hard labor, they have time to indulge in the luxury of intellectual speculation. In Ancient Greece this was the mark of the free man. In the Middle Ages, philosophy and the arts flourished within the castles of kings and bishops (who were feudal lords in their own right). And in our industrialized society, philosophy, the arts, culture remain a luxury of the rich. Hence, even theological reflection remains the luxury of professional clerics who do not have to soil their hands to earn a living. For it must be borne in mind as a matter of historical fact that in the division of society into classes the institutional church stands cn the side of the owning class.

What follows is a general outline of the dualistic philosophico-theological justification of the conditions of material life.

The material order's visible essential characteristic is its being finite. Whatever exists within the realm of matter has an end; it is limited. The world of finite material existence, therefore, cannot explain itself. Its existence can be explained only by positing another world, the realm of essence, which is unchanging. Ideal essence is the unchanging substance of things. Material existence is only an accident. And in the other world of unchanging essences one being not only has no beginning but has no end either, because its essence is its own existence. It is its own explanation, a being-by-itself. This is the prime mover, which causes the existence of both the unchanging essences and the material accidents of reality. In short then there are two worlds. Over and above the order of material existence is the order of ideal essence, which is the realm of ultimate reality, of meaning, of values. The material order has no reality, no meaning, no value apart from the world of essence. Plato's allegory of the cave describes this world as a world of shadows. The world of ideas, of essence, of being is the real world. The term "idealist metaphysics" is applied to this worldview, because it puts the order of reality not in the sensible, the material, the physical order but in the ideal, the spiritual, the metaphysical order. It is also sometimes referred to as the classical worldview or the two-planes theory.

If reality is fundamentally static and dualistic then the present social order is only an expression of that unchanging dualistic nature of things. Everything in fact, is a duality. Total reality is a duality of essence and existence, of the ideal (which alone is truly real) and physical (which is only a shadow), of the spiritual and material, of the infinite and finite. Society is a duality of the upper, ruling, owning class and the lower, ruled, non-owning class. Human beings are a duality of the body and soul. They belong to a duality of societies: the church for their souls, the state for their bodies. And this is an eternally decreed cosmic order.

Theology, strictly so called, is a product of slave, feudal, and capitalist societies. (What we had in the primitive-communal society is more properly termed theosophy.) Hence it understandably develops along dualist lines. What is claimed as Christian theology in reality has its basis in the conditions of material life of those societies. Christian theology does not determine how the social order is to be set up. On the contrary, the dualist setup of things determines theology and makes it dualist in outlook. It is Christian only in the sense that it is propounded by people who call themselves Christians. God might have made people in his own image at the start. But at a stage in history, people certainly make God in their own image. Christian theology simply applies categories in the attempt to understand faith and relate it to life.

Thus the God of theology is nothing much more than the prime mover, the being-by-itself of philosophy; and the heaven of theology, God's abode, is nothing more than philosophy's world of essence. Because individualism (later euphemistically called "free enterprise") is the rule of a bi-classist society, salvation becomes a private, indi-

vidual affair in the worst sense of the term. If the human body is
material, then it is worthless and meaningless. It can only be the
source of evil. Only the soul, which belongs to the spiritual world,
has value. It is the source of good in people. Hence the object of
salvation is the soul. The church, therefore, as the society entrusted
with human salvation, can only be responsible for the soul. It is not to
meddle in politics and economics because these are considered secular, material, and have relevance only to the body. Besides, if everything is only an expression of the unchanging essence or nature of
things, then such phenomena as the division of society into rich and
poor become in theological terms an expression of God's will. The
church has to respect this order of things and can only preach resignation to God's will. If people belong to the owning, ruling class, they
bless God for having willed their privileged position. In fact, in one
Christian sect, Calvinism, wealth is even considered a mark of the
saved, a sign of God's pleasure. But those who happen to be poor are
asked to be resigned, for there is another world of real eternal life,
without poverty. Thus religion becomes an opiate for the harsh
realities of a dualist society.

The material, the physical, is consequently despised as worthless
and as an obstacle to the growth of the spiritual. Salvation is described
as the process of an individual's going from this worthless world of
matter to the real world of the spirits. The more detached people are
from the secular, the closer they get to heaven, which, it must be
remembered, theology identifies with the eternal world of essence
dominated by God, the prime mover of philosophy. A system of
morality prevails that centers around the renunciation of the world, of
all worldly or profane activities.

With dualist theology, religion exerts a mystifying and alienating
influence. People are alienated both from themselves and from their
world. They give up all responsibility for what happens to them and
to the world and become safely captive of their passive resignation to
God's will. They cannot change the eternally decreed cosmic order of
things; they can only observe it. With such an attitude dominating
especially the lower classes, the bi-classist social order becomes secure
from any threat of change. Religion becomes a convenient tool for the
legitimation and the perpetuation of what in reality is a materially
based social order.

In fact, religions of salvation antedate Christianity. But these always grow in cities, i.e., in societies that are characterized by a certain accumulation of wealth and by a strongly individualist spirit. This phenomenon further confirms the contention above about the influence of social conditions on theology.

The Dynamic Worldview

Cutthroat competition in a capitalist economy forces owners of the means of production to put much financial emphasis on technological research. The consequent advanced technology produces highly sophisticated machines and/or systems of production that turn out a rapidly changing variety of consumer goods at an ever increasing volume and at relatively lower costs for big business. This stretches business's margin of profits and strengthens its stranglehold on monopoly capital. On the one hand these ultra-modern instruments of production are highly productive, thus affording more profits to the owners, and extremely expensive, thus being owned privately only by big monopoly capital. On the other hand, however, they are so complex that they require both a high degree of skill and education from the workers and a high degree of organization of their operations. Thus, whereas before one person or a few people with minimal education and skill operated simple machinery and made a product from start to finish, now a mass of well-educated workers with varying specialized skills operate different parts of extremely complex productive systems in a well-coordinated fashion and mass produce a commodity.

This situation heightens the contradiction between classes in post-modern capitalist society. The means of production are more securely owned but the social relations of production are increasingly more and more organized. Capital is concentrated in fewer individuals and more people become proletarians. (The use of modern machineries in agriculture has driven thousands of farm hands to seek jobs in urban industrial centers, swelling the ranks of the working class.) Above all, the new situation has created a new breed of workers. Although well educated and highly skilled, they remain proletarians since they still have to sell their labor at a price dictated by the owners and have no significant part in the decision-making of their respective productive communities. Although alienated from their labor, they are now mentally equipped to be aware of their alienation and its causes, to be aware of the contradictions of life in contemporary society. The dynamic worldview, therefore, registers for the most part in the consciousness of this group of people and in the consciousness of those who involve themselves in their lives.

The dynamic worldview grows from the conditions of material life that are rooted in the contradictions brought about by ultra-modern and sophisticated tools of production. It takes off basically from two contemporary phenomena, both of which modern technology is ultimately responsible for. The first is the increased concentration of wealth and power in the few individuals or groups (like multinational corporations) who alone can afford the price, and therefore benefit from the profits, of advanced technology; the proletarianization of more and more people is the consequence. The other phenomenon is the dizzying pace of contemporary living in general and yet the slowness of progress for the working class. The speed with which changes occur in post-modern life slowly erodes the foothold that the static worldview has in people's consciousness. Reality comes to be seen as in constant flux. Nothing is permanent except the abstraction of change itself. But if the average proletarians feel left out and helpless in the face of the many changes going on around them, they are nevertheless aware of the awesome influence and power of a few individuals on the quality and quantity of those changes. Hence, neither permanence nor change continues to be attributed to the irreversible will of a mysterious deity as in the first two worldviews. The conditions of life on earth begin to be slowly recognized as caused by historical material forces that are directly related to the will and power of the few who own and control the means of production. One, for instance, trembles at the admitted power of Exxon, the largest corporation in the United States, to influence the politics and economics of the countries where it operates.

People consequently shift the focus of their scrutiny from the ideal to the historical, from the other world to this world, from essence to existence, from God to human beings. They begin searching in earnest for the material historical roots of their economic deprivation and of their near-zero control over the concrete dynamics of change in post-modern living. Technological progress awakens them to the concrete possibility of becoming masters of creation. But they are stymied by a few masters controlling technology and hence life on earth for the many. Nevertheless, they also find hope in the knowledge, objective and scientific, that the present state of things is not an eternally decreed order, static and permanent, but the result of concrete historical material forces. They begin to be conscious of a world that is not a finished product but a seed that must be developed and brought to fruition by their own creative powers. Human beings are coming into their own.

In the church this initial insight into the dynamism of contemporary reality leads to, first, theology of the signs of the times, so called for its emphasis on the reading of events as a prerequisite to the reading of the gospel, its interpretation of traditional dogma, and its integration of faith with contemporary reality. Close on its heels is the theology of development, which sees salvation as human and the world's process of growth from being less to being more, with God as the dynamic beginning and end of the developmental process. Both theologies, arising from their existential confrontation with concrete realities, draw Christians closer into the hard-core economic, political, and cultural realities of life in the post-modern world. They read the signs of the times from the mainstream of social involvement in an effort to fulfil their responsibility of mastering the totality of life on earth. In the process, they get deeper into the power centers controlling people's lives. They run smack into the hard, thick, and high walls of oppressive social structures that systematically divide humankind into rich and poor, powerful and helpless, oppressor and oppressed. The liberation of the oppressed from these structures of domination comes to the fore as a prerequisite to development.

There can be no development without liberation. This explosive insight can be further investigated only by plunging deeply into liberating actions which, not from choice but from material exigency, are all political in nature. From the depths of this involvement in the struggle of the oppressed to liberate themselves from dominating structures are rising the clear outlines of a theology of liberation. Salvation is now the process of progressive liberation from oppressive structures that render the majority of people economically deprived, politically powerless, and culturally domesticated. Salvation becomes, moreover, total liberation, i.e., the liberation of the whole person, of all people, of all aspects of life, of total reality from all forces that lead to diminishment. God beccmes a liberator of the oppressed who intervenes in a people's history, as Exodus comes to typify. Political activity goes from taboo to extra-curricular activity to top priority action for Christians who want to live their faith and to take their responsibility to the world seriously. Christianity, which for a long time, as we have already seen, was used to justify the division of society into rich and poor, oppressor and oppressed, starts to regain its revolutionary character, questioning and changing the very structures that it helped to perpetuate and that it sees now as historically conditioned by material forces and events.

CHRISTIANS AND THEIR POSITION
IN SOCIETY: AN OVERVIEW

From the foregoing we see that the way Christians look at the world and relate to reality is not so much the expression of a strictly Christian outlook as the extension of a more fundamental worldview. In short, a specific system of theological thought is more the effect than the cause of the fundamental categories that Christians use to integrate their theistic belief with reality in a given historical moment. Many values, attitudes, orientations. and biases that are often presumed to be part of a distinctively Christian outlook simply stem from the conditions of material life of a particular social class in a dualist society. Christians, historically, first belong to a particular class with all its attending material conditions. This class position determines their basic outlook on reality. This class position forms the basic framework within which they interpret their faith and integrate it with reality. Thus, the dualist worldview of Christians belonging to the ruling class provides them with the categories to interpret religion, dogma, and the Bible in a manner that justifies the present social order and perpetuates their privileged position in that order. Since the institutional church is part of the propertied ruling class, it protects its vested interests against the challenge hurled at the system by Christians of the working class. All this is done in the name of upholding sound Christian doctrine. On the other hand, the dynamic outlook of Christians belonging to the working class is radicalizing their approach to Christianity, and not vice-versa.

10

Doing Theological Reflection in a Philippine Context

Carlos H. Abesamis, S.J. (Philippines)

THE MEANING OF THEOLOGY

I understand "doing theological reflection," quite generally, as the activity of reflecting on the contemporary human life-situation in the light of one's faith. Those who do theological reflection make an attempt to interpret the life-experience of their people or community today in the light of their Christian faith.

I take this way of doing theological reflection to be the most in keeping with the original spirit of our religion. For the main focus of our religion in its beginnings is a focus on life-experience and events in which our ancestors-in-religion discerned God's saving activity. We learn from certain of their basic religious statements (e.g., Deut. 26:5–9, Jos. 24:2–13, Deut. 6:21–23) that their religion was first and foremost concerned with the great saving deeds of Yahweh in their history as a human community. They proclaimed and confessed Yahweh's call and promise in the time of the Patriarchs, their deliverance from the oppression and slavery in Egypt, Yahweh's act to make them his people in the desert, Yahweh's activity in taking possession of a land broad and beautiful. And insofar as these saving deeds of Yahweh constituted a history of saving deeds, their religion and basic confession centered around the history of Yahweh's redemptive activity in their history as a human community. History—life-experience, events, history of events—is basic in the Mosaic religion.

Not only their basic credal statements but also their theology and theological reflection were quite naturally concerned mainly with events and history. The stuff of which much of their theology was made was the interpreted events and history of their life as a people, that is, God's redemptive activity and history with this people. We might recall as examples the religious production of the Yahwist, the Elohist, the Pentateuch itself, the Deuteronomic Historian.

What about our ancestors-in-religion in the early church, i.e., the first and second generations of Christians? Their basic confession also centered around history and events. They saw the works of Jesus in their time as the final and definitive saving deed of Yahweh in the history of Israel and the world. They testified that the last saving deed of Yahweh was to be found in the works of Jesus (healings, exorcisms, forgiving of sins, etc.), in his death and rising, and in his coming in glory in the parousia (cf., e.g., Acts 3:11–26). What about their theological reflections and theology? History—the works, death, resurrection, parousia of the Lord, in which Yahweh was exercising his last and definitive redemptive act—is the focus. This can be said to be the main focus of the writers of the body of religious literature we call the New Testament.

People are born, live, love, interact, struggle, hope, die in a given historical context. And God is involved in this concrete historical context. This is the level of concrete *life*. A reflection is made on this concrete life. This is the level of *theology*, more specifically, the level of "doing theological reflection."

THE CHRISTIAN FAITH AND THE HISTORY OF REDEMPTION

I described "doing theological reflection" as the activity of interpreting the contemporary human life-situation in the light of the Christian faith. I would now like to make this more particular by saying that doing theological reflection is above all else "describing" the present moment in the history of redemption (=deliverance, =coming into possession of salvific blessings, =salvation, which, by the way, is total salvation). Why is this? The answer to this question is first another question. What is the Christian faith about first and foremost? It is about the history of redemption. It is a history of salvific actions, of salvific events, especially of course the salvific ministry, death, resurrection, and second coming of the Lord. The salvific events of the promise of land and children, the Exodus, the covenant, the conquest of the land, etc., and the *history* that this chain of events formed constituted the main material of the religious confession of Yahwism and Judaism. This confession of salvific actions/events evolved into a hope for the final salvific action/event. This was the case with some of the prophets, the apocalyptic writers, the synagogue religion. (By the way, this salvific action/event, especially among the apocalyptic writers, was to affect not just the individual's soul in its life of sin and grace to prepare it for life after death; rather it was a question of the total salvation of the person—Semitically understood—of humanity, of all creation, from all evils, for all blessings.)

The early Christians confessed that this final action/event of total salvation had been inaugurated in the works, death, and resurrection of Jesus of Nazareth and would be completed in his parousia. These redemptive acts of Jesus, the Messiah and Lord, constituted for them the last phase of this history of salvation.

The Christian faith then is before all else about the history of redemption. (It is also about law, i.e., ethics, morals, law, but we will talk about this later.)

I suggest then that reflecting on today's human experience "in the light of the Christian faith" should mean first of all, though certainly not exclusively, "in the light of or within the context of the history of redemption." The theologian's primary task is to discover the meaning of the present moment, the 1970s and 1980s, within the context of a history of saving deeds/events, a history which begins in the first salvific deed of creation and will be completed finally in Christ's second coming when all things will be renewed in the new heaven and the new earth where there will be no more mourning nor tears nor suffering nor death nor pain (cf. Rev. 21:1–5).

THE TOOLS FOR "DOING THEOLOGY"

In this way of doing theological reflection, what the theologian needs are experience, analysis, and the Bible.

Experience

How can theologians reflect on and interpret the meaning of a particular human life-situation unless they have experienced it? Experience is important for doing theological reflection; and without this credential one like me should hesitate to make theological pronouncements today.

The doer of theological reflection is ideally the person whose daily life-situation is in all respects the life situation of the people. For example, a worker, not a university professor, is, from the point of view of the need for experience, ideally the best person to reflect on the life-situation of workers. Those who have a vicarious and occasional experience of the life of the worker could also (although as a poor second best) do theological reflection, but they must be acutely aware of their very, very serious limitations and be strictly on guard against them.

We should deal with this point more adequately, at least in parenthesis. It happens often enough today that in a dual society —consisting of those who occupy a social position that controls wealth-power-culture and of those who do not control wealth-power-culture (e.g., the worker)—those who do theological reflection are those who occupy neither position, i.e., they occupy a middle position and have little or no experience of the life of the poor. Can such people do theological reflection? Definitely. Will their theology be the theology of the worker, i.e., can it truly express the concerns, the frustrations, the hopes of the worker? Most likely not; in fact, the typical liberalism of their middle-class position makes them run the risk of betraying the worker's cause, not to speak of their penchant to unconsciously "apply" the western theology that they know "to the present situation" of the worker. Is the situation of middle-class theologians then hopeless? Not completely. Besides of course being able to produce a theology of the middle class for the delectation of the middle class, they can also produce a theology, which, though not a theology of the worker, carries an implicit message to the worker: "I support you and am in solidarity with you, and I invite others of my kind to be in solidarity with you." Or the worker may in effect say to the middle-class theologians: "You have been somewhat immersed in our life-situation and we, the workers. commission you to speak for us and with us, as long as you are aware of your limitations."

I would add here another parenthetical remark in response to an objection that could be raised in this present context: How can an ordinary uneducated worker do theological reflection? Passing over the condescending tone of the question, I would for now merely point to a distinction I would make between a theologian and a technician. A theologian reflects on and discerns the meaning of a contemporary human situation. Doing theological reflection is a creative task. It is an art. The technician is the one who has the skill and professional competence in, say, the Greek and Hebrew languages, or in the historico-critical method of exegesis, or in the social sciences (or, also, professional competence in patristics, dogma, history, canon law, etc.). The technician is at the service of the theologian. The theologian can be the same person as the technician, but this would be extremely rare and well nigh impossible. The task of doing theological reflection would generally be a collaborative task in which the theologians need the assistance of the technicians. So worker-theologians need not be technicians. Although, again, in an egalitarian society of equal opportunities, what would prevent them from being technicians as well?

In any case, my sincere hope is that in the Third World we middle-class "theologians" will be doing the necessary task of transition and then give way to the real theologians of the people. Our role is to fade away. Thank God, I see glimmers of this already in my country.

Analysis

In order to understand and interpret the total life-experience of the contemporary human community, the theologian needs, besides experience, a rigorous analysis of the total human situation of the community or society. This is the analysis not only of the intrapersonal and interpersonal (i.e., the psychological or Freudian) factors, but also, especially today, the historical and social (i.e., the economic, political, cultural, religious) factors. Technicians (in the sense I explained above) would ordinarily help the theologians here. Further, because there is no such thing as an objective, value-free social science, the theologians must know whether the tools of analysis being used are First World or Third World tools. They must make a basic option.

Bible

The theologians need experience and analysis. They also need the Bible. They must be able to situate the present in a history of salvation that has a past (the saving deeds of Yahweh, the final saving deeds of Yahweh through Jesus Christ), a present (including the reality of the risen Lord), and a future (the complete deliverance of people and creation from all bondage and decay). It is the Bible (which should be treated not as a dictionary of timeless truths, but primarily as a record of life-experiences with God, interpreted in faith, of a people who lived during the founding years of our religion) that contains the record of this redemptive activity and history, both as regards what has already been accomplished in the past and what is to be hoped for in the future.

Here the theologians need the help of other technicians, i.e., the exegetes and biblical scholars. However, even among biblical scholars there are different ways of treating the Bible. For example, one would see in the Bible an arsenal of incipient dogmatic truths. Another would see biblical study to be a handmaid in the service of systematic, dogmatic theology. Another would indeed reconstruct the meaning of the Bible by interpreting it against the background of the literary and the historical contexts, but without sufficiently seeing the broad scope of the history of redemption to which the individual books of the Bible are merely single testimonies through the course of the biblical centuries. Finally, there are the biblical scholars, who, as they do rigorous exegesis, open each book of the Bible as they would different single doors, and as they do so, open up to themselves and to others a whole panorama in which to contemplate the whole history of salvation with its past and its promise for the future. These last are the technicians the theologians are looking for.

THE HISTORICAL STAGES OF THEOLOGY

If doing theological reflection in the Judeo-Christian context, in keeping with its bias for history, is a reflection on concrete experience (i.e., the experience here among my people which is different from the experience elsewhere, say, in the western world), then theology, which is the product of theological reflection, cannot but be indigenous.

I would speak very broadly of three (perhaps there are more) major moments in indigenous theological reflection in the history of our religion, corresponding to three major indigenous situations of our religion: These are the Semitic, the Greek, and now the African and the Asian. The theologies of the Yahwist, the Pentateuch, the Deuteronomist Historian, Isaiah, of the Synoptics, John, even Paul, belong to the Semitic stage. The Greek and Latin Fathers, the Scholastics, the contemporary western theologians (like Rahner, Schillebeeckx), the theology contained in the great conciliar documents, including Vatican II, belong to the Greek stage. Two remarks may be singled out regarding this stage. First, the theology here was, for a long time and in a significant degree, metaphysical and thus ahistorical, i.e., it was often concerned with circumscribing the metaphysical nature of religious realities, e.g., the nature of God as Trinity, the essence of Christ as God and man in one nature, the divine motherhood of Mary, the nature of the sacraments, etc. Second, insofar as it has ceased to be significantly metaphysical and has become existential, experiential, or even historical, as in the case of contemporary western theologians and Vatican II, it remains a theological reflection arising out of a western and First World experience and the theological production remains, trunk and root, First World and western.

And now we speak, and rightly, of an indigenous African or Asian theology. What does this mean? I hope we are beyond the stage where "indigenizing theology" means translating the western theological works written in Latin, French, German, or English into our native dialects. "Indigenization of theology" is not a question of translation from language to language. Neither should producing an indigenous theology mean "applying" the theology of Athanasius, Ambrose, Pannenberg, Rahner, or Vatican II "to the local situation." Whether metaphysical or historical, their theological productions are western and we cannot produce our indigenous theology simply by taking over their reflections on their human situation and "applying" them to ours. How can I "apply" the "Theology of the Death of God" and the "Theology on the Use of Leisure" to the situation of my people for whom God is alive and life is difficult? Even the great theology of the historic Vatican II is a theology of the experiences of the First World church, and when it says, "The joys and the hopes, the griefs and the anxieties of this age, especially those who are poor or in any way afflicted, these are the joys and hopes, the griefs and anxieties of the followers of Christ" (*The Church in the Modern World*, no. 1), it is the First World church talking with compassion to or about the Third World. It is not the voice of the Third World telling of its own life-experience.

THE SEMITIC AND THE WESTERN STAGES OF THEOLOGY

Implied in what I have said (i.e., that the necessary tools for doing theological reflection are experience, analysis, and the Bible) seems to be a bracketing off of the western Greek tradition, i.e., the theological production in Europe and America from the second century to the present. Here, I make the following observations:

1. The Greek stage is one of the three major stages in indigenous theological production and it is a valid stage of indigenous theological production.

2. The authentic developments in this second stage are inspired and guided by the Spirit.

3. It is in a significant degree metaphysical in its concerns. For example, whereas, broadly speaking, in the biblical stage the question revolved around: "What is God *doing?*" the significant (and at the time necessary) question in the Greek stage was: "Who is God? What is his *nature?*" To say that theology becomes metaphysical is not necessarily to talk about a fault; it is to talk about a characteristic and a phase in the development of our Christian theological tradition.

4. During this stage the Holy Spirit helped the church to clarify points of doctrine and dogma. These dogmatic and doctrinal clarifications, insofar as they are proposed by the church as articles of faith, are inspired by the Spirit and should be assented to in faith and love.

5. The theological production of this age remains, as any other theological production, culture-bound. This means that the theological problem (e.g., "How do you explain the real presence of Christ in the Eucharist?") arises out of a concrete life-situation or culture, is reflected on in thought patterns and categories that are peculiar to that culture and articulated in a language peculiar to that culture (e.g., "transubstantiation").

6. One should study this stage seriously as part of the history of one's religion and should apply all the tools (e.g., scholastic

philosophy, contemporary western philosophy) necessary to understand it. A study of the development of the faith in the western Greek tradition is part of any theological education. This study can be done either thematically—Christology, Trinity, Mariology, sacraments, etc. Or it can be studied historically—the history of the development of Christian doctrine or dogma. Or both.

7. I make a distinction between doing theological reflection and studying theology, between a theologian and a student of theology. Students of theology must study exegesis, biblical theology, dogmatic theology (thematically or historically), the history of the church, canon law, etc. Theologians, on the other hand, must do theological reflection, that is, they must reflect on contemporary experience. Insofar as in certain and more common instances the students of theology must do the theological reflection, theological reflection becomes one of the tasks of the students of theology. In fact, in this instance, it is their most important task. And for this they need an understanding of the present life-situation of their people through experience and analysis and an understanding of the history of salvation through a study of the Bible. We must today both study theology and do theological reflection. But the two are not exactly the same.

8. Why is the western theological production not essential in doing our own indigenous African or Asian theological reflection? An initial and superficial answer is because you cannot produce an Asian or African theology by using or applying western theological production. But isn't the theological production in the Bible equally culture-bound? Yes, and let's not ever forget this point. Having said this and keeping it in the back of our mind always, we must go on to say that if theological reflection is done "in the light of one's faith," we must find this faith and its message somewhere. And anywhere it might be, it is culture-bound; and so we seem to have run into a dead-end. Or better, we are forced to choose one of the culture-bound theological expressions of our faith. I choose the Semitic for the following reasons:

a. The Semitic stage (Abraham, Moses, Jesus, early church) represents the primitive years of the founding of our religion. In God's providence, this world religion first took root in a Semitic life-experience and culture, and the original meaning and message of our faith was first expressed in a theological production that was Semitic.

b. In it I find the history of redemption depicted *in its integrity:* in its total breadth, i.e., the saving deeds in the history of a human community, from creation onward to the final saving deed(s) of Christ, finally to the full completion at the parousia. I find it *in its fullness,* i.e., in this stage I see depicted God's concern for total life and total salvation for the total person, humanity, and creation, God's concern for all forms of human ills, and God's concern both for this world and the world to come.

c. It is less interested in metaphysical descriptions of the nature of things and more concerned with history, i.e., with human events and God's involvement and activity in them.

d. It is more akin to our oriental spirit and to our Third World aspirations.

9. It is clear that the bracketing off of the western tradition pertains to the doing of theological reflection, not to the study of theology. Does this, however, mean that the western tradition is completely excluded from the activity of doing theological reflection? No. First, it could provide examples and models of theological reflection with which we can compare ours. Second, its theological insights could eventually be grafted into our indigenous theology. For example, the theology that comes out of the life-experience of workers would first come to certain core insights and then in the course of later reflections might ask about the role of the sacramental Christ in their lives. At this stage, the clarifications hammered out in the West regarding the Real Presence might prove useful. But one can see that the grafting on is natural, not violent. The procedure is not taking a western tree and transplanting it on African or Asian soil. Rather it is planting our own African or Asian tree and grafting on whatever is needed for its life and health.

THE MEANING OF CHRISTIANITY IN THE PHILIPPINE CONTEXT

In the light of the main outlines of our discussion, we can say that the theological question in doing theological reflection is this: What is salvation today? This is a briefer way of saying: What is the meaning of the present moment in the ongoing history of redemption?

This question can be taken narrowly as the first or core question. Or it can be taken as the broad umbrella that covers the whole process of theological reflection, including and starting with the first and core question. A hypothetical example will illustrate this. For one or other of the industrialized societies of the West, we might have:

WHAT IS SALVATION TODAY? (Broad Umbrella)

1. What is salvation today? (First and core question)

(Let us suppose that the hypothetical answer is: Deliverance from materialism and atheism.)

2. Then, what does it mean to be church in this situation of materialism and atheism?
3. What does God mean in such a situation?
4. What does grace mean?
5. What does wealth mean? or progress?
6. And so forth.

In summary, we may speak in terms of "method" and "tools" for theological reflection. The method calls for (1) knowledge of the present historical situation (the tools for this are experience and analysis), (2) knowledge of redemptive history (the tool for this is the religious literature called the Bible), and (3) the activity of interpretation or reflection itself.

In our Philippine human community we may say sketchily this: (1) The theologians would see that the present historical situation can be described as a lack of human life due to a social order in which human equality and justice are still mightily to be striven after, in a Philippine—not European, Latin American, African, Japanese, Vietnamese—context of life and meanings. (2) They would plant this situation in the history of God's redemptive activity for total life and total salvation. (3) They would arrive at an interpretation that salvation today means total human development, i.e., concern both for the life of sin/grace and for human dignity, human rights, human sufferings, human life, concern both for the world to come and for this world and its human concerns; and that this is to be done through the transformation of the social order in a Philippine context of life and meanings.

Then related questions will spontaneously surface. For example: What does it mean to be a Christian community in such a concrete setting? What is the meaning of poverty? Of wealth? How does one love? What is the role of the priest? The layperson? What is the meaning of suffering, of struggle, of self-sacrifice, of sharing, of community? Of Philippine values and spirituality? Of lifestyle? Liturgy or the Eucharist? Catechetics? Land? Work? Folk-religion?

I want to make one last remark which unfortunately must be brief. The Christian faith is first of all a *proclamation* of the history of God's redemptive activity. This is the gospel. Secondly, it is also a *teaching* about a way of life, an ethic, more particularly, the ethic of Jesus, and more concretely, the ethic of love. This is the law. And law follows gospel. A more adequate description of doing theological reflection would then be: reflecting on the contemporary human life-situation within the context of salvation history *and* in the light of the ethic of Jesus. Theological reflection is interpreting the meaning of life today in the light of the gospel and the law.

11

Between the Old and the New

Peter K.H. Lee (Hong Kong)

This paper, based on a talk I gave not long ago to a group of church leaders, is supposed to speak to the church situation in southeast Asia. Actually what is called southeast Asia is a very mixed region, and the situations vary widely from country to country (I shall deliberately leave out any discussion of the area known as Indo-China because the revolutionary changes there call for a special treatment). However, this is to be but a catalyst for our thinking, so that I need not pretend to be definitive, and I shall merely highlight certain points for consideration.

My presentation consists of three parts, asking the questions: (1) How shall we understand southeast Asia? (2) Is there anything wrong with the churches in that region? (3) What should the churches do in the present setting?

The Fading of the Old, A Taste of the New

Besides relative geographical proximity, what do the southeast Asian countries have in common? Certainly, they show immense diversity. Yet it requires no profound analysis to see that throughout the region an old order is crumbling and a new configuration of things is struggling to be born. Is this not true of the whole world? Yes, but there are at least two special features about the area in question.

First, the time-span in which the transition is taking place is relatively short. Prior to World War II most of the southeast Asian countries were colonies of western powers, and the majority of the people lived in tradition-bound ways. Within a generation, with but few exceptions all the former colonies have become independent nations. Once they achieve independence, the Asian nations want to develop themselves through modern means. So one viable way to characterize the region in our discussion is that the old and the new meet in heightened tension. It is this dramatic confrontation which makes the countries in question so volatile. What has taken the West three centuries or more to go through—from the Industrial Revolution to the Computer Age, from the modern democratic states to social welfare legislation—is compressed into three decades or less for the Asian nations.

Second, the new developments sought by the Asian nations have not evolved from their own ancient civilizations but have been transported from elsewhere. This means that the conflict of cultures is more acute than that in the West during the last two or three centuries. (The African nations are also going through excruciating cultural conflict, but certainly their indigenous cultures are very different from the Asian traditions, and this is not the place to go into the question.) The parliamentary form of government is quite novel to the Asians. Modern science is not native to Asian soil. No wonder the democratization of government as well as scientific and technological developments have in many instances run into obstacles.

What are the consequences of the heightened confrontation between the old, native traditions and the new, imported innovations? I would like to point out two paradoxical phenomena.

One paradox is that the people are awakened yet they remain frustrated. The Asian masses who were living in tradition-bound society have been awakened to their dignity as persons and to the demand for social justice. No longer will they accept deprivation of basic human rights or social inequality. With their attainment of independence the Asian nations have all given sanction to some semblance of citizens' rights and representative government and have at least given lip-service to the elimination of special privileges for a particular class.

Yet the realization of liberty, democracy, and justice in southeast Asian societies meets with far greater difficulties than those who were quick to shout slogans ever foresaw. The problem of political leadership has yet to be coped with adequately in most of these countries. There may not be absolutist monarchs anymore, but it is not uncommon for strong men, as military generals or even elected presidents, to usurp power at the expense of civil liberty. Due to long entrenched customs as well as freshly unleased forces, social and economic inequality remains glaring. The disparity between the rich and the poor is especially pronounced in the poor states.

Another paradox is that the more determined the developing nations are to catch up with the developed countries economically, the more they find themselves lagging behind. "Development" is spoken of a great deal in the Asian developing countries. They all have economic development plans, unless they are for the time being ravaged by wars. But the plans have not helped the nations as much as they were supposed to. Even where the gross national product has increased, that does not necessarily mean that the population as a whole has benefited. Where economic growth benefits a privileged few and the masses bear a heavy burden, the main economic problems of the nation are not solved.

Actually, development is found to be dependent not on economic factors alone; cultural forces and human values also come into play. Some Asians do not have a positive attitude toward work. Corruption, rampant in the great bulk of Asian countries, is detrimental to economic performance.

Further, the national Asian economies are intertwined with a larger international economic nexus. I have been impressed by Gunnar Myrdal's argument that capital movements and international trade have not been favorable to development.[1] We do not need a John Galbraith to tell us that there can be no glib talk of the poor countries catching up with the rich.[2] Hong Kong and Singapore are not poor, yet their lower-income groups have a hard time.

If the developing Asian nations are bent on aping the developed countries and reaching the same economic level, they are bound to be disappointed. The poor are still beyond the pale of a decent standard of living. The middle class have greater purchasing power than before, but they are forever discontented. They aspire toward more and more but they have to pay more and more, only to end up having not gained much.

So throughout Asia we find people having a taste of new values but still very far from being satisfied. Old values are no longer adequate. People are left in a spiritual vacuum.

There are signs of renascence in the ancient religions. The signs are by no means impressive as far as I can see, but they are indicative of some stirrings in the souls of the people (as well as of the use of a "native" religion to buttress national identity in certain instances).

Communism has not gained universal acceptance in Asia and is unlikely to in the future. However, in some quarters its appeal is strong. The People's Republic of China represents a very impressive alternative to other systems in Asia.

What about Christianity? I am certain that the Christian message has a great deal to offer to contemporary Asians, but many church-people themselves are confused about relating it to actual human situations. The Christian faith understands the paradox of the human predicament and it speaks to it in seemingly self-contradictory terms, but actually it has an apt approach to the complexity of life's problems.

In the parable of the Last Judgment, Jesus taught us to care for those who need food and drink, clothes and shelter, and are unjustly imprisoned. At another place he told us not to worry about whether we have enough to eat and to wear, but seek first the kingdom of God and his righteousness, and the rest will be added to us. Are these two sets of teachings contradictory? Of course not; they are meant for different situations. Unfortunately many Christians—in Asia as elsewhere—have the genius of applying Christian teachings in the wrong contexts. Where the people have a hard time meeting the bare necessities of life, the churches lightly pass them by and glibly talk about spirituality, by which they often mean something that has nothing to do with physical life or social living. At other times Christian leaders busily try to meet immediate needs or energetically tackle community issues, but they are helpless or quite indifferent when it comes to problems beyond what their eyes can see or their hands can handle.

The Christian message really has something wonderful to offer if we only know how to relate it to the predicaments in which people are caught. Where the standard of living is to be raised, the church can have the right words to say. The issue here is not simply economic in nature but involves the idea of justice. Indeed equality and justice should be essential components in development. Yet development, even in this larger sense, is certainly not the total concern of the gospel. Thus where the people and the government are intent on keeping up with the developed nations of the West, the validity of such a preoccupation is called into question by the biblical message. It is unnecessary for me to say more to impress upon you that the Christian faith is entirely pertinent to the needs of Asians in their modern setting. Indeed this is a marvelous opportunity for the church to announce the Good News to the Asian people.

What, then, is keeping the church from making the message of salvation known and acceptable to the people?

A Church That Is Neither Old Nor New

In a world where the old order is dying and new things are in the throes of birth, where do the churches find themselves?

The churches in the southeast Asian countries are certainly not "old" in the sense of being part of Asia's age-old native civilizations. The opening of the Asian nations to the West ushered in their modern era; Christianity did not figure in most of them in any notable way until the beginning of this recent period of their history, since Christianity's promulgation in Asia coincided with western penetration. As is well known, Christianity to this day remains a "foreign" religion in virtually all the Asian countries. If the Asian peoples are reasserting pride in their heritage they do not include Christianity in it.

The "foreignness" of Christianity to Asian cultures is an important problem in our consideration of the mission of the church in Asia today. Enough has already been said about this. Asian theologians in various countries are at work trying to develop indigenous or contextual theology by making use of their respective native thought-forms to respond to relevant issues. This should be high-priority work.

But western-packaged sectarian theological points of view and ecclesiastical traditions are still casting long and heavy shadows on the Asian scene. Earlier I pointed out the confusion the Asian churches have in confessing the Christian faith in concrete living situations. I referred, on the one hand, to high-flown spiritual talk when people are starving and sick and oppressed, and, on the other, the equation of social improvement with salvation. These and similar one-sided tendencies have their origins in western thinking. I mean the pietistic individualism that was stressed in some of the sectarian revival movements of the West of the eighteenth and nineteenth centuries or the shallow kind of social gospel, both of an earlier brand of liberalism and of a more recent form of activism.

Christianity is not new enough for the Asians of today in that it is still tied up with the colonial past. Colonialism as a political structure is all but gone, yet the colonial mentality still lingers in the churches. It is unfair to identify the missionary movement with colonialism completely. Strictly speaking Christian mission has a very different motivation from colonization. The accomplishments of the missionary movement should not be viewed in the light of western imperialism alone. Nevertheless the planting of churches in Asia was the work of western missionaries, not many of whom were imperialists at heart yet almost all of whom could not help transporting to Asians only what they brought with them, lock, stock, and barrel.

The image of the church that is held by Asian Christians to this day is very much part of the western package brought in earlier. The idea of Christendom still hovers in the vestibule of many an Asian church. This is certainly noticeable in an "established" church, as though the church were part of the establishment in Asia as it was in England. The overtones of Christendom are also seen in the sectarian churches that feel ready to conquer what they consider to be the heathen world. Whether the ecclesiology is that of an established church or that of a sect, ecclesiocentricity is the common characteristic. The starting point of mission is the church as an institution, and the final reference for missionary outreach is the institutional interest of the church. That God is at work in the world and that the church is called to participate in God's plan of salvation in history are ideas by and large foreign to the minds of the ecclesiastical authorities and functionaries. Where Christians are at best but a minority, as in almost all Asian countries, the assumption of a triumphalist posture does not look right somehow.

The church hierarchy is inclined to adopt the whole paraphernalia from the western ecclesiastical structures, whether or not they are suitable to the local circumstances. It cannot but seem out of place if the Asian Christian clergy take too seriously titles and ranks that came out of feudal Europe. Granted, a certain measure of continuity with the past is unavoidable, and order in the church structure is necessary; but the clergy should be willing to adapt according to the situation and should not lean heavily on a time-worn system for security or status. The main consideration ought to be the mission of the church for the sake of the gospel to the ends of the earth. Everything else is secondary. If ecclesiastical structure stands in the way, let us remake it.

Both ecclesiological thinking and ecclesiastical structure, in my judgment, are in need of recasting if the mission of the church in Asia is to flourish. As it is, the churches are less than fit to enable Asians to meet the challenge of the new days.

Whereas the Asian societies have broken away from the colonial era, the churches are still wrapped up in their imperial aura. The nations are beginning a new chapter in their history, but the churches keep turning back the pages to the past. I have said that the gospel offers the people of Asia a way out of their dilemmas. But the way remains closed to them unless the churches open their doors and go out to the people, getting involved with them in their aspirations and agonies, struggles and frustrations.

What I am saying here is nothing new to those who have been following theological ferments coming out of the ecumenical movement. But I am afraid that with the great bulk of the churches in Asia business goes on as usual as though they have heard nothing of the call to go out into the world. M. M. Thomas, who has spoken eloquently at meetings of the Christian Conference of Asia and who was until recently the chairman of the Central Committee of the World Council of Churches, had to admit in a lecture he gave several years ago that the churches in Asia are living spiritually and socially in what are called mission compounds, "Christian ghettoes" of their own creation, inward-looking and concerned with themselves.[3] I think that the same words are still applicable today, in most instances.

The churches in Asia must be renewed if they are to be equal to the task of presenting the message of salvation to the men and women of modern Asia.

An Old Church Made New;
Pointing Beyond the Old and the New

Every time the subject of the renewal of the church comes to the fore in my consciousness, I find myself wrestling with the question, "Where should renewal take place?" I seriously consider various possibilities. One possibility is to give up hope in the established church and start innovations outside of it. Sometimes the existing structure seems so backward, so cumbersome, so suffocating that I look at it in dismay, and it is a temptation to seek new life somewhere else. Another possibility is represented by activities carried on by ecumenical bodies like the Christian Conference of Asia. At the assemblies eloquent pronouncements are issued, and through the staff innovative projects are initiated. But how the ideas and experiments will be implemented by the churches is another matter. That leads to the third possibility, that in the final analysis no renewal efforts lead anywhere unless they move into the church setup. That is, new life must take roots in the church.

By temperament and experience I myself am very much a churchman. So here I am disposed to speak in terms of renewal within the church structure. I hope that what I am saying here is not out of place. In speaking of renewing the church, then, I do not mean that we start anew, cutting ourselves off from the past altogether. In fact, that is a historical impossibility. The church that is to be made new, in my understanding, is the church of the ages, an old institution, really, with all its grandeur and misery, its failures and potentialities.

In a moment, I shall sketch a kind of 'diocesan profile," one I would propose if I were in the position of a church leader or member of a diocesan council concerned about renewing the church. But first may I make two basic affirmations.

A fundamental requirement is that, if you are really serious about renewal, you must make a special effort to refresh the clergy on biblical theology. It seems to me no refresher course for the clergy is more fundamental than biblical theology—not just any biblical study but a course packed with insights into biblical scholarship of recent years. Reaffirmations coming out of research in the field of biblical theology undergird the call to the church to get out of its ghetto and go into the world where the living God is ever at work.

A concomitant prerequisite is that there should be repentance —repentance over the egocentricity of the churches. There is no renewal unless there is repentance. Writing on the renewal of the church almost two decades ago, Visser 't Hooft brought home this very point.[4] All great renewals in the history of the church, he noted, have been movements of repentance. Repentance is turning from the old world to the new, from the past to the future, from the closed world to the open heaven, from egocentricity and church-centeredness to God's kingdom. I am sure we all agree. But when will the churches actually repent? Besides biblical study, exposure to criticisms leveled at the churches is a sure way to puncture our complacency. Have you lately listened to the criticisms of the youth and the workers? Both these groups are especially vulnerable to the predicaments of contemporary Asians such as I characterized at the beginning, and they are uninhibited in telling us how the churches fail to reach the people.

Let me now draw my "diocesan profile" showing strategic emphasis in the church's effort at renewing itself. You will notice that renewal and mission will go hand in hand. My suggestions will relate to three levels—the articulate, intellectual level; the parish or congregational level; and the level of working with the oppressed. But at all these levels I would like to highlight the motif of development. "Development" is an overused word and it probably calls for re-definition. But I don't need to be too precise in the present context. I am speaking of "development" as a contrast to "liberation," if the latter stresses only freedom from something and does not have much to say about freedom to do what and for whom. Liberation theology from Latin America is attracting our attention. While I do not doubt that it is particularly pertinent in that part of the world in view of the oppressive structures there, I don't think we need to import the whole motif without qualifications. There are oppressive elements in Asia, yes, but they are not as entrenched as in South America. What the nations in our part of the globe need is not more revolution but building up the people.

Development is not just economic or social but both, and has other dimensions as well, including educational, psychological, cultural, and spiritual.[5] If the churches know how to employ them, the Christian faith furnishes amazing resources for development in its multiple aspects. A prerequisite is an affirmative cast of mind, a positive outlook, that enables the church, always being mindful of the need of the world for redemption, to take a creative part in constructive and reconstructive work in Asian society today. Of course, the work must be undergirded by sound theological thinking. Indeed the time is due for Asian Christians to recast their theology in light of stirrings on their continent. There is little chance for the inroad of a faddish North American "secular theology" that sheds the transcendent God; but to take out of historical context a classical doctrine such as justification by faith as the totality of the Christian message is likewise too wooden and intransigent and stifles human resourcefulness. However, let us hope that not all Asian Christians are paralyzed by such a theological "hangup." So let us move on.

At the level of *articulate, intellectual leadership*, I would like to see more thinking Christian men and women taking part in planning for national development. This may sound like wishful thinking, but I do not think it needs to be that. Having read fairly carefully the works of the sociologist Gunnar Myrdal and the economist John Galbraith, I have come to a fuller understanding of the methodology of the social sciences. These disciplines do permit and involve value considerations. It is specious scientism which keeps many social scientists from dealing with values. Social and economic studies as well as planning for national economic and social development unavoidably take into consideration value categories and presuppositions. The great Christian doctrines of creation, the person, justice, vocation, and so on, contain value assumptions that have implications for social and economic thinking. Not that Christians should insist on only one point of view; neither public policy nor social reality will allow that. But methodologically speaking, thinking Christians who are well-grounded in theology and well-trained in the social disciplines are actually in a position to offer valuable suggestions, along with those put forth by others, for the rebuilding of their nation. I really don't think that it is extravagant to hope that in almost every Asian nation, in almost every diocese, there be at least a few Christian intellectuals and leaders working in partnership or in dialogue with others on national and local development plans.

At the level of *parish work*, I would like to see the congregations take the development of people seriously. Earlier I mentioned factors affecting development, such as attitude toward work, corruption, lack of social responsibility. Parishes in the rural areas should have ample opportunities to help people to develop, all within the given framework of Christian teachings. In some parts of Asia the churches have become typically middle-class in outlook. Like the petit-bourgeois, these churches are among the most conventional-minded. The churches have nothing significant to offer unless they can help the people to break away from an individualistic-materialistic bourgeois ethic. I have learned from Paulo Freire not to despise the masses but to see great potential in them. What the People's Republic of China has done in developing the masses through "regeneration through self-efforts" (this is a more adequate translation of *tzu-li keng-sheng* than "self-reliance") has made me sit up and listen attentively. Some of you may think that the churches in the Asian countries are too small to serve as a base for the awakening of the masses. This may be true in some situations, e.g., Vietnam, Cambodia, Laos, but in other countries, like Indonesia, the Philippines, and Hong Kong, the Christian communities, though still a minority, are alive enough to be the sparkplugs. I dearly love the parable of feeding the thousands with five loaves and two fish. I believe that it is possible to work miracles in feeding the physically hungry as well as the spiritually starved, if only Christians as the small but creative minority know how to tap the resources of their faith. When the church can identify with the multitudes in their aspirations and frustrations and give them guidance and encouragement, it is fulfilling a function that few governments in Asia have succeeded or even tried. When that happens the church need not worry about having too few people to feed or having not enough to feed many folk. But of course that is expecting a lot from the Christian communities.

The level of *working with the oppressed* ought to receive major attention from the churches. It is an age-old tradition that the church has institutions to look after the weak and helpless. This is a noble tradition. But the time has come for the church to supplement the charity work of binding the wounds of the victims of a sick society with attacking the causes of social ills. I am afraid I am but repeating clichés. Some of you enlightened ones have heard this before. I do not wish to indulge in empty talk. To attack the cause of social evils requires the skilled diagnosis of social scientists, the prescriptions of wise sages, and the courage of the prophets. This is to say that it requires a good deal. It makes us humble. But if a triumphalist's air is out of place, neither is a defeatist's mood called for—by virtue of our grounding in the love of Christ. We should be "hopeful realists" in defending the weak against oppression. I am not trained for social work or social action, but I read with keen interest pioneering projects carried on by Asian Christians in a spirit of expectant realism to combat the forces of social injustice. And may I appeal to the bishops and other church executives to raise this kind of work to a high priority. If the entire constituency is made aware of the importance of working with the oppressed, there is a greater chance for raising the consciousness of the larger population to the sources of social evil.

So let the church work alongside of the strong, for the sake of building up everyone. Let the church strengthen the common people. Let the church defend the weak. In so doing we point beyond the old and the new in human terms; the churches will put off the old nature which is corruptible and put on the new nature, created after the likeness of God in true righteousness and holiness.

There are old and worn-out traditions and institutions that are repressive and retrogressive and ought to be discarded, but there may very well be old values that should be conserved or recovered. There are new ideas and constructs that will help people develop more fully, while there are others that are destructive. After all, the "new" as well as the "old," from a human perspective, are all fragmentary and fragile. What was deemed worthy in the old days may have become obsolete in the new generations. What is new and vital today will grow old and worn-out tomorrow. Above all, only if we die with the Old Adam and are born with the New Creation shall we recover what is of worth in the past and strengthen what comes to pass.

Take our relation to nature as an illustration. Traditionally Asians have taken a passive attitude toward natural forces, and this is not conducive to technological development. In contrast, Westerners in the modern era take an aggressive attitude toward the natural environment, and this does result in notable technological achievements. Is the old, Asian way all bad and is the new, western way all good? People everywhere are now alarmed at the tragic damage done by western science and technology to nature, and they are beginning to wonder if the Orientals' poetic feeling toward it does not have something to teach people today. If we go to the heart of biblical thought, we find that the Bible has a remarkably balanced view of nature. Human beings are the crown of creation, yes, but this is not to say that we have the right to exploit nature to suit ourselves at will; rather, reconciled with God, we are to help fashion the natural world in a way that glorifies the Creator and benefits his creatures. In this manner, a Christian believer in the Asian setting knows how much to adopt from western science's realistic attitude toward nature and how much to retrieve from the Orientals' sense of communion with it.

"From now on, therefore, we regard no one from a human point of view. . . . If any one is in Christ, he is a new creation; the old has passed away, behold, the new has come" (2 Cor. 5:16–17).

"In that new heaven and new earth," to quote Paul Devanandan when he was addressing himself to the theme of Christianity in relation to other faiths, "we will not be able to distinguish the new from the old. It is not for us to indicate what will be preserved and in what manner. For we cannot tell how God will bring his purpose for mankind and his world to a conclusion. But insofar as we identify ourselves with the will of God as revealed in Christ, we can be certain that we shall be working along the line of the purpose and not against it."[6]

NOTES

1. Gunnar Myrdal, *The Challenge of World Poverty* (New York: Pantheon Books, 1970), chap. 9.

2. John K. Galbraith, *Economics, Peace and Laughter* (New York: The New American Library, Inc., 1972), p. 198.

3. M.M. Thomas, *The Christian Response to the Asian Revolution* (London: SCM Press, 1966), p. 105.

4. W.A. Visser 't Hooft, *The Renewal of the Church* (London: SCM Press, 1956), pp. 95f.

5. Cf. Richard Dickinson, *Line and Plummet: Churches and Development* (Geneva: World Council of Churches, 1968), pp. 42–43, for a definition of "development."

6. Paul Devanandan, *Preparation for Dialogue* (Bangalore: The Christian Institute for the Study of Religion & Society, 1964), p. 192.

12

The Indian Universe
of a New Theology

D. S. Amalorpavadass (India)

If we want to talk about a new theological approach and a new vision of the church in India, then we must understand the reality of India and within that reality spell out the church's role and function.

India is the cradle of great religions that are ancient, alive, and have a long following.

India is in the process of liberation and development, yearning to weld this vast population into a well-integrated nation and create a just and human society.

Hence, while speaking of a new theology we have to take stock of the Indian universe in terms of ancient religious traditions and modern concern for development. These two factors are two signs of the times, among many others. So we have to recognize in them God's presence and discern God's designs for our times, and clearly spell out how the church must fulfill its prophetic mission with reference to this situation.

These two factors are the two main realities of India, the two sources of theology.

ANCIENT RELIGIOUS TRADITIONS

Theological Understanding of Religious Traditions

First, we want to consider the authentic teaching of Vatican II on the great religious traditions and its full extent and implications. Then we will take into account the advances made subsequently by international theological conferences, chiefly the Bombay Theological Seminar (1964), the Rome Sedos Theology Symposium (1969), and the Nagpur Theological Conference (1971). Of these, the last-mentioned has made the greatest advance and that on a sound footing; its declaration is comprehensive and creative.

1. The revelation and realization of God's universal plan of salvation for humankind is older than the church; it is wider than the narrow, linear, and limited Judeo-Christian history of four thousand years. Although its role is unique, and although it holds a special place in this history of salvation and has the fulness of the means of salvation, the church cannot limit to any time and space God's saving presence nor exhaust Christ's saving action through his Spirit. His presence and action as cosmic Christ, the Lord of the universe, the Savior of humankind, the Master of human history, and the norm and judge of human existence, are universally operative and effective both in time and space, hence before the foundation of the institutional church by Christ and outside it too today. Thus the religions of the world and the realities of the temporal order must be viewed as included in God's universal saving plan and its historical fulfillment. Consequently, the relation between the church and other religions can no longer be one of white and black, truth and error, good and bad, salvation and damnation, God and satan; it cannot be a relation of contrast and opposition, mutual exclusion and aggression, in view of conquest, subordination, or proselytization.

It is and must be a positive relationship, of mutual understanding and appreciation, respect and confidence, dialogue and cooperation. In a word, confrontation must yield to dialogue. This dialogical attitude must imply a new vision of a single world created by God's love, re-created by Christ's redemptive work and filled and led by his Spirit. It should also express recognition of God's universal presence and action through the Spirit of Christ in the world and history, in other religions and religious people.

2. Since other religions are not to be opposed to the church but are to be understood and evaluated in reference to it, we can no longer call these religions "pre-Christian," or "pro-Christian"—and much less "non-Christian." These three expressions in one way or other say that they are not or not yet "Christian." Instead we have acknowledged that Christ as the Lord of the universe and Savior of all humankind is present and active among all peoples, all religions, all realities, of all times and places. Hence, the right thing to do might be to see them as "Christian" in some way. However, for two reasons we cannot call them "Christian." First of all, by doing so we will not be able to distinguish terminologically Christianity from other religions. Second, other religions would not like to be styled "Christian" and thereby lose their identity; this could be an insult at another extreme. Hence we decided to call them simply "the religions," "the world religions," "the religions of the world" (Bombay Seminar) and "the great religions of mankind" or "the religious traditions of mankind" (Nagpur Conference).

3. The Nagpur Declaration rightly recognizes in other religions Christ's active presence and says that the mystery of Christ is operative in them as a reality (DNC, no. 12).

We see at work in them Christ and his grace. An ineffable mystery, the centre and ground of reality and human life, is in different forms and manners active among all peoples of the world and gives ultimate meaning to human existence and aspirations. This mystery, which is called by different names, but which no name can adequately represent, is definitively disclosed and communicated in Jesus of Nazareth. As there is a universal providence leading all men to their ultimate destiny and since salvation cannot be reached by man's effort alone, but requires divine intervention, the self-communication of God is not confined to the Judeo-Christian tradition, but extends to the whole of mankind in different ways and degrees within the one divine economy (DNC, nos. 13–14).

Vatican II offers us the ground for the above formulation: "These religions . . . often reflect a ray of that Truth which enlightens all men" (Nostra Aetate, no. 2), namely of Christ, the way, the truth, and the life. If we are Christians, we know Christ; we can and must also recognize Christ wherever he is. If we are really catholic (=universal) we will not deny this recognition. That is why we are asked by the very fact of our being Christians, "in witness of Christian faith and life, [to] acknowledge, preserve, and promote the spiritual and moral goods found among these men, as well as the values in their society and culture" (*Nostra Aetate*, no. 2).

The reality of the link with the paschal mystery—the saving Christ-event—"holds true not only for Christians, but for all men of good will in whose hearts grace works in an unseen way. For, since Christ died for all men, and since the ultimate vocation of man is in fact one and divine, we ought to believe that the Holy Spirit in a manner known only to God offers to every man the possibility of being associated with this paschal mystery" (*Gaudium et Spes*, no. 22). In an unseen way, the grace of Christ works in human hearts; in a manner known only to God—so unknown to us—the Holy Spirit associates the people with the paschal mystery.

"Thanks to his grace . . . those also can attain to everlasting salvation who through no fault of their own do not know the gospel of Christ or his Church" (*Lumen Gentium*, no. 16).

The Decree on Missionary Activity, basing itself on the above statements, concludes with reference to evangelization as follows: "God in ways known to Himself can lead those inculpably ignorant of the gospel to that faith without which it is impossible to please Him (Heb. 11:6)" (*Ad Gentes*, no. 7); for elements of "truth and grace are to be found among the nations, as a sort of secret presence of God" (*Ad Gentes*, no. 9). God is present and is already at work in people before the gospel is preached; this universal active presence of Christ is expressed by the Fathers as *semina verbi*, or "seeds of the Word"; God leads people to faith not only through the preaching of the gospel, but already through the seeds of the word. "The Holy Spirit, who calls all men to Christ by the seeds of the Word and by the preaching of the Gospel, stirs up in their hearts the obedient acceptance of faith" (*Ad Gentes*, no. 15).

4. It is not sufficient to say that Christ is actively present in them. We have to spell out in what ways this is so. Religious traditions can be defined as "any set of beliefs and practices, embodying man's ultimate values to which he commits himself in faith with the hope of finding through them his final fulfillment" (DNC, no. 12). Having

bodies and living in society, people can come into contact with God and respond to him and thereby attain salvation only through the historico-socio-religious phenomena "in the context of their religious traditions" (DNC, no 16). In other words, the beliefs and practices should have their origin in God. Hence we logically conclude that the reality of *revelation* is possible in their religious and life-situations; their Scripture must be *inspired* in some way or other (analogically at least), and their religious practices (e g., the *samaskaras* in Hinduism) may be visible means of *salvation:* Revelation, inspiration, and salvation should be granted and recognized in them in some sense or other, if we are open to and consistent with the Vatican II statements. This is what we declared in Nagpur: "The different sacred scriptures and rites of the religious traditions of the world can be in various degrees expressions of a divine manifestation and can be conducive to salvation" (DNC, no. 16). The workshop report on the subject was more categorical in its statement: "expression of divine revelation and means of salvation" (WNC, no. V).

We can have endless discussion as to the difference between divine "manifestation" and "revelation," between "milieus of grace," "occasions of grace," "channels of grace," and "means of grace," between "samaskaras" and "sacraments." Likewise we can debate the ambiguous character and inherent defects of the structures, signs, and formulations in a religion. In any case our present incapacity to formulate them adequately is no reason to deny them the reality of Christ's saving action through their socio-religious phenomena.

5. At the same time, we will be excessive and unwarranted in our conclusion if we go to the extent of saying that the other religions are equal or parallel to Christianity, or that those religions are the "ordinary," "normal," or "general" ways of salvation, while Christianity is the "extraordinary," "exceptional," or "special" way in keeping with the number of followers in each religion![1] In answer to this, we must state that the criterion is not the number of people in a religion or the presence of spiritual and supernatural values, but the positive and historical institution of the church by Christ as the fully adequate means of salvation, as the universal sacrament of salvation, as the animator and leader of the spiritual movement launched by Jesus Christ for the renewal and unification of humankind.

6. The main issue is how to understand and formulate, against this

background, the originality and uniqueness of the church, and how to find expressions for it in church structures and institutions, in its way of life and different activities, especially in evangelization and development. Likewise, the missionary motivation that was based formerly on the fact that the followers of other religions were not saved and that their religions could not be milieus of salvation should now find its source of inspiration in the fact that Christ's saving grace is operative in them. This is formulated in the Nagpur Declaration as follows: "This in no way undermines the uniqueness of the Christian economy, to which has been entrusted the decisive word spoken by Christ to the world and the means of salvation instituted by Him" (DNC, no. 16). It continues: "The recognition of the positive relation of the religious traditions of mankind to Christ does not in any way lessen the urgency of the Christian mission; rather it is recognized as more meaningful, more human, more universal" (DNC, no. 17) and more necessary. For, "it communicates the explicit knowledge of Christ and a deeper union with him, who is the central event of the history of salvation. Evangelization is necessary because Christian fellowship, being really universal and not bound by any culture, race or nation, is an indispensable factor for the peace and prosperity of the world, understanding between the peoples and universal justice. Evangelization is thus an expression of the Christian fellowship which communicates to others what has been entrusted to the Church to share with all men" (DNC, no. 22). The church thereby puts itself totally at the service of the urgent needs of humankind, in obedience to Christ who came to serve and not to be served. Finally, evangelization is necessary "because human history is not mere horizontal progress but contains an eschatological dimension of which the Christian is a minister" (WNC, no. V).

In the light of all that has been said above, there is no more room for the question, What need is there any more for mission if non-Christians can be saved outside the boundaries of the visible church, without the gospel preaching? Missionary activity today, as always, retains its power and necessity (*Ad Gentes*, no. 7). That is why Pope Paul reaffirmed that "the recognition that God has other ways of saving souls outside the cone of light—that is, the revelation of salvation—projected by him on the world, does not authorize the children of light to leave to God the unfolding of this secret economy of salvation, and to give up the efforts for the spread of the light."

Thus the Nagpur Theological Conference tackled boldly and earnestly a very crucial issue in evangelization. In doing so it was on the one hand faithful to the authentic teaching of Vatican II in a dynamic and creative way; and on the other, it took stock of the context of religious pluralism in Indian society and the daily vital contact of Christians with the people of other religious traditions among whom they live. We could come to this happy conclusion and make this original contribution because Nagpur was an attempt at a genuine act of theologizing, namely, a reflection in faith by the Christian community in India on their Christian experience in their society and in their living contact with the people of other religions. In so doing, the church in India has not only elaborated a relevant theology for its mission in India today in the place of imported bookish theology, but also has become mature and creative and thereby contributed to the universal church's theology of religions.

Dialogue

The mission of the church with reference to the people of other religious traditions could be either dialogue or evangelization or both. Let us take up first the question of dialogue.

The Nagpur Declaration, though it studies dialogue with reference to evangelization, did not fully settle the problem of the relationship between them. The Workshop that studied the question had therefore to make its options and point out the areas of disagreement. And they are pertinent to our consideration here: "For some, dialogue, although valid in itself, would be correlated to evangelization practically as its *praeparatio evangelica;* others, especially conscious of the suspicion that these conceptions might arouse in India, sought for a theological understanding in terms of polarity and tension between these two activities which, though connected in the practice of many Christians, remain theologically distinct." The latter conception was adopted both in the Workshop report and in the Conference Declaration. The polarity referred to is the polarity of the church's existence in the world as eschatological and pilgrim (WNC, no. VI).

The second clarification with regard to dialogue is on the meaning of the concept of "religious dialogue." Both the Workshop and the

Declaration took pains to emphasize that it must be understood in terms of the attitude of the partners rather than in terms of the subject matter of the dialogue. What matters is the spirit and mentality rather than the content and areas of dialogue.

In our personal relations with men of other beliefs, dialogue will be truly religious when, however different its object, its partners share a religious concern and an attitude of complete respect for one another's convictions and a fraternal openness of mind and heart. Religious dialogue, therefore, does not necessarily mean that two persons speak about their religious experiences, but rather that they speak as religiously committed persons, with their ultimate commitments and religious outlook, on subjects of common interest (DNC, no. 24).

It is not primarily an intellectual exchange, much less a controversy in a polemical and apologetic tone. The basic condition in the partners for a genuine dialogue is a spirit of openness and humility and a willingness to learn and receive from one another, from one another's religious traditions and values, insights and experience, in a process of sharing (DNC, no. 25). Dialogue is animated by the common hope of reaching mutual understanding and enrichment, communion and collaboration. Dialogue fosters communication and makes each other's faith intelligible. It edifies and enriches the partners. The mutual spiritual enrichment comes from the fraternal exchange of religious experience, from the fact that "in dialogue each partner listens to God speaking in the self-communication and questioning of his fellow-believers" (DNC, no. 27). It is through common searching and sharing that we come closer to the truth; such a sharing is part and parcel of our pilgrim situation.

The Christian wishes to learn of the religious values and experiences of others. The mystery of Christ is universal, yet this universality is at present realized only partially, and therefore the concrete life of the church, and much more that of the individual, is open to continuous enrichment. The partner in the dialogue may also be enriched, and Christians hope that they may be able to communicate to their partners something of the richness and strength of faith that is their own (SCNC). Dialogue leads to a spiritual growth and therefore to a kind of deeper metanoia or conversion to God, in a deep personal sense that we die to our narrow and selfish outlook in a new surrender to God, in response to his will and guidance (SCNC). It enables their mutual cooperation as well as their collaboration with people of various secular ideologies for a common cause of society. The areas of collaboration include concrete issues of society and the burning problems of the day (DNC, no. 28).

Above all, dialogue must not be undertaken as a means or bait for an ulterior end; it is good in itself like work for education, social justice, charity (DNC, no. 26). It gradually leads the partners toward that ultimate vision and perfect unification of all that can be discerned in the convergent aspects of the various religious traditions. The concrete goals of God's plans in history are beyond our calculation; we know only the final eschatological fulfillment in which "the elect will be united in the Holy City ablaze with the splendor of God where the nations walk in his light." We hope that in genuine dialogue we shall make progress in our move toward this final common destiny. From the side of the Christians, the dialogue supposes the standpoint of the believers' accepting Jesus Christ in faith as God's final and full revelation. It is in this faith that they know of the bounty of the divine truth and love which from the beginning of the ages is bestowed on all people in many forms. They also know that the fulness of the mystery of Christ will be revealed only in the end of time when all the treasures of spiritual insights and experiences will be manifest in the glory of Jesus Christ, that therefore it is their task to grow in the realization of the mystery of Jesus Christ through sharing with others (SCNC).

Such a dialogue is not to be limited to an elite group or urban areas, but must gradually extend to all levels and groups, both in urban and rural areas, so that every Christian community, wherever it may be, will be in fact a community in dialogue with others and so foster the universal communion of all.

DEVELOPMENT AND LIBERATION

If the first aspect of the Indian reality is the ancient and living religions, the second is its present process of development and liberation.

We are living today in a world where 15 percent of the people enjoy all the benefits of society, while 85 percent are deprived of them. The topmost 15 percent are the dominant, the lower 85 percent are the dominated. As Sheikh Mujibur Rehman pointed out in the Non-Aligned Meeting in Algiers recently, the division of the world is not a division into aligned and non-aligned, but rather into the oppressors and the oppressed. Whether they realize it or not, the topmost level of society is exploiting and living off the misery of the poor.

1. *The Indian scene.* If we turn to our home front, after twenty-five years of political independence India of the seventies does not present anything more than a dismal and frightful picture. Even a superficial analysis of the country's social, economic, political, and educational situation will reveal both our achievements of the last quarter century and the appalling condition in which the majority of our population lives. The daily papers headline the crucial issues: the spiralling prices, lack of essential commodities, hoarding and profiteering, black-marketing and food adulteration, the parallel economy of black money, the growing gap between the rich and the poor, increased production not resulting in equal distribution to all, the rapid growth of population, unemployment and underemployment, inefficiency and corruption in the administration at all levels from top to bottom, harassment of harijans and other weaker sections, infighting and factions in political parties and consequent political instability, chiefly in the states. The reaction of the people to all this takes the form of bandhs and strikes, including strikes in essential services, violence of all forms, mass looting, communal strife, student indiscipline, and the breakdown of law and order necessitating constant intervention of the police and the army.

All this is daily increasing the poverty, oppression, and suffering of the masses. All the achievements of the past twenty-five years have gone to raise the standard of life of the top 10 or 15 percent of the population, while the situation of the majority has remained the same or grown worse. Nearly half the population are below the subsistence level and hence live a life little worthy of human beings, subject to hunger, malnutrition, disease, lack of minimum shelter and clothing. The traditional passivity and fatalism is fast giving way to a mood of despondency and eruption of violence. An example of this is the resentment manifested by the city slum dwellers and rural population against the present process of development.

Education patterned on a colonial model tends to train bureaucrats. It domesticates people and makes them an elitist class to conform to and support the status quo of the established order. It is not at all geared to national development or to making the youth agents of social change. The hopes placed in the political parties and their election promises have been shattered to the ground. No party, including the New Congress, seems to be able to deliver the goods. Confidence in parliamentary democracy has been shaken. The prospects of leftist parties coming to power as an alternative to the right centrist New Congress are bleak; a brief spell of a presidential form of govenment at the center or military dictatorship are also envisaged as alternative solutions.

From all this one concludes obviously that this miserable state of affairs is due basically to the present economic, social, and political structures of the country. They are oppressive and unjust, basically incapable of bringing about any change for the better, especially since they are backed by vested interests determined to preserve the status quo. Our brand of socialism, in spite of tall talk and radical language, is in fact a camouflaged form of state capitalism with a view to neutralize and absorb leftist tendencies.

It is obvious that work for development and liberation implies commitment to bring about a radical change in the structures of society, and this calls for structural changes in the church as well.

In this situation, Christ the Incarnate Word, the Liberator of humankind, is present. What will he do? What has he done in similar situations? Or what does he ask his church to do now?

2. *Various approaches.* In spite of a decade of discussion in books and reviews, meetings and seminars, there is a lot of confusion in the mind of many Christians, chiefly bishops and priests, with regard to the relation between evangelization and development. My first reaction to this is to wonder whether a discussion about it is not idle academic talk, an evasion of the reality and a lack of commitment to do something about it. However, since a clear understanding can lead to committed action, let us examine this issue. We notice several groups among us. A few see in theology as well as realize in their own praxis a good integration of evangelization and development; and they remain faithful to the identity and specific aspect of both. Some are engaged in developmental activities that neither they nor others see as acts of evangelization. In some others, they are acts of evangelization for those who are engaged but they do not appear so to others. A vast

majority cannot yet see any connection between evangelization and development, though they appreciate the value and meaning of each activity separately. If they see any connection at all, they consider them as two different activities, one specifically the duty of the church and the other a common task of everyone. The church can help the latter if it has the time, resources, and personnel after having attended to evangelization. And even if the church were to be engaged in development, it would not be part and parcel of evangelization but only a part of its general mission.

There is a second problem flowing from the first. Even those who consider involvement in the development and liberation process as a part of the church's mission find it hard to recognize it as a specific duty of the clergy and the religious. The tension experienced in life is serious; the dichotomy felt in thought and practice is real. This may lead eventually to polarization in the church and consequently to a split in communities and institutions. On the one hand, those who accept development as a valid form of evangelization are opposed to those who reject it as evangelization and want to dedicate themselves to so-called direct evangelization; on the other hand those who believe that priests and sisters should be in the forefront of development as part of their priestly and religious ministry are opposed to those who flatly deny that it is their business and would like that it be purely under lay auspices. This problem calls for a theological understanding and a genuine Christian vision of the world.

3. *Christ the liberator in the India of the seventies:* Christ in his person, by his preaching and doing, has ushered in the eschatological kingdom of God. This consists in the recapitulation of the whole of creation and in the salvation of all of humankind, the resurrection of the whole person and every person in all aspects and dimensions, so that all things thus made new and brought together may belong to Christ; and since Christ himself belongs to God, God may thus be all in all (Eph. 1:3–12; 1 Cor. 3:23; 15:29). This salvation of the whole person and of every person and the re-creation of the earth consists of the humanization of people across the whole gamut of their relationships—familial, social, economic, political, and cultural. It means liberation from all forms of alienation—psychological, existential, social, ideological, and cosmic—and the redemption of all the realities of the temporal order. In this way, everything will come

under the cosmic leadership of Christ; everything will be imbued with his Spirit and orientated to the Creator, toward the eschatological unity and fulfillment of God's kingdom. Christ identified himself with this cause, both by his word and deed and gave his life fully for it as a suffering servant (Isa. 52–53; Mark 10:41–45).

4. *The church as the living sign of Christ's liberation for today.* The church has no other mission but to be the sign of Jesus Christ here and now, to make present his liberating action in the frustrating situation of our country, by its own involvement in the common struggle of our people for liberation from the unjust and oppressive structures of our society. Its witness demands that like Christ it identify itself with the suffering masses, that it be in solidarity with the concrete situation of the society in which it lives, placing itself entirely at its disposal as a servant and as an embodiment of Christ's all-embracing love. Fulfilling its prophetic function, it should interpret the signs of the times and show the exigencies of the Lord's designs for social change, for a new order of things, for building the new society, for assuring a better future for our people. Its prophetic function includes a critique of society, a denunciation of its evils and unjust structures, and a positive mobilization of forces and efforts to effect social change. This requires charismatic leadership within its ranks to show the revolutionary implication of the gospel for structural changes in an emerging socialistic society. This must include a positive appreciation of all human efforts by underlining their meaning and contribution to the progress of liberation. Its influence is not from outside, but from within. It will therefore act as the animator and conscience of the world; it will inspire all people to review their lives in terms of an existence for others and of being for others. As educator, it will make all Christians and people of good will aware of their social responsibility for their neighbors. As a dynamic force it will urge all to commit themselves to action. Ultimately, its whole ministry must take on the form of humble service and become a witness to the love of Christ and its redeeming power shown through the cross and resurrection.

Seen in depth thus,

evangelization and development far from being in opposition, or even being separated from one another, compenetrate each other in one redeeming movement of human progress and salvation. Both are integrated into the one all-embracing salvific function and mission of the Church. If we sense a certain polarity in their relationship, a certain tension and dialectic, we also believe that the tension is full of life and dynamism, full of inspiration and excitement (WNC, no. IX).

The work of integral development when motivated by the love of Christ and understood in this sense of integral development is a genuine way of realizing the values of the Gospel. Its thrust goes beyond the individual to the whole of mankind, beyond the visible to the invisible, beyond time to eschatological fulfillment (DNC, no. 30).

5. Notion of development. The development that we speak of is, in a Christian understanding, an integral human development. This implies the progress and advance of the whole person and the whole society in all human dimensions: economic, social, political, cultural, educational, religious, and spiritual. People must grow conscious of their human dignity, exercise their freedom, and play an active role in developing themselves and helping others to advance in authentic development, not as objects and passive recipients, but as subjects of their own development, taking initiative, freely deciding, sharing responsibility, and actively collaborating.

Social justice and self-reliance are just as important as economic growth. In countries like India increased productivity should receive very high priority. In this perspective of the integral development of all men, we realize and implement the love which Christ has brought and taught us. Development is the liberation of people from the various forces that constrict and stifle their human existence, so that they are free to grow to fullness. The economic dimension of development has great significance. Development includes creation and promotion of structures that foster and maintain the best human relations, sensitivity and openness with compassion to one another. Development is not the concern of one section of the community for another but of all for each and each for all. Its universal aspect needs underlining as ultimately development of all mankind is one. There is a dehumanizing aspect in the selfish and isolated development of nations independent of one another. This phenomenon can happen to classes, groups, communities, religions and individuals within nations also.[2]

The work of development has two aspects. First, it involves liberation from unjust structures and oppressive powers by a radical transformation of social attitudes, by the change of socio-economic structures, and by the realization of social justice. The church must join forces in the struggle for liberation. Second, the church must contribute to humanization and community building, by having human dignity, freedom, and equality recognized; to economic growth and social justice by increased production and equitable distribution of wealth; to the removal of poverty, illiteracy, unemployment, disease, and suffering; and to building a new society that will make real the ideals of human communion, justice, and peace. The credibility of the institutional church's witness today is chiefly connected with its championing of social justice and with an all-around involvement in the nation's struggle for human dignity and freedom, justice, and communion. What Julius Nyerere said needs to be taken seriously:

The church should accept that development of peoples means rebellion. Unless we participate actively in the rebellion against those social structures and economic organizations which condemn men to poverty, humiliation, and degradation, then the church will become irrelevant to men. . . . Unless the church—its members and organizations—expresses God's love for man by involvement and leadership in constructive protest against the present condition of man, then it will become identified with injustice and persecution. If this happens it will die, and humanly speaking deserves to die, because it will then serve no purpose comprehensible to modern man. . . . The development of peoples at this time in man's history must imply a divine discontent and a determination for change. What all this amounts to is a call to the church to recognize the need for social revolution and to play a leading role in it.[3]

6. Both these aspects of development call for *political action*, for it is by participating in politics that one can hope to bring about the required change of the economic system. At the same time we cannot disregard other forms of involvement and efforts.

7. With regard to the supposed conflict and tension between evangelization and development in *the ministry of the clergy and the religious*, I shall repeat what I already said in my address to the Zonal Consultation on Evangelization in Bombay in September 1969:

Though evangelization is a task of the whole Church, and as such it is carried out by various groups (the clergy, religious and lay people), the task in the temporal order belongs especially to the laity. Hence the laity should involve themselves more in the work of development, especially work of a technical nature, while the priest should keep to spiritual animation, guidance and inspiration and formation of the lay people. In regions where there is not as yet a Christian community, or where it exists but is unable to undertake such activities, it is the duty of the priest to initiate them. However, at the earliest opportunity he should hand it over to the laity and other agencies and devote himself to the Christian animation of the community, which is his basic and permanent task. With regard to priority in the lives and ministry of the priests, it matters little where one starts from; it will depend very much on the circumstances, aptitudes and needs of the community and the times; but whatever be the field in which one engages oneself, the dynamism of one's commitment should be such as to take him to the others.[4]

The Memorandum of the CBCI to the Synod of Bishops held in October 1971 says the same:

Concerning the relation between Evangelization and Development we suggest the following: The priest is not confronted by a dilemma between two mutually exclusive alternatives, viz. either evangelization proper or development, either christianization or humanization; but he is expected to embrace both as integral parts of the Church's global mission. Development, understood in all its aspects and dimensions, will not be complete without the fulfillment of man's spiritual destiny. A priest, as minister of the Church, will dedicate himself to the tasks of development, and by the very involvement of his spiritual freedom, will bear witness to the universal Lordship of Jesus Christ over the world and be gradually led to make explicit and interpret his commitment. On the other hand, the priest, while announcing the good news of salvation in Jesus Christ, cannot but be led to discover the implications and exigencies of the Christ-event in the heart of this world and in the course of history, impelling him to join forces with all men in their struggle for their total development. In this way his Christian proclamation will not only get credibility but will also sound relevant and meaningful to his audience.[5]

CONSCIENTIZATION AND EVANGELIZATION

Finally, no genuine commitment to development and liberation on the part of anyone is genuine and valid unless it is translated into what is known as "conscientization."

1. Conscientization is to be understood as a method and strategy of liberation in the context of a society divided into two groups, the oppressed and the oppressors. Its ultimate aim is to realize the humanization of dehumanized people caught up in dehumanizing structures and to bring about the liberation of the oppressed culminating in the liberation of the oppressors themselves by unleashing the power that is in the oppressed masses to change their situation and to convert the oppressors themselves by a process of love.

It is a long process and implies the following, according to Paulo Freire:

a. One must realize that one is oppressed and that one can liberate oneself if one transforms the concrete situation where one finds oneself oppressed.

b. This calls for a "critical insertion into a process; it implies a historical commitment to make changes."

c. This bids one "to adopt a utopian attitude toward the world, an attitude that turns the one conscientized into a utopian agent"; utopia is not something unrealizable, but the dialectization in the acts of denouncing the dehumanizing structure and announcing the structure that will humanize.

d. The creation of liberating structures calls for courage and committed action: "to join the action historically by genuinely loving, by having the courage to commit oneself."

e. Only those who announce and denounce, who are permanently committed to a radical process of transforming the world, only they can be prophetic.

In other words, conscientization is

an awakening, a growing awareness through a dialectic of action and reflection on reality. It involves an accurate and realistic awareness of one's locus in the real situation. It calls for the capacity to analyze the causes and consequences of this locus. . . . It involves the basic and constant attitude of questioning which precipitates tension and in practice leads to conflict. Our efforts, therefore, should not be geared to neutralize tension and conflict nor to reconcile what cannot be reconciled. . . . Conscientization is directed not only towards changing oppressive structures; it involves also and right from the beginning of the process a transformation of people, their society and culture, mobilizing all their resources for a genuine awakening.[6]

In short, "conscientization is the process whereby one learns to perceive the social, political, economic, cultural and religious contradictions and begins to take action against the oppressive elements in his environment through critical involvement, total identification and committed action in favor of the poor, the destitute, the outcaste, the victimized, the voiceless."[7]

2. This conscientization is obviously related to evangelization. Far from replacing evangelization in the mission of the church, conscientization is part and parcel of any genuine effort at evangelization today. Without a serious effort to enter into the life-situation of the masses of the poor and oppressed, without a serious effort to initiate the process of action-reflection that will lead to the liberation of the

oppressed and the conversion of the oppressors and will bring justice and peace to society, the preaching of the gospel will be meaningless in face of the realities of today's world.

3. What this entails in practice may be spelled out in the following concrete suggestions:

a. All the members of the church should be made aware of the explosive and revolutionary situation in the country today; they should be inspired by a relevant theology and spirituality to involve themselves in activities for development and social change.

b. No real knowledge is possible without living with people and getting involved in the situation of the oppressed and having a dialogue of life with all classes of the poor, the workers, the peasantry, slum dwellers, youth, and students. This applies to various groups in the church; those under formation, for example, in seminaries, novitiates, and juniorates, should have opportunities and facilities in their life-schedule for a living contact with existing social realities of India.

c. All Christians, especially church leaders, should change their lifestyle so that, without being any more identified with the privileged and elite, they can be more one with the poor and the oppressed—shedding their image of wealth, ridding themselves of surplus property, privileges, and symbols of high living, and accepting the legal limitation of property rights and implications of labor laws.

d. All Christians must be involved in the building up of the human community and resisting apathy and fatalism, exercising initiative and responsibility, and acquiring technical competence and skills by training.

e. A healthy secularity must purify our piety, religious practices, and the liturgy; instead of serving as evasion from hard work and commitment or as a source of pacifying the conscience, these should give effective motivation, elan, and inspiration for committed service to society.

f. Our educational institutions—schools and colleges—and all our communications media should be geared to create this awareness, to lead to involvement, and to offer training for it.

g. The church, besides working through its own institutional structures, should endeavor to become a vital movement of dedication, of pioneering service and collaboration with other agencies, and join in the development efforts undertaken by the wider local communities, such as village, neighborhood, and even larger units.

h. Initiative and directives should not come from above; rather local initiative and responsibility must be encouraged in view of promoting self-reliance and genuine community building.

i. Enlightenment of the masses and their involvement (conscientization) alone will not be enough. An alternative power structure would seem necessary so that they will be able to defend themselves.

j. The urgency of the needs and the variety of situations will call for diversification in the apostolate and for change in our lifestyle, for different forms of organizing and living community life and for creating new structures.

k. Above all, this new type of participation in nation-building, far from being a romance, will call for a total identification with Christ and his cross, and hence will make demands on our generosity and cause us suffering, leading us to risk our lives and to face failures. This itself is part and parcel of the process of liberation as well as its authentic sign and pledge; for it is by dying to our selfish comforts and personal security that we can rise up with the masses to a new life of freedom and communion of all people.

We have reviewed the prevalent Indian situation of which the two major aspects and dimensions are an active religiosity of the people and their common struggle for liberation and development. These are not contrary and mutually exclusive concerns. Modern India's relentless and all-out effort for development and liberation is nothing but a modern expression of its age-old spiritual quest for *moksha* and *mukit*, a process of self-realization through the discovery in the depth of one's being to identification of one's self with the self of the universe.

These two aspects call for dialogue and conscientization on the part of the church. In this context, evangelization too will be most human, meaningful, and necessary, provided it is linked with a correct understanding of the religious traditions of humankind and integrated with the process of conscientization.

NOTES

1. H.R. Schlette, *Towards a Theology of Religions* (New York: Herder and Herder, 1966).

2. Report of Workshop on Theological Understanding of Development at the All-India Christian Consultation on Development, New Delhi, February 23–27, 1970.

3. Conference delivered by the President of Tanzania to the Chapter of Maryknoll Sisters at Maryknoll, New York, October 16, 1970.

4. *Theology of Development* (Bangalore: NBCLC, 1969, 1973), p. 22.

5. *Priestly Ministry*, booklet published by the CBCI Commission.

6. Asian Seminar on Religion and Development (ASRD), Report of Workshop X on Conscientization, *Word and Worship*, October 1973.

7. *The New Leader*, September 16, 1973.

13

Development of Christian Theology in India: A Critical Survey

J.R. Chandran (India)

This paper is an examination of some of the attempts at theological reformulation in India with a view to understanding how in India today Christian theology can serve the renewal of the church for its mission. It is the task of Christian theology in every situation to interpret the Christian faith commitment to the gospel of Jesus Christ, both for the purpose of deepening the understanding of the faith and for communicating the faith in a manner that calls for the response of faith.

Christian theology in India illustrates some of the important insights in the history of Christian thought down through the centuries. On the one hand is the confirmation of the insight that there is no perennial theology, no formulation of any universally relevant doctrine. This insight has been affirmed by several western theologians who have reflected on the meaning and role of theology. John Dillenberger puts it as follows:

Theology too is inextricably immersed in the problem of changing orientations and cultural shifts. That all genuine theological statements contain truth is not thereby denied; but the radical contingency of all theological work is affirmed. Both the statement that cultural shifts cannot be explained, and that all theology is relative to the situation, can be interpreted as matters for despair or for hope. Such approaches are psychologically difficult to accept for those who must be sure, and a source of laziness for those who must be assured of certain results. It is a source of hope for those for whom the situational aspects of truth provide multitudinous facets by which truth may be known.[1]

Jaroslav Pelikan, discussing the problem of doctrinal change, refers to a traditional patristic view that change is something that can happen only to heretical doctrines and says,

Unfortunately for the simplicity of such a criterion, the closer one studies the various texts, the more evident does change become, with the result that none of the Fathers appears to have been exempt from the inexorable reality of change. By a strange but unique irony, the dogmatic method of treating the phenomenon of theological change can move with great rapidity into the very relativism it seeks to avoid.[2]

He concludes by saying,

The continuity of Christians with one another both within a period of history and between periods is neither indentical with doctrinal agreement nor separable from it, but it is a function of that unity which the Church finds not in its members but in its Lord. . . . There is an ecumenicity in time as well as an ecumenicity in space, and this calls for a doctrine of the unity of the Church that will take up into itself both the fact of theological variety and the fact of doctrinal change.[3]

On the other hand, even if we recognize changes and variations in theology, the historical development of theology raises the question of identity and continuity of the faith that theology seeks to understand and interpret. What is the faith "once for all delivered to the saints" (Jude 3)? In what sense are the apostolic affirmations about the uniqueness and finality of Jesus Christ normative and unchangeable?[4] The apostolic confession that Jesus, the man of Nazareth, is the Christ, the one in and through whom we have the saving knowledge of God, is the substance of what theology seeks to interpret. It is the meaning of this confession that has to be brought out in a challenging manner in the formulations made in the context of different social, political, cultural, and philosophical backgrounds.

The Contribution of Missionary Theologians

Confronted with the Indian religious, cultural, and philosophical situation, many missionaries from the West recognized the need to modify the totally negative approach to other faiths and cultures with which the western Christian missions had started. Earlier they had held that the Indian church should accept the theological formulations made in the West. It took a long process before this attitude could be effectively challenged and a more dynamic approach adopted.

One of the earliest to raise the question of adopting indigenous forms for expressing the Christian faith was the Roman Catholic Jesuit *Robert de Nobili*, who came to India in 1605.[5] According to the traditional policy of his mission, the more Indians who discarded their ancestral customs and the closer they adhered to Portuguese ways, the better Christians they would be. But de Nobili said that it was unjust to require people to change their national customs, to give up caste and other forms of social and cultural life. The only way to make Christianity acceptable to caste Hindus was to present it as a universal religion, not as the religion of the *Parangis*.[6] He wanted to replace Latin with Sanskrit. He advocated Christian participation in Hindu festivals like Pongal, suggesting that Christians might cook their newly harvested rice at the foot of the cross planted for the purpose. His approach, however, was mainly directed to making Christianity look least objectionable in external forms. He made no attempt to modify any part of his theology, which was the Tridentine theology of his time. He rejected the Hindu practice of the repetition of the divine names, calling it a prescription from the Devil, and ridiculed the doctrines of Karma and rebirth.[7]

The first Protestant missionary, *Bartholomeus Ziegenbalg*, who arrived in India in 1706, also shared the prejudices and assumptions of European Christians of that time, and in his conferences with the Brahmins he used such terms as "you heathens," "your blindness," "the bondage of idolatry," "gross ignorance," "extremity of madness," etc. After his study of Hindu scriptures, however, his attitude clearly changed. In 1710, in his unprinted *Remarkable Voyage*, he wrote, "I do not reject everything they teach, rather rejoice, that for the heathen long ago a small light of the Gospel began to shine." He wanted his reader in Europe to see "how far they had come by the light of their reason in the knowledge of God and of the natural order, and how by their natural powers, they often put to shame many Christians by their upright life, also showing a much greater striving for the future life."[8]

But such sensitivity to facts did not find much encouragement from the official sponsors of the mission. What *A.H. Francke* (1663–1727) said expresses the general attitude of the western Christian missions for a long time. "The missionaries were sent out to exterminate heathenism in India, not to spread heathen nonsense all over Europe."[9] Even Ziegenbalg and generations of missionaries after him, on the whole, shared a spirit of certainty not only about the superiority of the gospel of Jesus Christ but also about the unchangeableness of their own doctrines.

The discovery and interpretation of the Hindu, Buddhist, and other religious Scriptures by the great orientalists like *Max Miller, Paul Deussen, A.A. Macdonnel, Berridale Keith* and others did have an impact on Christian missionary thinking. But while this started a process of rethinking of the Christian approach to other faiths, few missionary theologians considered it necessary to revise their formulations of the basic Christian doctrines such as those of the authority of the Bible, the person of Christ, the work of Christ, the Trinity, the sacraments, and the church. Even for a scholar like *J.N. Farquhar*, whose thesis was that Christ fulfills the unfulfilled longings and aspirations of Hinduism, the positive appraisal of several aspects of Hindu faith and practice was based on the acceptance of the traditional Christian doctrines as the criteria for evaluation.[10] This was true also with several other missionary theologians in India such as *T.E. Slater, Sydney Cane, E.W. Thompson,* and *A.G. Hogg.* For some of them the issue was not only the normativeness of the doctrines but also the givenness of the Hebrew-Greek-Roman heritage. Even a person like *H.S. Hayland,* who was known to be very sympathetic to India and Indian culture, writing in *The Young Men of India* in August 1927, assumed that India did not possess any heritage comparable to what was contributed by Plato and Socrates and that by accepting Christianity India would also be accepting the Hebrew-Greek-

Roman cultural values. *A.J. Appasamy* rightly challenged such a view and wrote,

The first and most natural reaction that a good many Indian Christians may have to his suggestion is one of resentment and criticism. With our deep love for the heritage of India, we may find it difficult to believe that it has to yield to Greek philosophy. We readily acknowledge the uniqueness of Jesus and bow humbly and willingly before him, but when we are told that we must learn from Plato before we can learn effectively what Jesus taught we hesitate and wonder.[11]

Theological Response Outside the Church

When we turn from the western missionary theologians in India to Indian theologians we need also to recognize the contribution of those who did respond to the message and the person of Jesus in a very profound way, without either joining the Christian church or subscribing to the traditional formulations of the Christian faith. Only a few of these may be considered here.

Two of them, Ram Mohan Roy and Keshab Chandra Sen belonged to the Brahmo Samaj movement, which stood for a radical reform of Hindu religion and society. *Ram Mohan Roy* (1772–1833) had come under the influence of western rationalism and Unitarian Christianity. His most significant book, *The Precepts of Jesus*, is evidence of the appeal the person and the teachings of Jesus had for him and his faith that a moral reform of Hinduism could be brought about by calling people to accept the teachings of Jesus as the moral expression of their faith in one God. The doctrines of the divinity of Christ, the Holy Spirit, Trinity, and atonement, as presented by the missionary theologians of the time, particularly the Serampore group, appeared to him irrational, and he rejected them. At the same time he gave centrality of place to Jesus' ethical teachings in his movement and accepted titles like "Son of God" and the doctrines of the Virgin birth and the resurrection, interpreting them in his own rationalistic manner; this is evidence of a depth of faith that, though far removed from the traditional form, has had great theological significance in India.[12]

Keshab Chandra Sen (1838–1884) made Jesus Christ even more central to his faith and experience than Ram Mohan Roy had done. His form of the Brahmo Samaj was known as the Church of the New Dispensation and had much resemblance to the Christian church, including the rites of initiation and communion. His interpretation of the person and work of Christ and the doctrine of the Trinity also came much closer to orthodox Christian doctrines than that of Ram Mohan Roy. To interpret the person of Christ he used the concept of *logos* as involved in the creation, evolution, and final perfection of the world as well as the concepts of divine humanity and kenosis. Even though some of his statements about the work of Christ sounded like moral influence theories, he also called Christ "the Mediator" and spoke of the "atoning medium." In an appealing speech he said, "Behold, I am reconciled to all through the blood of him crucified. Fellow-countrymen, be ye also reconciled through him."[13] He definitely moved away from Ram Mohan Roy's unitarian interpretation of the Brahman and expounded a trinitarian doctrine relating the Trinity to the Indian description of Brahman as Sachidananda (Sat, Cit, Ananda). For him the confession of God as the Father, Son, and the Holy Ghost also implied the "whole philosophy of salvation," because it means a God who comes down to humanity and carries it up to heaven.[14]

In spite of all this he was not regarded as a Christian, nor would he call himself a Christian. This was because the criteria for Christian orthodoxy and membership in the church had been derived from the formulations of the West, and the church in India, which Keshab Chandra Sen described as denationalized, had no freedom to reformulate. Today, however, looking back on the theology of Ram Mohan Roy and Keshab Chandra Sen we are faced with the question of redefining the boundaries of Christian orthodoxy and membership of the church of Jesus Christ.

Others like *Swami Vivekananda* (1862–1902) and *Sarvepalli Radhakrishnan* made their response to Jesus Christ in the context of their reaffirmation of Advaita or non-dualistic Vedanta. They interpreted Jesus Christ only as one manifestation of the universal reality of the Vedanta to be understood on a par with many other such manifestations. *Mahatma Gandhi* (1869–1948) approached the question of the person of Christ from a different perspective, namely, that of the ethic of love, which he interpreted in terms of *ahimsa* or nonviolence. From this perspective he did recognize his indebtedness to the teachings of Christ and the example of Christ's life and death on the cross. However, he believed that all religions had a common goal in promoting an ethic of love. Such a response, calling Christianity to take its place within a harmony of all religions, is by no means new or unique to the Indian context of Hindu renaissance. The early church had been challenged with such a demand by Celsus. But the Indian church could not simply depend on the theological apologetics of the past. Fresh answers had to be given from within the Indian context.

Christian Theology from Within the Indian Church

Many Indian Christian theologians have attempted to reformulate Christian theology in a manner relevant for the Indian context. These attempts have produced different models, depending on the particular framework and the concerns of the gospel expressed through that framework. Only a few representative theologians have been chosen for this study.

Brahmabandhav Upadhyaya (1861–1907) was a Bengali Brahmin by descent, who at first championed the principles of the Brahmo Samaj, was baptized in the Anglican Church in 1891, and in the same year joined the Roman Catholic church. [15] His original name was Bhavani Charan Bannerjee. Brahmabandhav is the Sanskrit rendering of Theophilus, the name he assumed at baptism. He had inclinations toward the ascetic life, and after becoming a Roman Catholic he adopted the yellow robe and chose the life of an ascetic. He shared the nationalist aspirations of his generation of Indian intellectuals and at the same time was deeply committed to the gospel of Jesus Christ. Therefore he wanted to express the Christian faith and life in a manner indigenous to India. He was trained in Thomistic theology and, applying its framework, proposed that in India the philosophy of Aristotle could be replaced by the Adavita philosophy of Sankara. For him, Indian philosophy was as much a part of natural theology as Plato's or Aristotle's. He further proposed an integration of the social structure of India into the Christian way of life, the establishment of an Indian Christian monastic order, and the recognition of the Vedas as part of the Old Testament for the Indian church. He wrote,

Indian thought can be made just as useful to Christianity as Greek thought has been to Europe. . . . The truths of the Hindu philosopher must be baptized and used as stepping stones to the Catholic faith. . . . The European clothes of the Catholic religion should be laid aside as soon as possible. It must assume the Hindu garment which will make it acceptable to the people of India. This change can only be effected by Indian Missionary Orders who preach the sacred Faith in the language of the Vedanta.[16]

He worked out his theology very systematically along the lines of Thomistic synthesis and went to Rome to present it to the Vatican. Unfortunately the Vatican authorities rejected his proposal and held that the traditional Catholic faith in worship, morals, spirituality, and theology should be continued in India. Now, however, both Catholics and Protestants in India have a more positive appraisal of Brahmabandhav's contribution to theology.

In his interpretation of the Trinity, he indentified the Thomistic idea of God as pure being with the Vedantic absolute, the *Brahman;* God the Son, the Logos, with *Cit;* and God the Holy Spirit, with *ananda,* the boundless bliss. He even found the doctrine of *maya* consistent with the Christian doctrine of creation. At the same time, because of his faith in Christ as the unique incarnation of God, he rejected the use of the *avatara* concept for interpreting Christ. He believed that without compromising on any of the essentials of the Christian faith Christian theology could be reformulated in India using the categories of Indian philosophy.

A.J. Appasamy (1891–1975) had been greatly influenced by his father, who was a convert from Hinduism and continued to have great regard for the Bhakti tradition. He had the opportunity of studying theology in the West, at Hartford Seminary, Harvard University, and Oxford University. At Oxford, he studied under Canon B. Streeter and made a special study of Sadhu Sunder Singh. Later he became a bishop of the Church of South India and was very much involved in the promotion of revivalism and evangelical piety in his diocese. He wrote many books, the most important ones being *Christianity as Bhakti Marga* (1928) and *The Gospel and India's Heritage* (1942).[17]

Like Brahmabandhav, Bishop Appasamy also believed that Christian faith can be interpreted in India using the categories of the Indian religious and philosophical tradition. Whereas Brahmabandhav had turned to Sankara's advaita philosophy for his Indian framework, Appasamy turned to the *visishtadvaita* (qualified non-dualism) philosophy of Ramanuja and the related Bhakti tradition of personal devotion to the deity. Accordingly, communion with God rather than the mystical union of non-dualism is the goal of the religious quest that is fulfilled by Christ. He finds parallels in Bhakti Hinduism to several Christian concepts, particularly to the union of the human and the divine in Christ, and to the relationship between divine immanence and transcendence. But he does not simply accommodate the gospel to the Indian heritage. On the contrary, he boldly rejects whatever is contrary to the Lordship of Christ, such as caste, transmigration, fatalistic interpretation of Karma, idolatry, and the like. The main point of his approach is that the gospel of Jesus Christ can be reformulated in India in the framework of India's religious heritage and that the gospel can help to reinterpret and renew India's heritage.

P. Chenchiah (1886–1959) hailed from a family of converts from the Brahmin community. By profession he was a lawyer and he served as a judge in the High Court of the princely state of Pudukottah in South India. Even though he was not a trained theologian and did not write any major theological book, he was the most creative and stimulating member of the "Rethinking Group."[18] He had two major concerns in the understanding and interpretation of the Christian faith in India. The first is expressed in his own words as follows:

The convert of today regards Hinduism as his spiritual mother, who has nurtured him in a sense of spiritual values of the past. He discovers the supreme value of Christ, not in spite of Hinduism, but because Hinduism has taught him to discern spiritual greatness. For him loyalty to Christ does not involve the surrender of a reverential attitude towards the Hindu heritage.[19]

Second, he was equally concerned about giving real evidence for the uniqueness of the Christian faith. In his spiritual quest as well as theological interpretation he was influenced by Aurobindo Ghosh who reinterpreted Vedanta in terms of integral yoga, using the categories of the Bergsonian philosophy of emergent evolution. Under this influence Chenchiah found the New Testament concepts of the new creation and the new man most appropriate to provide the key to the interpretation of Christ. He believed that Jesus Christ was the first of a new species of humanity brought about by the work of the Holy Spirit.[20] The purpose of the Christian faith was to reproduce Christ in human lives. This was to be achieved through the appropriate discipline for making the Holy Spirit operate in human lives, which might thereby become a Christian yoga similar to the yoga of the Aurobindo movement. Chenchiah's theology has close similarities to process philosophy and the theology of Teilhard de Chardin. But the main poles of his theology were what he described as the Raw Fact of Christ, the concrete historical reality of Jesus of Nazareth, and the concept of the new man or new being, suggesting both the apostolic teaching and the goal of the integral yoga of Aurobindo.[21]

Like Brahmabandhav, Chenchiah also stressed the importance of restating the Christian faith in Indian categories, liberating Christian doctrines from the language of Greek philosophy and the categories of western thought and culture. He also raised the question of whether the Old Testament could not be replaced or supplemented by Indian religious scriptures.

The Call to Dialogue

A conviction has become increasingly evident through the efforts at interpretation of the Christian faith by Indian theologians, namely, that a theology that will serve the cause of the church's mission in India has to take account of, on the one hand, "the faith once for all given," received through the different theological formulations of the past, and, on the other, the discernment of the reality of the Risen Christ on the different frontiers of the church's mission.

One of the most obvious frontiers of the church's mission in India is the meeting with people of other living faiths. The assumption of a past era that the church's goal on this frontier is simply to seek the displacement of other religions by Christianity has proved inadequate and superficial. The situation has demanded deeper theological reflection and understanding. In the fulfillment of the evangelistic and missionary task of the church on this frontier, the evangelists or missionaries do not simply carry the reality of Christ with them. They go to witness to the reality of the gospel of Jesus Christ, and this process includes the discernment of the presence of that reality in the frontier situation or even in the other faiths. It is this realization which has been expressed through the dialogue approach.

In India one of the theologians who made a significant contribution to the preparation of the churches for the dialogue approach was *P. D. Devanandan* (1901–1962). He had been a professor of Christian Ethics and History of Religions before he became the director of the Christian Institute for the Study of Religion and Society (CISRS). He had come under the influence of Barthian theology. Yet he was quite sympathetic with the Rethinking Group. He saw the importance of understanding the contemporary religious and cultural movements as well as the concerns of those who profess other faiths. He realized that this process of understanding could not just be one of academic study. It had to be promoted through living dialogues with individuals and groups. With this in mind he initiated programs of dialogues and colloquiums under the auspices of the CISRS. Through his writings also he sought to promote the dialogue approach.[22] He wrote, "The real problem in Hindu India is to effect a synthesis between traditional worldview and contemporary secularism. Thoughtful Hindu leaders are wrestling with this problem and it is in relation to this concern that the good news of God incarnate in Jesus Christ will have to be spelled out."[23] He pointed out that, "In our task of missionary preaching we have yet to take the dominant philosophical and religious concepts of the non-Christian faiths and make them into instruments of interpretation of the Gospel. . . . If God's redemptive activity in Jesus Christ is a fact with which we shall reckon in every human situation, it is not so much by total destruction that he manifests His power, but by radical renewal of what we cherish as valuable."[24] It was Devanandan's conviction that Indian Christian theology would develop its own distinctive character only through the interpretation of the "once for all delivered faith" in dialogue with people of other faiths and for the purpose of meeting their needs.

Another great advocate of the dialogue approach to Christian theology is *Raymond Panikkar* (1918–), a Roman Catholic theologian, born of a Hindu father and a Spanish Roman Catholic mother and brought up in close acquaintance with both Hinduism and Christianity. He shares the fruit of his theological reflection in several of his writings, particularly in two of his books, *The Unknown Christ of Hinduism*[25] and *The Trinity and World Religions.*[26] Both these books combine the technical terminology of Thomistic philosophy and Vedanta. In a spirit of genuine dialogue he seeks to understand Hinduism from within and comes to the conclusion that Christ is already present in Hinduism, though he is not known as Christ. He says, "Christ has not unveiled his whole face, has not yet completed his mission there. He still has to grow up and to be recognized. Moreover, He still has to be crucified there, dying with Hinduism as he died with Judaism and with the Hellenistic religions in order to rise again, as the same Christ (who is already in Hinduism), but then as a risen Hinduism, as Christianity."[27] Similarly in his book *The Trinity and World Religions*, which he describes as a meditation rather than an erudite study, he expounds the three traditional *margas* of Hinduism, namely, the *Karma Marga*, the *Bhakti Marga*, and the *Jnana Marga*, as being related to the three persons of the Trinity. He describes the synthesis of these *margas* as a "theandric synthesis," which, according to him, helps both to deepen the understanding of the trinitarian Christian faith and to recognize the possibility of such a synthesis in other faiths, though the key to the fullness of revelation of the Trinity is Christ.

In the methods of dialogue implied in Panikkar's writings as well as in some other Roman Catholic theologians, the emphasis is on the common ground of the interiority of the religious experience. Such a recognition of the reality of the presence of Christ is certainly an important and legitimate starting point for dialogue. However, for the dialogue approach to be truly faithful to the mission of Jesus Christ it cannot be exclusively limited to the sphere of interiority of religious experience. Personal as well as corporate religious experience has to be related to the total human experience, including the social and political struggles of the human community.

The Theology of Liberation and Humanization

The development of the dialogue approach to other faiths in India has also been closely associated with an interpretation of the gospel in terms of the Christian concern for the struggles for liberation. *M.M. Thomas* (1916–), till recently the Director of the CISRS, is a good representative of the theological trend in India in which the central concern is the role of the gospel in the struggle for justice. For many years Thomas had been involved in the ecumenical movement, first through the World Student Christian Federation and later through the World Council of Churches, of which he was the chairman of the

Central Committee from 1968 to 1975. While he made a significant contribution to ecumenical thinking on social questions, the ecumenical movement also contributed to the shaping of his views.[28] The following statement of R. H. S. Boyd is a fair indication of the theological orientation of Thomas:

> In carrying forward Devanandan's experiments in dialogue, Thomas speaks of three different levels at which dialogue with Hinduism must be carried on. First there is the dialogue which studies the contribution of each faith to man and society—a secular conversation which should lead on to the possibility of a common culture—not a "Christian" culture, but an "open" culture based on a common humanity. Secondly, there is the type of dialogue which seeks to come to grips with the central theological issues of each faith. And thirdly, there is dialogue at the level of interiority—the dialogue "in the cave of the heart" of which Abhishiktananda writes. All of these are necessary, but Thomas' own special interest is in the first type, where Christian and Hindu meet together in the context of modern secular India in order to find common fields of action and service for the good of the nation as a whole and of individual persons.[29]

His faith is deeply rooted in the affirmation of Christ crucified and risen as the basis for the hope of salvation for the sinner. He is critical of religious as well as secular systems of thought that fail to recognize the tragic character of sin. But he understands sin and salvation in terms of the loss and the restoration of true humanity. He rejects the separation of theology from anthropology and interprets salvation as essentially humanization. The christological affirmation of Christ as the true man is the basis for his interpretation of the work of Christ as humanization. He says that "the mission of salvation and the task of humanization are integrally related to each other, even if they cannot be considered identical."[30]

Conclusion

This brief survey has shown that there is no single pattern or model for the development of Indian Christian theology. But the main key to Indian theology is the discernment of the reality of Christ and his mission on frontiers of the church both with other faiths and with the struggle for justice. What is important for Indian theology is not just the form in which different doctrinal formulations are made about God, Christ, Holy Spirit, the church, the sacraments, salvation,

Christian hope, and the like. It is true that doctrinal formulations have helped the understanding of the faith and its communication to those within the church as well as to those outside. But the basic fact for Christians is not the possession of these doctrines or the institutions and sacraments of the church interpreted by these doctrines. The basic fact for Christians is the reality of Christ whom they confess as the risen Lord. Traditionally even this fact has been modified into a doctrine of the resurrection, and Christians have been tutored to believe in resurrection as a historic event of the past and to hope for a bodily resurrection in the same way as the bodily resurrection of Jesus. The New Testament testimony, however, is something much greater. God's power related to the resurrection faith is not just illustrated by a past historic event. It is the continuing event of the church's faith that God has raised Jesus from the dead and that the ministry of Jesus is therefore continuing.

According to the New Testament the historic event was not the resurrection of Christ. The risen Christ was seen and experienced only by the believing church, not by his enemies or nonbelievers. The resurrection faith, which is the key to the confession of Jesus as Christ and Lord, is also related to the affirmation that the mission that Jesus began in Galilee is being continued, and the apostles are called to meet Jesus and manifest this ministry. This is the significance of the testimony of Mark. The Pauline interpretation of the Last Supper as well as the Johannine interpretation of the washing of the feet try to state the same thing, namely, that the church of Jesus is to continue the ministry of Jesus, knowing that through the Holy Spirit the risen Lord has made the church to be his body. Therefore for Christians, in dialogue with others the subject for testifying is not just a past event. They are to testify about a continuing event of which they and the believing community to which they belong are an integral part.

The question this affirmation raises is to what extent can we discern ourselves and the churches to which we belong as the continuing event of the resurrection, carrying on the mission of God begun with the mission of Jesus of Nazareth. Believing in the God who has revealed himself in Jesus Christ does mean taking a stand for a righteousness, peace, and justice in human affairs that would lead to a certain polarization. But the polarization brought about by Christian mission is not that between Christians and non-Christians. The polarization is between, on the one hand, those who accept the concern of Jesus Christ for liberation from everything that enslaves and distorts human dignity as the basis for forging new structures of social and political existence, those who therefore will promote movements that seek such liberation as part of their religious commitment, and, on the other hand, those who interpret their religion in a way that makes them knowingly or unknowingly support the structures of economic and political life that continue to enslave people and distort their human dignity.

Such a theology cannot simply remain in abstract formulations. If it is genuinely expressive of the discernment of the reality of Christ crucified and risen in concrete human situations, then it will inspire the believers to get involved with others, whatever their religious faith or ideologies, for the liberation of individuals and groups from all forms of dehumanizing bondages and oppressive structures. In other words, true theology is not just a process of formulation of doctrines, but a process of doing, a process of participation in the real presence of Christ with two poles, one the sacramental participation and the other a contemporary re-enactment of the exodus-covenant experience for people suffering from different forms of oppression. It is when this dimension becomes the real basis of Indian Christian theology, grappling with the totality of the Indian religious, social, and cultural situation, that Indian Christian theology will share in the universal concern of Christian theology.

NOTES

1. John Dillenberger, *Contours of Faith: Changing Forms of Christian Thought* (Nashville, New York: Abingdon Press, 1969), p. 22.

2. Jaroslav Pelikan, *Historical Theology: Continuity and Change in Christian Doctrine* (London: Hutchinson, 1971), p. 26.

3. Ibid., p. 161.

4. See Heb. 1:1–2; Eph. 4:13–14; Col. 1:15–20; John 20:31; Acts 4:12; etc.

5. See C.B. Firth, *An Introduction to Indian Church History* (Madras: CLS Press, 1961), pp. 107–19; R.H.S. Boyd, *An Introduction to Indian Christian Theology*, rev. ed. (Madras: CLS Press, 1975), pp. 11–14; Vincent Cronin, *A Pearl to India: The Life of Robert de Nobili* (London: Hart Davis, 1959); S. Rajamanikam; *The First Oriental Scholar: Robert de Nobili* (Tirunelveli: de Nobili Research Institute, 1972).

6. Cronin, *Pearl to India*, p. 168.

7. Boyd, *Introduction*, p. 13.

8. E. A. Lehmann, *It Began at Tranquebar* (Madras: CLS Press, 1956), pp. 31–32.

9. Quoted in ibid., p. 32.

10. J. N. Farquhar, *The Crown of Hinduism* (London: Oxford University Press, 1915).

11. A. J. Appasamy, *International Review of Missions*, 1928, pp. 472–82.

12. For a fuller discussion of the theology of Ram Mohan Roy, see Boyd, *Introduction*, pp. 19–26; and M. M. Thomas, *The Acknowledged Christ of Indian Renaissance* (Madras: CLS Press, 1970), chap. 1.

13. Quoted by Boyd, *Introduction*, p. 33.

14. For a fuller discussion of Keshab Chandra Sen's theology, see Boyd, *Introduction*, pp. 26–39; and Thomas, *Acknowledged Christ*, chap. 3.

15. See B. Animananda, *The Blade: Life and Work of Brahmabandhav Upadhyaya* (Calcutta: Roy and Son, probably 1947); K. Baago, *Pioneers of Indigenous Christianity* (Madras: CLS Press, 1969), pp. 26–49, 118–50; Boyd, *Introduction*, pp. 63–85.

16. Quoted by Boyd, *Introduction*, p. 64.

17. Some of his other books are *Temple Bells* (1930); *Church Union: An Indian View* (1930); *What is Moksha?* (1931); *The Johannine Doctrine of Life: A Study of Christian and Hindu Thought* (1934); *My Theological Quest* (1964); and *The Theology of Hindu Bhakti* (1970).

18. They were called so because of the book they published under the title *Rethinking Christianity in India* (Madras: CLS Press, 1938). The other members of the group were G. V. Job, V. Chakkarai, and D. M. Devasahayam. This book was written as a critical response from India to H. Kraemer's book, *The Christian Message in a Non-Christian World*.

19. *Rethinking Christianity*, p. 48.

20. Ibid., pp. 62, 158–68.

21. For a fuller discussion of Chenchiah's theology, see D. A. Thangasamy, *The Theology of P. Chenchiah* (Madras: CLS Press, 1966).

22. Several of his books are specially relevant for this theme, namely, *The Gospel and the Hindu Intellectual* (Bangalore: CISRS, 1959); *The Gospel & Renascent Hinduism* (London: SCM, 1959); *Christian Concern in Hinduism* (Bangalore: CISRS, 1961); and *Preparation for Dialogue* (Bangalore: CISRS, 1964).

23. *Preparation for Dialogue*, p. 38.

24. Ibid., p. 191.

25. London: Darton, Longman & Todd, 1964.

26. Madras: CLS Press, 1970.

27. *Unknown Christ*, p. 17.

28. His major books are *The Christian Response to the Asian Revolution* (London: SCM, 1966); *The Acknowledged Christ of the Indian Renaissance* (London: SCM, 1969); *Salvation and Humanization* (Bangalore: CISRS, 1971); *The Realization of the Cross* (Madras: CLS, 1972).

29. Boyd, *Introduction*, pp. 311–12.

30. *Salvation and Humanization*, p. 8.

LATIN AMERICA

14

The Political and Ecclesial Context of Liberation Theology in Latin America

Enrique Dussel (Mexico)

The context of the history of theology in Latin America is the history of the theology of the "center," originally Europe and today, by extension, the United States (since Russia contributes little today to theological creation). The context of the biography of the son is the biography of the father, which is not to say that the son is the father but rather that the father is his context Latin American theology is the child of European theology, yet it is different; it is separate; it is another avenue of the same tradition, because it evolves in a "peripheral" world within first the modern mercantile period and then the monopolistic imperial period. It is the theology of a colonial or neocolonial world which often simply reflects the theology of the "center"; but in its more creative moments it has produced a new theology that has risen up against the great traditionally constituted theology.

In other essays we have proposed a periodification of the history of the church in Latin America.[1] It is not my purpose to discuss again here the entire history of theology in Latin America. However, a brief chronological outline of the periods in Latin American theology would be as follows:

1. Prophetic theology confronting the conquest and evangelization (from 1511)
2. Theology of colonial Christendom (1553–1808)
3. Practical-political theology in neocolonial emancipation (from 1808)
4. Conservative neocolonial theology on the defensive (1831–1931)
5. Theology of the "New Christendom" (1930–1962)
6. Latin American liberation theology (from 1962)

This paper will strive to develop the last two periods of this chronological history. In order to understand the development of Latin American liberation theology, we must first examine what was happening in the theological world from 1930 to 1962.

My discussion will be limited to a Catholic perspective of these two periods. Another paper included in this volume will treat the Protestant churches during this time.

THE THEOLOGY OF "NEW CHRISTENDOM" (1930–1962)

After 1930 there was a transition from the traditional theology of the landowning classes (whose enemies were bourgeois liberalism, communism, Protestantism, and "modern times") to developmentalist, reformist theology. This theology adopted the bourgeois ethos within the tragic context of dependent capitalism (at least in the most "advanced" countries, because the majority of our nations have not even reached the level of capitalism; they remain mere neocolonies for the exploitation of raw materials with no national bourgeoisie, in the strict sense of the term).

The crisis of 1929 had had repercussions in the "periphery," especially in Latin America. In certain areas, such as the Southern Cone (Argentina, Uruguay, Chile), central Brazil (between Río and São Paulo), and Mexico, the response was industrialization based on import substitution, a trend which increased during the Second World War. But at the same time there were popular social movements (the first of which was the Mexican revolution of 1910, later skillfully taken in hand by the bourgeoisie of that country) which made it impossible for the neocolonial bourgeoisie to exercise power. Thus a military class arose in nearly every country, first in the name of the landowning classes and later in the name of an ambiguous unity between the national bourgeoisie and the working classes. This meant the end of militant, lay, positivist, anti-clerical liberalism and the beginning of overtures toward the traditional, conservative Catholic church. This permitted the organization of gigantic Eucharistic Congresses but, more important, the foundation of *Acción Católica* and similar institutions, based on the theoretic theological formulation of "New Christendom."

In 1928 the priests Caggiano (later cardinal of Buenos Aires) and Miranda (later cardinal of Mexico City) went to Rome to study the organization of *Acción Católica*. From 1929 on it became slowly institutionalized in all our countries. This theology clearly distinguished between the "temporal" and the "spiritual." The layman was responsible for everything temporal, worldly, material, and political; the priest was the "spiritual man," the vicar of the kingdom of Christ. The role of the Christian people, the militants, was to fulfill the "apostolate." This "sending" or mission was defined as a "participation in the hierarchical apostolate of the church." In this way the sacrament of orders practically suppressed the meaning of charisms and the sacrament of baptism.

The laity could be politically active in parties of "Christian inspiration." So, for example, there arose in Chile in 1936 the "Falangist" group, which after the Second World War, through Italian influence, was called "Christian Democracy" and flourished especially from 1950 to 1970. The laity could be active in labor unions, also of "Christian inspiration." Thus was organized the Latin American Confederation of Christian Syndicates (CLASC), which were in most cases reformist unions. The laity could teach, but in "Christian schools." Their task was to reconvert the Latin American nations to Catholicism. The kingdom of Christ required the recognition of the Catholic religion as the majority, official religion. The church dreamed of recovering the power it had lost in the nineteenth century after the crisis of Christendom, with militant lay people as the means to that end.

This theology of "New Christendom" was not academic but militant. It was not directly political but rather dualistic with regard to the temporal and the spiritual; the state and the church were perfect societies, each on its own level and not in conflict.

The step toward a *developmentalist theology* did not come until 1950. That is when Christians, or some of them, decisively adopted the bourgeois—and petty bourgeois—goals of expansion and development. Clearly there was as yet no awareness of the problem of *classes* and of the *dependence* that the Latin American continent was suffering under the economic, political, and military power of the United States.

Theologians were now trained not only in Italy; the most progressive went to France, land of the pastoral teams, of catechetical and liturgical experiments, of spirituality, of the "worker priests." The "social doctrine" of the church permitted many to dedicate themselves to workers or marginal groups of society.

In this era many new theological schools or centers were founded at universities, for example in Bogotá (1937), Lima (1942), Medellín (1945), São Paulo and Rio de Janeiro (1947), Porto Alegre (1950), Campinas and Quito (1956), Buenos Aires and Córdoba (1960), Valparaíso and Guatemala (1961). Theology, European style, enjoyed an academic atmosphere in which it could grow while it awaited its creative moment.

Ecclesiastical praxis was growing, too. *Acción Católica*—founded in Argentina and Chile in 1931, in Uruguay in 1934, in Costa Rica and Perú in 1935, and in Bolivia in 1938—eventually moved into a lukewarm "social struggle." Groups such as "Economía Humana," inspired by Lebret, or the Bellarmine Center in Santiago, Chile, were building awareness. The Centers of Social and Religious Research, founded in Buenos Aires, Santiago, Bogotá, and Mexico, permitted the beginning of a certain "sociographic" (not sociological, much less economic-political) vision of Latin American reality.

No less important was the establishment of the Latin American Episcopal Conference (CELAM) in Rio in 1955, under the inspiration of Bishop Manuel Larraín. CELAM facilitated the coordination of apostolic movements and became the training ground for the militant theologians of the next period. In 1958 the Latin American Confederation of Religious (CLAR) appeared, and little by little all sorts of movements were organized: schools of theology, theological seminaries, *Acción Católica* movements, labor unions, etc.

The basis was also being laid for the biblical movement. The

Protestants with their Bible societies and the Catholics through seminaries, periodicals, and new editions of the Bible were opening the way for biblical renewal.

Nevertheless, it must be said that even after World War II, theological production was by imitation and application of European methods, with no real, historical understanding of Latin America.

LATIN AMERICAN THEOLOGY OF LIBERATION (FROM 1962)

The most recent period has three clearly discernible stages: the first (1962–68), from the beginning of Vatican II to Medellín, a time of preparation and of a still rather developmentalist position; the second (1968–72), a time of formulation of liberation theology and an attitude of euphoria; the third (beginning on the Catholic side in Sucre in 1972, with the restructuring of CELAM, and on the Protestant side in UNELAM [Unión Evangélica Latinoamericana]), a time of maturation, of persecution, of new awareness that liberation was to be a *long* process; a time of exile, of captivity. If the previous stage emphasized the Exodus, this stage is characterized by a rethinking of Second Isaiah and the other books of the Babylonian captivity. This period, then, is the time of passage from *developmentalist* to *liberation* theology.

But we must not fool ourselves. As Luiz Alberto Gómez de Sousa explained in the theological encounter of Mexico (August 1975), within dependent capitalism there coexist a traditional theology (of the classes linked to agriculture), a developmentalist theology (of the bourgeois and petty bourgeois classes), and a theology of liberation (which expresses the faith of the emerging classes—workers, peasants, the marginalized groups, and the radicalized middle sectors). The theological confrontation in Latin America is not between the traditional and liberation theologies, but between the progressive developmentalist theology (inspired in the best contemporary European thinking) and the theology of liberation. The criticism that liberation theology often makes of the best of European thought (political theology, the theology of hope, etc.) in reality is directed against those among us who use the European theologies to discredit a *real* and *critical* Latin American theology. European reformist theology may be valid for the world of the "center" but it is profoundly ambiguous and ideological on the "periphery." Even if the European proposals are reformist there, here they may be reactionary and antirevolutionary, in short, allied with frankly traditionalist theologies (like that of *Opus Dei*).

The theology of liberation was not the product of spontaneous generation. Its history goes back to Bartolomé de las Casas in the sixteenth century. Among the youth movements of *Acción Católica* (JUC, JEC, JOC) in the last stage of "New Christendom," there was a discovery of the responsibility of the layperson as such and the requirement of political commitment. Coming from the middle sectors or from workers or peasant leaders, these groups were radicalized in the 1950s. No longer did they accept the alliance with the industrial bourgeoisie and the landed oligarchy. Many were students with uncomfortable consciences because they did not naturally belong to the oppressed classes. So they often rejected their own class, moved from reformism to revolution, and frequently adopted an anticommunism—not of the right but of the extreme left (communist parties were reactionary from their viewpoint). And they sometimes fell into a romantic, Zealotist approach because of their lack of political realism. This utopianism can be observed in the heroic, but neither practical nor operable, positions of Camilo Torres in Colombia or of the "guerrillas of Teoponte" in Bolivia.[2] In the face of the unlikelihood of change, they were trying to do everything at once. It is not surprising that the armed groups of the Peronist left in Argentina (the *montoneros)* were founded by former leaders of JUC, or that the leftist MIR in Chile had the support of most of the "Group of Eighty" priests. Nevertheless liberation theology is far from being the expression of guerrilla or extremist groups. Quite the contrary, it indicates a profound and fruitful reflection on reality. Consequently persecution increased, Latin American Christs were martyred, hundreds gave up their life for their faith—in concrete political situations, murdered by parapolice or police, armies, or groups linked to the CIA and its partisans (the soldiers of Pilate!).

The Time of Preparation (1962–68)

Developmentalist theology was based on the myth of the "development" of the underdeveloped peoples, which was supposed to occur with the help of the technical assistance and the capital of the powers of the "center" (principally the United States and Europe). This myth reached its highest expression in Kennedy's "Alliance for Progress." The *theology of development*[3] is the reflection of a faith that in socio-political and economic matters proposes partial social reforms. It has a "functionalist" spirituality: The "grace of one's state" helps one to fulfill one's duty and to give "good example." This theology is up-to-date with whatever is coming out of Europe. It stresses becoming "incarnated" in the world (without ever discovering the conflictive nature of that world, because it is considered good or positive from an a priori viewpoint). This is the "world" of the bourgeois, and the conflict is never discovered because the Christian has been educated within the bourgeois ecclesiastical culture.

Vatican II must be situated within the cultural process of the European center and of the peaceful coexistence between the United States, Western Europe, and Russia (which continued to grow until the recent Helsinki meeting). The participation of the Latin Americans at the Council can be considered, theologically speaking, virtually nonexistent. This was understandable considering the immaturity of theological reflection on our continent since the beginning of the century.

In 1963, during the Council, Manuel Larraín, bishop of Talca, Chile, was elected president of CELAM (a position he held until his accidental death in 1966). The movement led by Larraín culminated in the Second General Conference of the Latin American Episcopacy, which took place in Medellín in 1968. Medellín was the end of the preparatory stage; its vocabulary was developmentalist (speaking of "human promotion," "development") as well as liberationist ("international tensions and external neocolonialism," "the flight of capital," "international monopolies or the imperialism of money"). It was the fruit of a long process.

Starting with the post-war years, groups of young seminarians and theologians studied in France and then in Austria and Germany and the United States. At the beginning they did nothing but parrot what they had learned. But little by little they began to describe their reality, thanks to organizations like FERES,[4] founded by François Houtart, or DESAL,[5] founded by Roger Vekemans in 1961 (both Belgians, who later moved in very different directions). ILADES[6] was established in Santiago, Chile, in 1961. Religious sociology was followed by general and pastoral sociology. Thus ICLA[7] was founded in the south (1961) and in the north (1966), and somewhat later the Latin American Institute of Pastoral Liturgy was established (1965); OSLAM[8] provided courses for seminary professors; IPLA[9] opened its doors in Quito in 1968 and trained more than 500 pastoralists, having begun its itinerant work in 1964 under the inspiration of Bishop Proaño and a group of theological activists. Theologically this developmentalist period culminated in a meeting in Mexico, September 24–28, 1969, under the slogan of "Faith and development."

Because theology was discussed among representatives of all the Latin American countries (from Mexico and the Caribbean to Brazil, the Andean countries, and the Southern Cone), the theologians went beyond parroting what they had learned in Europe, broadened their discourse to Latin American reality, and began to deal increasingly with the anguishing problem of the poverty and injustice that afflict the continent.

The Latin American theologians of this period were, among others, Juan Luis Segundo[10] and José Comblin—a Belgian resident in Latin America for twenty years.[11] His book *L'échec de l'action catholique* (1959), based on his experience in Brazil, was the end and the first authorized critique of the theology of "New Christendom." Simultaneously, as a passage to the next stage, during these years there was talk of a "theology of revolution,"[12] a theme suggested in ecumenical circles where Latin American theologians were already participating.[13]

Formulation of the "Theology of Liberation" (1968–72)

A long process had been gestating in Latin America. In 1959 a group of guerrilla fighters overthrew Batista in Cuba. Fidel Castro and Che Guevara appeared as a worldwide symbol of the process of liberation from North American imperialism. The organization of liberation movements began everywhere. In Chile, with the Popular Unity, the process showed new vitality (1970). The return of Perón and the goals of liberation of the popular movement in Argentina (1972–73) inspired great hopes. It seemed possible to organize a continental movement of liberation. CELAM played a part with the organization of its institutes. There were study meetings of religious, bishops, and laity. "Grassroots" movements multiplied. Priest groups sprang up in nearly every country; the most important were "Priests for the Third World" in Argentina, the "Group of Eighty" in Chile, ONIS in Peru. University students became politically committed within a socialist perspective.

There was an epistemological split in the human sciences beginning around 1964: The socio-economics of development was transformed into a theory of liberation by means of a diagnosis that included a "theory of dependency."[14] In short it said: It is impossible to develop the underdeveloped countries because their underdevelopment is due to their systematic despoliation by the nations of the "center." The "periphery"—as Raúl Prebisch discovered when he was economist with ECLA, in the 1964 meeting of UNCTAD I—sells its raw materials at lower and lower prices, while the cost of the manufactured products sold by the "center" become more expensive. The imbalance is progressive and structural. Thus developed the sociology of liberation and with it the new economics.[15]

It is not surprising, therefore, that by 1968 theology adopted the experience and aspirations of the "grassroots" [*las bases*] and the hypotheses of the human sciences: Thus was born the "theology of liberation." Gustavo Gutiérrez, advisor to student movements in Peru, raised the question: "Theology of development or theology of liberation?"[16] Richard Shaull asked the same question at the ecumenical level,[17] Rubem Alves within Brazilian Protestantism,[18] and Lucio Gera within Argentine populism, which was rising up against the theology of secularization.[19] The praxis of liberation was the basis for a critique of the theologies of revolution, of the "death of God," of secularization. Hugo Assmann differentiated liberation theology from political theology and the theology of hope,[20] and the movement became more consistent—beginning around 1970–71. This was when history and philosophy also began to support the nascent Latin American theology of liberation.[21] Theologically, the Encounter of Escorial (Spain, July 1972) was the first meeting where the participants of this movement could carry on a dialogue.[22] Also present there were Míguez Bonino,[23] who had risen through the World Council of Churches, and Juan C. Scannone of Argentina.[24] *Víspera* (a periodical published in Montevideo), led by Borrat and Methol Ferre, provided a uniting link,[25] as also was provided by MIEC's Documentation Service in Lima. Periodicals such as *Stromata* (Buenos Aires), *Teología y Vida* (Santiago), *Christus* (Mexico), *Pastoral Popular*, *Revista Brasileira de Teología* (Petropolis), *Sic* (Caracas), and *Diálogo* (Panama) all contributed to this new line.

This euphoric stage was begun in a way by the Archbishop of Olinda-Recife, Helder Camara, and sixteen other bishops from the "periphery," in a document which appeared in *Témoignage Chrétien* (Paris, July 31, 1966). They declared that "the peoples of the Third World constitute the proletariat of the contemporary world." The position was confirmed by the Secretary of CELAM, Eduardo Pironio, when he said in New York that "our mission, like Christ's, consists of proclaiming the good news to the poor, proclaiming the liberation of the oppressed" (Maryknoll, 1971).[26]

This was a theological reflection that considered the *concrete* political commitment of Christians, in their geopolitical situation in the "periphery" and their social position as the "organic intellectuals" of the oppressed classes (in the case of the theologian) or as full participants in the risks involved in the liberation of those classes. The "struggle" is not what is desired; the "struggle" is the fruit of sin: it is perpetrated by the oppressor (the sinner) and suffered by the oppressed.

"Captivity" and "Exile" as Stages of Liberation (since 1972)

The theology of liberation—which had been primarily inspired by positive events of liberation (and therefore by Moses' departure from Egypt)— discovered, through the hard reality of praxis, the themes of "captivity" and "exile." (I was forced out of my own country and am writing these lines from a real, concrete exile.) It is not hard to understand why the theme was suggested by Brazilians, Leonardo Boff,[27] among others. The liberating Christ is also the "suffering servant."[28]

The shadow of repression and imperial domination covers practically the entire continent (with the exception of one island in the Caribbean). Groups are redefining themselves in the face of external oppression (that of the police state) and internal oppression (that of the church itself), and the theology of liberation begins its coming of age on the cross.

With the failure of the "Alliance for Progress," the United States changed its policy toward Latin America. Thus for example the CIA in Chile opposed the Popular Unity party in 1963, the same year that William Rogers was named the new assistant secretary of state for Latin American affairs and ten million dollars were delivered to a certain Belgian priest to support the propaganda of Christian Democracy.[29] The coup d'état in Brazil came in 1964, under the theoretical and practical leadership of Golbery, who was trained—like the military officers who led the coups in Uruguay (1971), Bolivia (1972), and Chile (1973)—in the United States or in the School of Panama (Canal Zone). The "Rockefeller Report" (1969)[30] confirmed this hard line by indicating that in the name of the "security of the western hemisphere" (of the United States) it was necessary to help the military leaders, even when in fact they are dictators (this, obviously, was left unsaid) to fulfill their role as defenders of order and of the values of "western, Christian civilization." Among those Christian defenders are the presidents of Brazil, the Uruguayan military rulers, Banzer, Pinochet, etc. The empire no longer talks about freedom and democracy in its neocolonies; now it is "order" and "security" and "in God we trust," with God looking more and more like the god Mars, the god of war, who gives victory to the oppressors.

It is clear that the political imprudence of the guerrilla groups justifies the transformation of the armies into occupying forces on behalf of the Empire. Church groups support this tendency and sacralize this ultra-rightist line. It is important to note that allied with these positions are the "progressives," reformists, and post-conciliar developmentalist theologians inspired by the best of European theology. They all criticize the theology of liberation and some develop, with the help of German Catholic agencies, specific projects to carry out their criticism. The argument is simple: The theology of liberation is identified with the "extreme left" (which is untrue) and with guerrilla groups; it is then criticized as being the strategic, Marxist-Christian support of those violent groups.[31]

The meetings of Bogotá (November 1973)[32] and Toledo (1974),[33] for example, were directed against the theology of liberation, but they only partially achieved their goals. On the other hand, beginning with the meeting at Sucre in November 1972, it was decided to close the Pastoral Institute in Quito, the Liturgical Institute in Medellín and the Catechetical Institute in Manizales, and to establish a fourth institute with a different orientation—excluding Comblin and myself, among others, from its classrooms. In Belgium the old *Lumen Vitae* Institute, where numerous Latin Americans had participated, was closed, and little by little the list increased of closures of institutes, seminaries, and groups oriented to the theology of liberation.

Between the left and the right, in the "center," there were certain theological movements that we might call "populist"—especially in Argentina, on account of the euphoria caused by the return of Perón—which in 1974 began to realize the ambiguity of their position. This situation impelled them to define more carefully their notion of "people" and to understand the difference between reformist and revolutionary positions. Now the confrontation, as we have said, was between European-style progressives and liberation theology groups—a confrontation which was clearly revealed in the above mentioned meetings in Bogotá in November 1973, called by CELAM, and in Lima in September 1975.[34]

Meanwhile the theology of liberation was maturing through persecution, and its number of tried and proven participants was increasing. Expelled from their places of work (like Comblin from Brazil, Assmann and others from Chile, etc.), persecuted at times by their own church, they increased in quantity and quality. Thus appeared, besides those already mentioned, the figures of Ignacio Ellacuría and Jon Sobrino in El Salvador,[35] Luis del Valle in Mexico,[36] Virgilio Elizondo among the Chicanos of the United States,[37] Raúl Vidales working in Lima,[38] Rafael Avila in Colombia,[39] Ronaldo Muñoz in Chile,[40] Antoncich and Cussianovich in Peru.[41]

The theology of liberation took with increasing seriousness its involvement in popular liberation movements and remained united with its brothers and sisters in the struggle—the martyrs of the Latin American Church: Antonio Pereira Neto, murdered in Brazil (1969), Héctor Gallego, who disappeared in Panamá (1972), Carlos Múgica, gunned down in Argentina (1974), Ivan Betancourt, killed in Honduras (1975).[42]

Christians for Socialism, which had held its inaugural meeting in Chile in 1972, by the time of its second meeting in Quebec found itself to be a world-wide body showing a real maturation, greater precision in its interpretative categories, and greater distance from the Chilean event. It represents an important contribution of Latin American theology to universal Christian theology.[43]

The first Latin American Theological Encounter, held in Mexico in August 1975,[44] constitutes a pause in the new stage of the theology of liberation and a clear confrontation with positions, in this case mainly "functionalist" North American positions, that again show their lack of awareness of our concrete Latin American reality. And the Theology in the Americas meeting, held in Detroit the following week, made possible the first global contact between Latin American theologians and North American exponents of the movements of black, feminist, and Chicano theology, and with other theologians critical of the system.[45] Through the present dialogue with other theologians of Africa and Asia, the theology of liberation can now open its scope to the broader world.

We can say then that the theology of liberation has discovered the *political moment* of captivity, of prudence, of patience. But in order that it not be converted into reformism, it will have to keep very much in mind the strategic goal of liberation.

NOTES

1. See Enrique Dussel, *History and the Theology of Liberation* (Maryknoll, New York, 1976).

2. Cf. Hugo Assmann, *Teoponte: Una experiencia guerrillera* (Oruro, Bolivia, 1971). The leader of this group was Nestor Paz, poet and medical student, a former Catholic seminarian (1963–66); he died on October 8, 1970, at age 25. In English see *My Life for My Friends: The Guerrilla Journal of Nestor Paz, Christian* (Maryknoll, New York, 1975).

3. See, for example, F. Houtart and O. Vertrano, *Hacia una teología del desarrollo* (Buenos Aires, 1967); Hugo Assmann, "Die situation der unterentwickelt gehaltenen Länder als Ort einer Theologie der Revolution," in *Diskussion zur "Theologie der Revolution"* (Munich, 1969) (the "theology of revolution," however, represents a clear break with the "theology of development" and a kind of passage to the "theology of liberation"); Rubem Alves, 'Apuntes para una teología del desarrollo," in *Cristianismo y Sociedad* 21 (1969).

4. International Federation for Studies of Religious Sociology.

5. Center for Economic and Social Development in Latin America. This center helped inspire the Chilean Christian Democratic party. The "center" moved to Caracas in 1970 and from there to Bogotá. In Bogotá it established the review *Tierra Nueva*, in which the first article of the first issue was written by Alfonso Lopez Trujillo ("La liberación y las liberaciones," pp. 5–26). It says: "Whatever is not revolution (presumably violent) is catalogued as developmentalism, a useless and fallacious effort." The theology of liberation is identified with extreme and guerrilla-oriented positions and is

The Context of Liberation Theology

distinguished from the liberation that occurs above human, political contradictions. In the July 1975 issue (p. 27, note 16), we are accused of utilizing the ideological hermeneutic method with regard to theology (A. Lopez Trujillo, "El compromiso politico del sacerdote"), without the author's realizing that the subject was raised by Christ himself (Luke 23:34). Thus began the criticism against liberation theology.

6. Latin American Institute of Doctrine and Social Studies, founded by Jesuits coming from *Action Populaire* (Paris), such as Pierre Bigo of France, now in Bogotá, who did not adopt the liberation line.

7. Latin American Catechetical Institute.

8. Organization of Seminaries of Latin America.

9. Latin American Pastoral Institute, which carried out a praiseworthy effort of conscientization, publications, and meetings. It suffered severe criticism at the hands of the most conservative groups.

10. Born in 1925. Author of *Berdiaeff: Une conception chrétienne de la personne* (Paris, 1963); *La Cristiandad, ¿una utopía?* (Montevideo, 1964); "L'avenir du christianisme en Amérique Latine," in *Lettre* (Paris) 54 (1963):7–12; and somewhat earlier *Función de la Iglesia en la realidad rioplatense* (Montevideo, 1962); later, the five volumes of *Teología abierta para el laico adulto* (Buenos Aires, 1968–72) [Eng. trans.: *Theology for Artisans of a New Humanity* (Maryknoll, New York, 1973–74)], (along the lines of Vatican II, prior to the theology of liberation). More recently, see Segundo's *De la sociedad a la teología* (Buenos Aires, 1970); and *Liberación de la teología* (Buenos Aires, 1975) [Eng. trans.: *The Liberation of Theology* (Maryknoll, New York, 1976)].

11. Born in 1923 in Belgium, but resident in Latin America since 1957. Among his works: *Théologie de la paix* (Paris, 1960–63); *Théologie de la ville* (Paris, 1968); *Le Christ dans l'Apocalypse* (Paris, 1965); *Teología do desenvolvimento* (Belo Horizonte, 1968); *Théologie de la révolution*, 2 vols. (Paris, 1970–74) (only in vol. 2 does he adopt some of the theses of liberation theology).

12. See a bibliography on the subject in *Desarrollo y revolución*, in the bibliography of CEDIAL (Bogota, 1974), pp. 73–95; and Hugo Assmann, "Caracterização de una teología de revolução," in *Ponto Homen* 4 (1968), pp. 6–58. In part the problem developed in the "Church and Society" meeting of the World Council in Geneva in 1966. The works of Richard Shaull contributed to it, and also the rich Latin American experience.

13. It should be emphasized that the "theology of liberation" later showed that the "theology of revolution" is only an *application* of certain themes of moral theology to the revolutionary situation—a kind of "green light." It is not a complete restating of theology but rather a kind of "opportunism."

14. The most creative group originating this doctrine were the Brazilians, beginning with Guerreiro Ramos (*La reducción sociológica* [Rio, 1958]), and centered around people like Helio Jaguaribe, Cándido Mendes, Alvaro Vieira Pintos, who did research in ISEB. Celso Furtado, Theotonio dos Santos, and others later joined this group. The theory of dependence was formulated between 1968 and 1970, a period in which most of the related works appeared (cf. the bibliographies of CEDIAL and *Fe y cambio social en América Latina* [Salamanca, 1973]).

15. See the works of the African economist Samir Amin, *L'accumulation à l'échelle mondiale* (Paris, 1970), and others of his works that follow the line of the Latin American "theory of dependence" and state it as a hypothesis of world economics.

16. Born in 1928. Among other works: *La pastoral de la iglesia en América latina* (Montevideo, 1968); *Hacia una teología de la liberación* (Montevideo, 1969); and his book

Teología de la liberación (Lima, 1971) [Eng: trans.: *A Theology of Liberation* (Maryknoll, New York, 1973)]; plus many periodical articles.

17. In his short work "Consideraciones teológicas sobre la liberación del hombre," in IDOC (Bogotá) 43 (1969); and in "La liberación humana desde una perspectiva teológica," in *Mensaje* 168 (1968), pp. 175–79.

18. Born in 1933. See "El protestantismo como una forma de colonialismo," in *Perspectivas de Diálogo* 38 (1968), pp. 242–48; *Towards a Theology of Liberation* (Princeton, 1968); *Tomorrow's Child* (New York, 1972).

19. Among other works. *La iglesia debe comprometerse en lo político*, JECI (Montevideo, 1970); "La misión de la Iglesia y del presbítero a la luz de la teología de la liberación," in *Pasos* 8 (1972), p. 21. He was principal editor of the document *Sacerdotes para el Tercer Mundo: historia, documentos, reflexion* (Buenos Aires, 1970). With Rodríguez Melgarejo, "Apuntes para una interpretación de la iglesia en Argentina," in *Víspera* 4 (1970), pp. 59–88. As for the investigation of popular religion, we should mention the work of Aldo Buntig (born in 1931), *El catolicismo popular en Argentina* (Buenos Aires, 1972), and *Religión-enajenación en una sociedad dependiente* (Buenos Aires, 1973).

20. Born in 1933. See a bibliography in *Fe y cambio social en América latina* (Salamanca, 1973), p. 403. His most important work is *Teología desde la praxis de la liberación* (Salamanca, 1973) [In English see *Theology for a Nomad Church* (Maryknoll, New York, 1976)]. Together with the work of Gustavo Gutiérrez, his is the most original in the movement.

21. I was born in 1934. *Hipótesis para una historia de la iglesia en América latina* (Barcelona, 1969); *Para una ética de la liberación latinoamericana* (Buenos Aires, 1973–); *Historia y teología de la liberación* (Buenos Aires, 1972) [Eng. trans.: *History and the Theology of Liberation* (Maryknoll, New York, 1976)]; *Etica y teología de la liberación* (Buenos Aires, 1974); *Método para una filosofía de la liberación* (Salamanca, 1974).

22. The papers were published under the title *Fe y cambio social en América Latina* (Salamanca, 1973). There have been other encounters along the line of liberation theology (beginning at first with developmentalism): In Mexico, November 24–28, 1969, a meeting was held on the subject "Faith and Development" (Mexican Theological Society, *Memoria del primer congreso nacional de teología: Fe y desarrollo* [Mexico, 1970]), still in a context of the "theology of development." In Bogota, March 6–7, 1970, there was an international meeting, the report of which was titled *Liberación, opción de la Iglesia en la década del 70*, "Simposio sobre Teología de la Liberación" (Bogota, 1970). In Buenos Aires, August 3–6, 1970. ISAL brought together some twenty theologians, some of whose papers were published in *Fichas de ISAL* 26 (1970), and in *Cristianismo y Sociedad*, 23–24 (1970). Again in Bogota, July 24–26, 1970, there was the Second Encounter on Liberation Theology (published in the bulletin "Teología de la Liberación" [Bogota, 1970]). In Ciudad Juarez, Mexico, October 16–18, 1970, there was another "Seminar on Liberation Theology" (the papers were mimeographed and can be obtained through IDOC, Via S. Maria dell'Anima 20, 00186 Rome). In Oruro, Bolivia, December 2–19, 1970, there was a pastoral course on "liberation theology." There was a study week in August 1971 on "the dialectic of Latin American liberation," published in *Stromata* [Buenos Aires] 1–2 (1971), which was also the birthplace of the philosophical movement of "philosophy of liberation" (originally Argentinian; see *Hacia una filosofía de la liberación latinoamericana* [Buenos Aires, 1973], with such authors as Osvaldo Ardiles, Horacio Cerutti, Julio Dezan, Enrique Dussel, Anibal Fornari, Daniel Guillot, Juan C. Scannonne). There have been more encounters and meetings on "liberation theology." Europeans do not understand that this theology is not the fruit of academic discourse, but rather the expression of a grassroots ecclesiastical and political move-

ment, which is supported by thousands of religious, priests, and laypeople in the most diverse situations. The "discourse" of liberation theology is not intra-theological but arises out of a historical praxis. As Rosino Gibellini of Brescia expressed it, "There is still no ecclesial movement of the theology of hope, nor of political theology. Yet here there is such an ecclesial movement. . . . The European who reads a text of liberation theology understands conceptually the point of liberation theology, *but does not understand that it is a movement of the church* (in *Christus* [Mexico] 479 [1975], p. 9).

23. Born in 1924. See "La théologie protestante latino-américaine aujourd'hui," in *IDOC International* 9 (1969), pp. 77–94; "Nuevas perspectivas teológicas" in *Pueblo oprimido* (Montevideo, 1972); *Doing Theology in a Revolutionary Situation* (Philadelphia, 1974).

24. Born in 1931. See "Hacia una dialéctica de la liberación," in *Stromata* 17 (1971), pp. 23–60; "El actual desafío planteado al lenguaje teológico latinoamericano de liberación," in *CIAS* (Buenos Aires) 211 (1972), pp. 5–20; "Ontología del proceso autenticamente liberador," in *Panorama de la teología latinoamericana*, SELADOC (Salamanca, 1975).

25. Especially note the articles of Methol Ferre, "Iglesia y sociedad opulenta: Una crítica a Suenens desde América latina," in *Víspera* 12 (1969), pp. 1–24; and the defense, for Third World political reasons, of the encyclical *Humanae Vitae* in *Víspera* 7 (1968); and the works of Hector Borrat, "Para una teología de la vanguardia," in *Víspera* 17 (1970), pp. 26–31; or "Hacia una teología de la liberación," in *Marcha* (Montevideo) 1527 (1971), pp. 1–15.

26. Cf. Eduardo Pironio, "Teología de la liberación," in *Criterio* (Buenos Aires), 1607–1608 (1970).

27. Born in 1938. Among his works are *Jesucristo libertador* (Petropolis, 1974); *Vida para Além de Morte* (Petropolis, 1974); *O destino do homem do mundo* (Petropolis, 1975); *A vida religiosa e a Igreja no processo de libertação* (Petropolis, 1975). He has collaborated with many of the authors already named in the issue of Concilium 96, June 1974.

28. This theme, however, is not new to contemporary Latin American reflection. See in my work *El humanismo semita* (Buenos Aires, 1969; written in 1963), the appendix: "La misión en los poemas del Siervo de Yahveh." Christ as the Servant of Yahweh, suffering, crucified, *politically* persecuted, has a very concrete meaning in Latin America. The oppressed people (socially, politically, and economically oppressed for five centuries: by the European or the North American empire, by national oligarchies) has been identified for centuries with the bleeding Christs of our baroque and colonial churches. He is the Christ of the people, despised by the theologians of secularization and by our dominating oligarchies.

29. Father Roger Vekemans *appears* to have received from the CIA ten million dollars for the campaign against the Popular Unity party (Cf. *The Washington Star*, July 23, 1975, reporting statements by Fr. James Vissard).

30. *The Rockefeller Report on the Americans* (Chicago, 1969).

31. This type of argument has been wielded against the theology of liberation. Cf. Hugo Assmann, *Teología desde la praxis de la liberación*, pp. 238ff.

32. The results of this meeting were published under the title *Liberación: diálogos en el CELAM*, CELAM (Bogota, 1974); worthy of special note is the article by Buenaventura Kloppenburg, "Las tentaciones de la teología de la liberación," pp. 401–15, in which one can see all the attacks that are brought against the theology of liberation; also Jorge

Mejía, "La liberación, aspectos bíblicos," which argues from an exegetical viewpoint (pp. 271–307); and A. Lopez Trujillo, "Las teologías de la liberación en la América latina" (pp. 27–67) distinguishes between 'good" and "bad" (Marxist) theologies of liberation.

33. Proceedings were published under the title *Teología de la liberación: Conversaciones de Toledo* (Burgos, 1974), with the participation of Jiménez Urresti, Congar, Lopez Trujillo, and others. It speaks of "as many theologies as there are authors," "the integral liberation of man and the universal liberation of all men" (pp. 295ff). There is no awareness of the conflict that exists in a situation of sin; the domination of one nation over another (imperialism), of one class over another, etc. "Universalism" conceals the contradictions of sin.

34. Under the theme of "Social conflict in Latin America and Christian commitment," September 6–13, 1975. There was not a single theologian of liberation among the speakers or panelists. On the new orientation of CELAM since 1972, see F. Houtart, "Le Conseil épiscopal d'Amérique latine accentue son changement," in ICI (Paris), 481 (1975), pp. 10–24.

35. By Ellacuría, see "Posibilidad, necesidad y sentido de una teología latino-americana," in *Christus* (Mexico), 471 (1975), pp. 12–16, and 472 (1975), pp. 17–23. An excellently prepared philosopher, we can expect of him some important theological work, and also of Sobrino who has made an important contribution on "The death of Christ," along the lines of liberation theology.

36. Author of many articles in *Christus* (Mexico), he is one of the theologians of the "Priests for the People" movement (now called "Church in Solidarity") in Mexico.

37. His first theological-pastoral study has been published by Our Sunday Visitor publishing house. He is the founder and director of the Mexican American Cultural Center (San Antonio, Texas), the first Chicano theologian.

38. See *La Iglesia latinoamericana y la política después de Medellín* (Bogota, 1972), as well as numerous articles in *Servir, Christus,* and *Contacto* (Mexico). In the last of these there is a theological analysis of the language of Gilberto Jiménez, "El golpe militar y la condenación de Cristianos para el socialismo," in *Contacto* 1/2 (1975), pp. 12–115.

39. A Colombian layman specializing in catechesis and the author of several works on that subject.

40. Born in 1933. His best known work is *Nueva conciencia de la Iglesia en América latina* (Santiago, 1973).

41. A book worth noting by Cussianovich is *Nos ha liberado* (Salamanca, 1973), aimed at teaching "grassroots" groups to think in terms of liberation theology.

42. On the recent Latin American martyrs, see *Scarboro Missions* (Ontario), June 1975; among others I cited Carlos Múgica (Argentine priest, 44 years old); Maurice Lefèbvre (a priest assassinated in Bolivia, 49); Henrique Pereira (Brazilian priest, 28); Tito de Alencar (a priest tortured in Brazil, who died in anguish in France, 29); Juan Alsina (killed in Chile in September 1973, 31); Hector Gallegos (died in Panama, 28); and Ivan Betancourt, who received a doctorate from the University of Buenaventura in Bogota, was born July 28, 1940, and martyred on June 23, 1975, near Jutigalpa in the diocese of Olancho. They were all *explicitly* aware of giving their lives for Christ the Liberator. They are *saints* of our church, just as the martyrs of the Mediterranean church were during the first three centuries.

43. The encounter was held April 23–30, 1972. For documentation in English see

Christians and Socialism (Maryknoll, New York, 1975). See also Gonzalo Arroyo, "Católicos de izquierda en América latina," in Mensaje 191 (1970), pp. 369–372.

44. The material from the Encounter has been published as Liberación y Cautiverio (Mexico, 1976). On the influence that it is having in Mexico, one can already read the articles of Vicente Leñero, "Teología de la liberación," published on the front page of Excelsior (Mexico), and reproduced in Christus 479 (1975), pp. 62–70.

45. This meeting, held August 18–25, 1975, began to overcome the incommunication with black theology (as could be seen in Freire-Assmann-Bodipo-Cone, Teología negra, teologia de la liberación [Salamanca, 1974], the result of a meeting of the World Council of Churches: "A Symposium on black theology and the Latin American theology of liberation"). At Detroit there was a fruitful dialogue between black and Latin American theologians, and similarly with some feminist and Chicano theologians. The dialogue was centered on the so-called principal contradiction: the "center-periphery," that is, U.S. (Empire)—Latin America (neocolony). Documentation of the meeting has been published as Theology in the Americas (Maryknoll, New York, 1976).

15

New Visions of the Church
in Latin America: A Protestant View

Beatriz Melano Couch (Argentina)

The assignment proposed to us was to compose an "outline," a term
which well describes the schematic nature of this presentation.[1] A
schema or outline may have two purposes: either to summarize a
study, and therefore it comes at the end of a longer and more thorough
investigation, or to serve as a stimulus to open up discussion. Our
hope is that this will serve as the latter. We are faced with an initial
limitation, that is, the lack of a serious investigation of the many
sources where one can trace the evolution of Protestant theological
reflection and of the church's approach to its mission in Latin
America. This material is dispersed in church documents, theological
journals, books, reports of conferences, etc., produced since the
beginning of this century all over this vast continent. One of the
results of the absence of an inclusive and rigorous historical analysis of
the Protestant phenomenon in Latin America is that it is generally
unknown outside the circles where reflection and action have taken
place. The scarce knowledge of it is fragmentary and lacks the objectivity and sense of continuity needed to grasp the meaning of any
historical movement. I am indebted to José Míguez Bonino, whose
essay on "Vision of Social Change and Its Tasks from the Perspective
of the Non-Catholic Christian Churches" has served me as a frame of
reference.[2]

There is a historical fact that makes a fundamental difference between the establishment and influence of the Roman Catholic church and that of the Protestant churches in Latin America. While the Roman Catholics exported mainly from Spain one church with one *corpus* of doctrine, one liturgy and cultural form, there are different kinds of "Protestantisms" imported from diverse countries of Europe (German Lutherans; Swiss, French, Hungarian, and Dutch Calvinists; Scotch Presbyterians; English Episcopalians; Welsh Methodists; Italian Waldensians), which represent waves of European immigration at the end of the last century and the beginning of this one. To these different ethnic groups we must add those that came into being through the missionary enterprise coming from Europe and the United States and which represented the traditional and free churches and also the sects. All of these groups of immigrants and missionaries brought with them their own culture, their own church structure, doctrine, liturgy, morals, etc. As we try to outline a short history of the development of theology in Latin America, we have to keep in mind this fact, which means that at least two or three different approaches to mission and different theological trends are juxtaposed in any given historical moment.

MAIN THEOLOGICAL TRENDS AND
APPROACHES TO CHURCH MISSION

The main concern of the so-called *free churches and sects* is the evangelization of this continent, conceived mainly as the conversion of souls.[3] The stress is on the otherworldliness of Christianity and on a dualism expressed in a strict differentiation between world and church, body and soul, worldly and spiritual matters, evil and the kingdom of God (interpreted in eschatological terms as the kingdom to come in the other life, or in the other world). This particular theological view meant the following emphases:

1. The conversion of the soul is a "change of life" and this means a change in individualistic moral conduct. The change of heart implies also that one changes behavior. This has led to pietism and to legalism in ethics.

2. In terms of church mission, it means mainly proselytism. Religion is not inherited. One must be converted. On a continent first

evangelized with "the sword and the cross," where popular religiosity was a mixture of Christian beliefs and superstitions and where the people had little or no instruction in the meaning of the Christian faith, there is an insistence on the personal, rational, and emotional acceptance of Christ.

3. In terms of the relation between this approach and the Latin American culture, it means the importation of cultural forms foreign to the expression of the people and therefore creates to a certain extent an "uprootedness" of the people from their own cultural background.[4]

4. The liturgy is an expression of the mother church's liturgy, with centrality of the sermon, which often becomes a lecture for the indoctrination of the people and a fervent polemic against the Roman Catholic church with regard to its belief and practices.

In summary, the new converts do not belong to this world, which is under the power of evil; therefore they do not associate with the people "of the world," nor with politics and social matters, which are considered "dirty business" in the realm of evil. One finds a new home and a new family within the church, which not only provides for religious life but also for social life and the education of the young.

Another theological trend is expressed in the marriage of a certain kind of *pietism with the social gospel.* According to this view the gospel has to do with a change of heart but also with the change of society. The aim is the modernization of society according to Christian values which are expressed politically in democracy, socially in the achievement of human rights, and economically in a system that respects the values of human beings, their dignity, and individual freedom. Society must be "just, modern, and democratic." The Protestants launched themselves into the "conquest of liberal rights" for this continent (they fought for freedom of worship, freedom of the press, lay education, the creation of state records offices for marriages —before, only the Roman Catholic ceremony had official validity —cemeteries open to all religious creeds, etc.).

1. In terms of church mission, this means not only the conversion of the soul but the creation of social living conditions that enable individuals to exercise their freedom and to develop their human potentials. So Christian responsibility is seen in terms of promoting just salaries, safe conditions, equal rights for labor, education for all,

freedom of choice and of expression of the individual, caring for the needy, etc. In turn, this is expressed in the creation of institutions that embodied these ideals such as hospitals, health centers, schools, Bible institutes, seminaries, centers for social welfare, etc.

2. In terms of the relation between the mission of the church and culture, we cannot underestimate the influence of this liberal project in Latin America. There are profound discrepancies among historians in their interpretation of the meaning of this project on this continent. Even though it coincides with the expansion of industrial capitalism in the West, we cannot afford to fall either into an oversimplification of this complex phenomenon, and dismiss it as solely an imperialistic enterprise of the bourgeois ideology of the eighteenth and nineteenth centuries, or into a failure to acknowledge its impact in terms of a *de-sacralization* of traditional society, monolithic and rigid, inherited from the Spanish colonization.

I venture the hypothesis that liberal philosophy and Protestant liberalism coincide at a number of points, but they are not exactly identical. The Protestant version carried a slight critique of the socio-economic system, on the basis of democratic liberalism over against a semifeudal type of society, especially in the rural areas. It therefore represented a subversion of the traditional conservative order in its beginning, but later became the ideological justification of an unjust social order. Its emphasis on the dignity and liberty of the individual was a dynamic element vis-à-vis a static and passive conception of Christianity. Roman Catholicism was identified with the Hispanic culture and with national politics. This is the inheritance of what Enrique Dussel describes as a *temporal Hispanic messianism*[5] that today appears in the form of a *nationalistic Catholic messianism*. Country, tradition, and Catholic faith are equated; to defend the country is to defend both tradition and Catholicism and vice versa.

The liberal national leaders tried to break this schema and secularize, or as they put it, "modernize" society by separating church and state. In some countries like Mexico and Uruguay this meant a drastic break with the Roman Catholic church. Protestantism fought in the same direction, but the churches, consciously or unconsciously, accommodated themselves within an economic system: capitalism (supported by an individualistic philosophy); a political system: democracy; and a cultural aim: secularism (supported by pragmatism).

It is true that the Pan American Evangelical Congress (Panama, 1916) equated Christian and liberal values; Protestantism thus (unconsciously) became a vehicle of an Anglo-Saxon neocolonialism. Nevertheless, the First Latin American Evangelical Conference (CELA I, Buenos Aires, 1949), in spite of inscribing itself in the same framework, showed some awareness of the dangers of neocolonialism. For instance, it declared that *"any political, social, or economic system that diminishes human personality, uses it in any sense as a mere object or prevents its free expression, is anti-Christian and anti-human."*[6]

In this sense I believe that we can say that Latin American Protestantism carries with it at the same time and in the same process the radical critique of the gospel and the liberal ideological critique of traditional society. Because this is so, it carries the seed of its own crisis and the possibility of reaching a new historical project. . . . Liberalism represents a new conception of the relation of man to the world; it bears a humanistic impact, an openness to the new in a crucial moment in Latin American history. It is in this sense that it is not enough to *unmask* liberalism. It is also necessary to *reclaim* and to *recover in a critical form* what liberalism—and in particular Protestantism—means for a new social, political, and religious project in Latin America.[7]

As Míguez points out, there is a coincidence of the theological approach with the ideology inherited from positivism and liberalism; this meant a slight denouncement of imperialistic tendencies and the stress on the need for the Christian to be part of the process of becoming a "universal brotherhood," a "new human society," following liberal lines. This approach is "articulated theologically in the freedom of grace, the sovereignty of Jesus Christ, the power of the Spirit—and not exclusively in the autonomy of the individual —which transcends the liberal critique and points to a more profound subversion."[8]

Still a third theological trend and approach to mission is represented by the so-called *transplant churches.* These are the product of European immigrations. They are ethnic enclaves with a strong tendency to be closed in on themselves. They preserve the linguistic and cultural tradition of the fatherland. Their worship is conducted in their mother tongue—English, French. German, Hungarian, Lithuanian, Swedish, Norwegian, etc. Their function is to serve those foreign communities, providing some of the atmosphere of their country of origin, to preserve their cultural, theological, and ecclesiastical heritage, and their mission is practically limited to this function. Theologically they maintain a clear-cut division between church and world, like the sects and conservative missionary churches. This means two things: First, they have not done evangelization; there is no outreach to the Spanish-speaking public; their ministry has been only inward. Second, they have ignored the Latin American socio-political problematic. Their social concern is limited to charity, but this work does not perturb their structures, liturgy, theology, or outlook on society. They keep themselves separate. This type of concern does not raise questions for them about the unjust social structure that produces poverty, abandonment, exploitation here. Church affairs have nothing to do with the worldly economic-social-political problems of this continent. (Curiously, most of these churches in the fatherland have a rather well-developed sense of Christian responsibility in society.) This has permitted them to maintain a foreign identity alien to the national identity; they are not integrated into the historical reality of this continent. Therefore this reality has not been able to enter their temples. We can call them the churches of the closed doors. Since the process of acculturation has been nil or slow, their membership has decreased as their offspring have begun to merge with the Latin Americans through marriage. "A great portion of Latin America is foreign in its own land."[9]

CRISIS AND CREATIVITY

During and after the Second World War the crisis of liberal ideology began to be seen in deep fissures in the political and economic structures of the world and in a special way in the Third World. The liberal ideals of a "just, modern, and democratic" society began to fade in the face of economic dependency of the Third World on the developed countries of the western hemisphere; an increasingly wider gap has grown between the developed countries of the North Atlantic and those on the periphery. In Latin America military regimes in many cases have taken the place of feeble democracies. As someone said, Latin Americans became aware that they were "beggars treading on gold fields."

On the other hand, the seed was already sown that would produce the crisis of liberal theology under the influence of post-liberal European and U.S. theologians—such as Karl Barth, Emil Brunner, Rudolf Bultmann, and Reinhold Niebuhr. Therefore, the crisis is twofold; it involves the bankruptcy of liberal ideals and the disillusionment of liberal theology.

Both crises made Latin American thinkers become aware of the inadequacy of their message to respond to the particular historical moment. As we will see in the brief outline of the development of a new type of theological reflection and new approaches to the mission of the church, what is now called Latin American theology of liberation was born out of a concrete historical struggle. It involved a rather slow and painful process of becoming aware of the meaning of the crisis and of the historical and social dimensions of the gospel. We are convinced that only as people become conscious of the injustices of this world, of the situation of exploitation and dependency that produces subhuman conditions for the vast majority of the masses, are they moved to commit themselves to bring about needed changes. Out of this engagement for change, in the midst of concrete struggle, they begin to perceive God's message and action in a new light. This theology was not born of a priori party lines, nor of a transference of illusionary hopes, but out of a painful search to respond to three fundamental concerns: How can we be faithful to Jesus Christ in our time and in our own particular historical crossroads? What is the church's mission in the midst of economic and political oppression? What is the meaning of Christian hope for those who are kept marginated by the rest of society through exploitation and discrimination?

This painful process, as all processes of growth, evolved through prophetic insights as well as errors, tactical mistakes, naiveté, the overlooking of reality. But it shows a steady awareness of the meaning of God's justice and love, judgment and redemption. Interestingly enough, it is a collective enterprise where denominational lines tend to disappear, and both reflection and action become ecumenical.

At least two characteristics make this approach different from customary academic theology. The emphasis is not on individual achievement or on competitive schools of thought; it is rather a communal search for truth and action in solidarity with Christians and non-Christians. Its hermeneutic makes use of the social sciences as necessary tools to analyze historical reality and take serious account of the human dimensions that are brought to light through experience and suffering. It is therefore not a dogmatic and closed theology but rather an open one; it is still being worked out. That is why there are few books produced but hundreds of essays and articles, quite a number of church declarations and many more unknown testimonies written in lives dedicated to the literal task of liberation (the *actus primus* in Gutiérrez's terminology). This is one reason why only a few names will appear here; also liberation theology involves only a small minority of the whole Protestant community.

I believe it would be fair and descriptive to designate the three decades, the fifties to the seventies, as follows: (1) The crisis of liberalism (the 1950s); (2) the awakening of reflexive consciousness (the 1960s); and (3) the creative commitment to change (the 1970s).

The Crisis of Liberalism (the 1950s)

We have already stated that the influence of post-liberal European theologians contributed to the crisis of liberal theology in this hemisphere. In 1956 there appeared an issue of *Cuadernos Teológicos* dedicated entirely to Karl Barth; this theological periodical was published in Argentina but had a wide distribution all over the continent. One of Barth's disciples, Emilio Castro (from Uruguay), contributed an article entitled "The Theological Situation in Latin America and the Theology of Karl Barth." He stated that the debate between modernism and fundamentalism was an imported theological struggle—foreign to us—and that theology had been reduced so far to a polemic with the Roman Catholic church. He pointed out further the "theological poverty" of Latin American Protestantism as well as two facts as signs of hope: the appearance of the magazine *Reforma* in the River Plata (whose contributors had overcome the tendency towards anti-Catholic apology); and the beginning of translations into Spanish of the church fathers as well as the publication of Spanish Catholic mystics.[10] But the most significant questions raised in this article were concerned with the relevancy of the Christian message and the problems of our continent—"What is the essential message we must preach *to our people today* . . . ? What is the meaning of Barth's thinking in relation to South American problems?"[11] (italics mine)

The presence of neo-orthodoxy in the 1950s is very important for the future development of Latin American theology. As Castro states in his article, the whole debate around the meaning of the Bible as the Word of God is central, especially the emphasis that "it is not independent of God but subject to God." The Barthian doctrine of the Word of God helps therefore in the important debate between fundamentalism and modernism concerning the doctrine of the inspiration of the Scriptures; this doctrine was the product of a seventeenth-century mentality and "was born in the fight against rationalism, but in itself was a product of the same rationalism."[12] The other Barthian emphasis that carries weight in today's thinking, albeit in another way, is the centrality of Christology. The meaning of Christianity proceeds from the event of Jesus Christ; his love does not contradict his justice, nor does his grace contradict his law; love and grace help us affirm his justice and his law. Today precisely these issues of hermeneutics and Christology are main concerns in Latin American theology.

Two significant features in the crisis of liberal ideology and theology in the fifties were the presence of neo-orthodoxy, especially in the southern cone (Chile-Argentina-Uruguay), and the First Evangelical Conference of Latin Americans (CELA I), mentioned above. This conference met in 1949 in Buenos Aires with representatives from all over the continent, making the following theological emphases: a timid denouncement of political, economic, and cultural imperialism from the West, related to a revaluation of the human being. (The reference to the marginated people was centered on the Indian population, exploited and subdued on many levels since the sixteenth century.[13]) This revaluation was based on an emphasis on a *full* salvation (the term "full" is vague, yet it points to something more than the salvation of the soul), on the universal love of God, and on the kingdom's signs that are visible in a new type of human society.

The new humanity was still envisioned as the product of educational development, the establishment of just laws to protect the laboring class, freedom for all, respect for each individual's dignity. As we see, it was still within the framework of liberal ideology. Ethics became the central theme both in the beginning of the development of native theological thought and in terms of the church mission. From then on ethics would be a predominant concern, slowly evolving from a mere individualistic endeavor to a communal approach that later would embrace the whole of society in all its aspects—political, economic, social, and cultural. The theology of the kingdom in relation to concrete historical situations acquires new meanings in terms of the understanding of God's action in the world and human responsibility. We can call the development of Latin American theology a slow and painful process of *incarnation* in our own continent's problematic. The social gospel and the ideals of democracy and personal freedom became inadequate to cope with unjust and oppressive structures on our continent. During the next two decades we faced the search for the concretization of God's justice and love in our world, a concretization that would lead us from a theology of development to a theology of revolution and liberation, from mere denunciation of the evils of political structures to an engagement for revolutionary changes of structures.

The Awakening of Reflexive Consciousness (the 1960s)

During the sixties there is the awakening of what Míguez calls "reflexive consciousness." I would say that Emilio Castro is the first prophetic voice calling for a relevant theology for Latin America, a theology intimately related to local situations, which he envisioned but never fully developed. In another publication of *Cuadernos Teológicos* (no. 38, April–June 1961), Castro had an article entitled "Theological Thought in Latin America." There he stated that the task of theology is "the encounter between the world and the Word of God," and he declared that this task is a duty of Christian obedience. He called for a theology not enclosed in local provincialism, because the truth of the gospel is too rich and too universal to enslave it in local formulas, but rather related to reflection on Latin American problems. This *incarnate theology* should make its own the human situation where God is speaking, and reflect on this situation starting from the word of God and vice versa. He also appealed to the church to define itself before the concrete problems of this continent. Furthermore, he criticized the alliance between the so-called Christian and liberal principles and added:

What is the existing relation between individual honesty and social justice? (What does Niebuhr mean when he speaks of *Moral Man and Immoral*

Society?). . . . A better understanding of the gospel leads us inevitably to ask ourselves, what does it mean that Jesus Christ is the Lord of the world? What is the meaning of the incarnation in "worldly matters"? How do we discover the actual relevance of the prophetic message? In what sense is justification by faith something more than a doctrine applied to the salvation of souls, which becomes the foundation of a social and political ethics?[14]

Castro goes on to relate three very important points: *incarnate theology*, the *mission of the church* (which should see its task independently from the direction given from abroad), and *worship*. "Worship has lacked the sense of mystery, of all expectancy of a miracle. The gospel has been ready in packages to be delivered; what has been important is how it was delivered; the content of the deliverance was assured and sealed by the country of origin. Worship was then converted into a lecture and a call to decision with the insistence of an auction of souls."[15] He states one of the main concerns of the hermeneutical task, that is, the unmasking of the ethos of liberal ethics accepted (consciously or unconsciously) by our Christian communities, an ethos that has permeated our approach to the Bible and its interpretation.

The Second Evangelical Conference of Latin Americans (CELA II), which gathered in Lima in 1961, and the Presbyterian Confederation of Latin Americans (CCPAL: Comité Central Presbiteriano de América Latina), which gathered in Chile in 1962, are landmarks in the development of our Protestant theology. Both conferences express a new kind of social awareness. The themes treated in Lima speak for themselves: social injustice, agrarian reform, economic imperialism, the Indian population, etc. There is a search for a way to change the unjust social structures. Immediately after this conference, two interdenominational working groups, already formed in Buenos Aires, met a few miles from Lima, in Huampani, with a wide representation from the whole continent.

The birth of the Commission on Church and Society in Latin America (ISAL: Iglesia y Sociedad en América Latina) is one of the outcomes of this historical event. It drew together an ecumenical group of the most outspoken thinkers from different Latin American countries. It became a pioneer in the development of a new type of theological methodology and content. A Commission on Christian Education, assembled at the same time and in the same place, launched the call for a new philosophy of Christian education that would take seriously the problems of the continent and relate them to Christian instruction. The idea of a new Commission on Christian Education for Latin America was put forth and worked out. This is the seed of the later organism called CELADEC (Comité Latino-americano de Educación Cristiana). Its purpose was the unification—continent-wide—of catechetics, based on a relevant theology and using a curriculum adequate to our own idiosyncrasies instead of translating and reproducing foreign material imported from the United States.

We are at this point in the presence of what can be described as a *theology of development*, whose aim is the reflection on the reformation of society. This type of reflection had not yet cut its moorings from liberal idealism; the very words used, "development" and "reformation," point to this fact. An effort was made to overcome the pietistic individualism and the otherworldliness inherited from the *revival*, yet the theologians were still trapped in a liberal type of humanism. There is also an effort to analyze the concrete situation of Latin America, where the church is called upon to serve; but I would venture to say retrospectively that this effort lacked a historical understanding of the evolution of Latin America. Even though it recuperated to a certain extent a sense of direction in our history, this was only seen partially and in the long run it maintained the old liberal ideals inscribed in a new social reality. Therefore it was anachronic. The ideals of *Hispanic messianism* (inherited from the sixteenth century) and the ideals of *liberal messianism*, reproducing Anglo-French philosophy and North American pragmatism, failed to recognize the situation of dependency of this hemisphere. Nevertheless it would be unfair to underestimate the effort to understand the meaning of underdevelopment and the attitude of solidarity with our peoples expressed during this decade. The search was for a *structural* change, but the reforms proposed were economical and educational; they did not advocate a political rupture with the sources of oppression.

Theologically speaking, the transcendent nature of the church was maintained (a neo-orthodox type of transcendency), together with the call for a concrete expression of solidarity with the oppressed. Three theological premises were central to the debates: the sovereignty of Jesus Christ, the divine initiative in God's presence in this world, and the unity given in Jesus Christ. This theology is already ecumenical in its content and outreach. By ecumerical we mean not only the overcoming of Protestant denominational lines, but a new openness to Roman Catholicism. José Míguez Bonino made a significant contribution by the very theme of his doctoral dissertation, "Scripture and Tradition in Recent Roman Catholic Theology" (1960), and particularly by his intervention as an observer at Vatican Council II. Roman Catholicism was taken seriously at a scientific level and new roads of understanding between Protestantism and Catholicism were expressed both in ecumenical meetings of different kinds and in a variety of publications. I would say as a way of summary that Latin American ecumenicity was born and developed not only as a consequence of the new openings that Vatican Council II represented, but in the midst of the struggling and suffering borne together by many members of the Christian family in this hemisphere. Out of this shared struggle and the new awareness that was produced by the situation itself, new bonds of unity were discovered and expressed in concrete ways. Officially the churches were still separated; existentially they found their oneness. Officially they still declared themselves apolitical (a position that always unconsciously sustains the status quo), but existentially, groups of Christians here and there began to see the need for political commitment to be able to participate in solidarity with their own oppressed peoples.

The Church and Society Committee became the mind and the voice in the development of theology. It increasingly functioned as the speaker for the most radical wing of the Protestant church. The evolution of its reflection, in spite of representing a small minority, is very significant.

In February 1960 there was organized in Buenos Aires the first Argentine National Conference of the Student Christian Movement (MEC: Movimiento Estudiantil Cristiano), with delegates from both Argentina and Uruguay. The very program of this conference spoke of the search for concrete historical answers to questions regarding the church's mission. University professors and experts on sociology, economics, and political science were invited to analyze the situation; the evenings were dedicated to bringing this information together with the Bible studies and theological lectures that took place during the day. The main concerns of the conference are reflected in these questions: Where does the Bible and the analysis of the situation lead us here today? What directions in reflection and action should we take to be faithful to a God of history? Many of the students present later became continental and ecumenical leaders. The presence of Joseph Hromadka was extremely significant. The theology of Dietrich Bonhoeffer gave a basis to open up new roads of Christian political commitment to many.

A second meeting of the Church and Society Commission was held in El Tabo, Chile, in 1966, and represents a decisive moment for the theology of Latin America and for the new visions of the church's task. Here was born what we can call a theology of history, precisely because a concrete analysis of the "sociology of dependency" was introduced with a pronouncement for revolutionary change. As Míguez points out in the article mentioned above, there was a "vacillation between revolution and development," a search for the concreteness of the Christian commitment to social change and at the same time for the preservation of the transcendence of the church. Two names should be mentioned here: Richard Shaull and Paul Lehmann, whose thought greatly influenced Latin American thinkers. Eleven years earlier, Richard Shaull had already produced a book called *Revolution and Reconciliation*, where he stated the need to read "the signs of the times" in order to obey the Christ of history. Lehmann, with his insistence on the contextual nature of ethics and on the Christian concern to make this earthly life truly human, found echoes in this part of the world.

What does the "humanization of man" mean? How can we keep human life truly human in a continent where subhuman conditions alienate and dehumanize? The call for a "full salvation" in 1949 acquired an existential and dramatic dimension.[16] "Only through the liquidation of a system of oppression will man be able to be truly [man], free from all alienating limitation," said Julio de Santa Ana later on.[17] If God is a God of history, and God's intervention is always liberating and humanizing, then Christian responsibility is to join in a divine-human project. Theologically speaking, the transcendence of the "Other," separated from humanity, is overcome by the "Spirit among us." The human being is responsible for collaborating actively in what God is already doing in the world, and this is expressed in a secular language instead of in traditional theological wording. Theology searches for a new language and sees its task as a reflection-action enterprise that is done in the midst of the struggle for liberation. Sociological tools become necessary instruments to understand better the situation in which we are immersed; engagement is a prerequisite of reflection; and Christian faith provides the impulse, together with the awareness of injustice, for this commitment. A Marxist type of social analysis is related here to the traditional biblical language of exodus and liberation, captivity and deliverance.

Another landmark in the development of Latin American Protestant theology was the conference in Piriápolis, Uruguay, in 1967. This conference had as its background the meeting of the Department of "Church and Society" of the World Council of Churches held in Geneva in 1966. The French newspaper *Le Monde* published a front-page article reporting on the Geneva meeting and entitled: "The Prophets Come from Latin America." It would be difficult to overestimate the impact of the Latin American thinkers on this meeting and therefore on the programs later sponsored by the World Council of Churches as it developed a theological view of the church's relation to social-political-economic reality.

In Piriápolis, three different groups met at the same time and in the same place: the Church and Society Committee (ISAL) and a group of women and another of youth of the Evangelical Union of Latin Americans (UNELAM: Unión Evangélica Latinoamericana). Church and Society moved at this time from theological reflection to a clear-cut call for social-political engagement. The mission of the church was defined in terms of praxis, that is, of a complete participation in the Latin American process of liberation at all levels (universities, unions, politics in the broad sense of the word). And here there appeared what I might call a new prophecy of Emilio Castro. He promoted a meeting of women from all over Latin America under the auspices of UNELAM to reflect on the theme, "The role of women in church and society."[18] He was the first to see the need to incorporate women into the struggle for liberation and, significantly, called this meeting at the same time as the men were gathered for the "Church and Society" assembly. If the women's problem has not yet been fully assumed into the theology of liberation, either Catholic or Protestant, this meeting stands as a symbol for the need to assume it and in so doing to lead it toward fulfillment.[19] The third group present in

Piriápolis was the young people, who assumed the same goals as Church and Society.

Church and Society as a movement disappeared around 1972, and when we talk about it we speak about past history in a sense; but it would be unwise to underestimate its impact on the decade in which we are living.

In 1969 the Third Evangelical Conference of Latin Americans (CELA III) met in Buenos Aires. It showed clearly some of the directions of reflection and the problematic that today our churches express in their life experience. The theme was "Debtors to the World." The climate of this conference can be presented briefly in three main points:

1. Sociologically, the diagnosis of the historical situation coincided with the analysis made by the Latin American Episcopal Conference at Medellín, Colombia (Roman Catholic, 1968): The source of under-development and social injustice on our continent is economic dependency on the West and on the national elite that produce exploitation; the reaction against this injustice is revolution, and its counter-reaction is political oppression.

2. Theologically, it showed polarization in the conception of the mission of the church confronting the actual historical situation. It stated that the "transformation" of society into a "new humanity" calls for the prophetic voice of the church, for an "incarnate Christian presence" in the struggle toward the humanization of subhuman life; yet although the aim is semantically accepted by all, there is a fundamental difference in content and strategy. On the one hand, this transformation still is conceived within a reformist framework, supported by liberal ideals. As a consequence of this position, there is an open rejection of the idea of assuming political definition, since "all political options are relative." This position can be qualified as a kind of resignation vis-à-vis the evil of the world.

In another context Rubem Alves speaks of the displacement of frustration by resignation.

This is the mood one finds over and over again in the writings of the old Niebuhr. "The liberal world manages to achieve a tolerable life in a kind of confusion of purposes," he says, "which is better than the organization of the whole resources of a community for the achievement of false ends." There is a profound pessimism here. The best that can be achieved is "a tolerable life in a kind of confusion of purposes." The possibility of organizing the whole resources of a community for the achievement of true ends is not even mentioned. Social creativity is dismissed as either a utopian dream or an ideological demon, with its ultimate roots in man's selfishness and self-deception.[20]

If all political options are relative, the church cannot take sides; the prophetic mission is reduced to condemn the actual oppressive structures and to reject violence, yet there is not an open and frank involvement to bring about basic changes in a situation of institutional violence whose daily death toll is criminal.

3. Another theological trend is expressed in the youth document, which, recognizing the situation described in point one, calls for a militancy with the oppressed for their liberation, for the redemption of structures as well as individuals.

Creative Commitment to Change (the 1970s)

The decade of the seventies is what I would call *the time of more creativity* in Protestant theological reflection. If we only follow the titles of the publications of the magazine *Cristianismo y Sociedad* and of many books, we will find evidence of this fact. First of all, the pedagogy of Paulo Freire is launched for the whole continent. His first writings are published under the title "Concientización." Freire's work is launched not only by the publications but by the very process of education carried out by teams in different countries of Latin America.

Theological reflection is "to be born on the march." Historically this point of departure that guides both reflection and action coincided with a political movement in Bolivia (Torres), the Popular Unity in Chile, the coalition of leftist parties and segments of the traditional parties called "The Common Front" in Uruguay, etc. This was a moment of euphoria: With a certain naiveté the emergence within the decade of a humanistic socialism for Latin America was envisioned. The option was a new type of socialism, not a copy of Russian or Chinese Marxism, but a new kind of Latin American socialism that would express the Latin American idiosyncrasy. It was a *time of building and of new hope.* Books such as the following appeared between 1970 and 1973 (I am translating their titles literally): *The*

Churches Have the Word; Cultural Action for Freedom (Paulo Freire); *Popular Education and the Process of Conscientization; Education and Life; Education for Social Change; Pedagogy of the Oppressed; Theology of the Oppressed; Consciousness of Revolution; Hilda: A Mother's Protest; Oppressed People, Lord of History; Faith, Ideology, and Revolution in Latin America; On Society and the Church; Protestantism, Culture, and Society; America Today.* Three facts should be pointed out. (1) Sociologists and theologians worked as teams and published their essays together. (2) They dealt with the description of the same reality in its different aspects—political, economic, social, cultural, educational. (3) The main theological themes were strictly related to the situation and can be summarized around two foci: Christian political ethics (exploration of the meaning of exodus, captivity, deliverance, the kingdom of God and history, humanization); and the relation between ideology and theology (the search for a new theological language that might serve to express the ideological socialistic utopia).

Rubem Alves's doctoral thesis, *A Theology of Human Hope*, published in English in 1969, appeared in Spanish under the title *Religión ¿ Opio o instrumento de liberación?* (1970). Alves starts from the theology of exodus and moves on to the theology of hope, of a new human hope. Parallel to this literature there appeared the declarations of the Methodist Church of Bolivia in 1970, of the Methodist Church of Argentina in 1971, and of the Lutheran Church of Chile in 1970, which not only denounced the injustices of the structures that oppress the Latin American peoples, but called for Christian engagement in the changing of those structures.

In 1971 the last meeting of the organism Church and Society took place in Naña (Peru) with the suggestive theme "Popular Mobilization and Christian Faith." The very wording "popular mobilization" speaks of an ideology and a strategy assumed as necessary to bring about the structural changes needed for liberation of the oppressed and the building of a new humanity. Julio de Santa Ana has been one of the main thinkers in the exploration of social dependency. Rubem Alves and José Míguez Bonino are the main theological writers of this decade. Historically, these years represent a real breaking away for the Protestant theologians of liberation; they cut moorings from both ideological liberalism and European theology even though some themes treated in the North Atlantic are apparently similar (political theology and the theology of hope). What makes a tremendous difference is its methodology (dialectical social analysis is included in the hermeneutical circle), its content (marked by political engagement leading to reflection and vice versa), and—what I consider of crucial importance—its source: the concrete struggle for liberation of the Latin American peoples. Praxis, reflection, and action, committed to breaking down the oppressive structures and to creating new ones, assumes to a great extent the existential meaning of God's judgment and redemption of society, where humans are called to participate. Engagement for revolutionary change is no longer an academic question but a mandate of Christian obedience, a sign of faithfulness.

I would like to call attention to two phenomena, an existential one and a theological one. The existential phenomenon is precisely the price that was paid by Christians who were persecuted, incarcerated, tortured, and killed, because they were involved in popular movements. As a friend of mine said, "We lived in a strange paradox; the more conservative elements of the church rejected us and labeled us 'Communists,' 'Tupamaros,' 'extremists,' . . . and the common people who belong to the popular organizations accepted us and looked for us precisely because we were Christians. We did not engage with them to sell our faith, but *in the name of faith* we tried to be instrumental toward political love; in other words, a love that meant political involvement for the overthrowing of the structures that oppress our society."

The theological phenomenon in the present situation is polarization and conflict.[21] Both characterize our churches and are present, more than in the theology written and taught here and there in Latin America, in the approach of the church to social, political, and economic problems—that is to say, in the implicit theology of the preaching and liturgy and work of the church today. For one thing, we still live under the impact of the dualistic theological approach described at the beginning of this paper, characterized by "otherworldliness" and the emphasis on the salvation of the soul and on individual morality; this view is associated with an aggressive, conservative militancy in the political field. On the other hand, sections of the church all through Latin America believe in the call for a revolutionary praxis. "They denounce such dualism as an ideological obfuscation in itself—with a residue of liberal idealism that has not been overcome—and call for the total "emptying" of the love of God in the love of neighbor, of faith in ideology, of ecclesiastical practice in a political commitment."[22]

Míguez Bonino poses the following theological question to the approach described above which, semantically speaking, may be different from the questions posed by some radical evangelicals,[23] but which in its essence is exactly the same in my understanding:

If we are involved in a political practice . . . do we not subordinate the specificity of Christianity to the ideological, strategic, and tactical option to such a degree that the theological datum, the continuity and the universality of the people of God, remains totally absorbed? . . . On the other hand . . . the "confessional" theology of the tactical-strategic level results in a sectarian fragmentation almost without limits that menaces "the Christian left" as well as the leftist position in general. Curiously enough, it thus abandons one of the functions that the Christians engaged in the revolutionary process have at times accomplished with great efficiency: intercommunication and openness between groups having the same strategy but different tactics. . . . The political sectarianization does not seem to be the best contribution of Christians to the Latin American revolutionary process.[24]

But we have to ask ourselves whether the church can remain on the level of the mere denunciation of the social evils that attack our society, the mere denunciation of the institutional violence that we suffer every day, and the condemning of the system. Can the church remain ideologically neutral? Or better, Is there a church that is ideologically neutral? Should the church—with all the critical reservations that one must keep in mind—be willing to accept a concrete historical project such as socialism as a better solution for Latin America than capitalism?

There is a new group of theologians who have been described as "'radical evangelicals" and there are university groups that follow their lines of reflection. They represent an effort to break the theological dualism of the conservative churches and to overcome "otherworldliness" by the analysis and immersion in the Latin American problematic. Their aim is to conscientize the most conservative Protestant elements in order to produce a renewal of the church; their point of departure is a rigorous biblical exegesis and they are moving toward a realistic understanding of the social, economic, political, and cultural situation of Latin America. Their position, represents a new evangelical social ethics. They expose and denounce the structures of oppression and dependency and call for Christian commitment to bring about needed changes. For most of them the concrete political option for Latin America is a democratic type of socialism, yet they are very suspicious of the social class analysis used by the theologians of liberation and strongly criticize it. They denounce it as neither scientific nor objective; they say that it represents a veiled Marxist ideology to be exposed and is as dangerous as the capitalist ideology that preconditions the hermeneutics of the conservative approach to theology.

Even though this group criticizes the hermeneutics and theology of the liberationists as well as their revolutionary commitment, they duly acknowledge the legitimacy of the effort of the Church and Society people to awaken the Protestant consciousness to the problematic of our continent.

We can reject the philosophical premises of the movement [Church and Society]. We can object to many of their theological statements. We can question the relevancy of their strategies. . . . And, nevertheless, are we going to ignore the legitimacy of the Church and Society project as an effort to deal with the situation of the Latin American people and to "theologize" starting from that situation? The only theology that the Bible knows is a "functional" theology, that is to say, a theology in dialogue with the concrete reality, a theology at the service of praxis. The only way to live an authentic Christian life is to take seriously Jesus Christ's incarnation. Here lies the greatest challenge of Church and Society: in its call to reflect in the context of a concrete engagement and make theology an instrument of transformation.[25]

These radical evangelicals represent a new theological opening that is significant. They are a kind of bridge between the conservative and the most radically engaged Protestants. To ignore their contribution or simply dismiss them would be a lack of vision—in terms of strategy alone—if we believe that we are facing a period of conscientization and mobilization of our peoples. They have been suspected both by conservatives, who are afraid of their "leftist" tendencies, and by leftist Christians, who consider them developmentalists and reformists. In brief, this small group "proposes a theological alternative more strictly related to the classical evangelical biblical theology,"[26] aimed at forming a critique of both capitalist and Marxist ideologies in the search for a missiology that would be relevant to Latin America's problems. Some well-known Protestant theologians of liberation have collaborated with them in encounters, dialogue, and publications.

The themes of Protestant theological works stress precisely the need for a *realistic attitude* in the understanding of the world and a *realistic understanding of hope*, the rediscovery of the temporal and the worldly in the relation between the kingdom, history, and the church. Faith, suffering, and love are the leitmotifs in many pieces of work, participation in a "solidarity kind of love" for the creation of the new humanity. They speak of the need to transform reality by a "creative act," of the re-creation of reality and the total reorientation in the understanding of reality through faith and political engagement. They speak of the creation of new values, of new criteria for judgment and reasoning. They speak of a new time, a new space, and a *new humanity*, re-created by the hope that is based on the promises of God who was at work from the very beginning, through the people of Israel, through Jesus Christ himself, and through the church to the end of time. They also speak about *human rebellion* before the present situation and the need to interpret our ethics in terms of a fresh biblical understanding of the meaning of history and the kingdom.

If Alves is the philosopher, Míguez is the ethicist of the Protestant reflection on liberation. In Alves the present world reality of dependency and oppression is described as "insanity" (especially in his later writings). Míguez portrays it as an "unjust" social order contrary to the kingdom's purposes expressed in the Scriptures. For both, the future is certainly not the perfection of the present or the reformation of society, but the *eruption* of a *new society* that will concretize the visible signs of the kingdom. They are far from the developmental theology of the fifties and sixties and from liberal ideology. That means, politically, an option for socialism, and, theologically, an option for ethical commitment to the struggle of liberation as a sign of Christian obedience. Lately Alves describes the oppressive structures with the word "organization," which symbolizes both western capitalism and the technological culture that dominate and dehumanize. Míguez describes it as the anti-kingdom, which oppresses and renders human life impossible. The former theologian speaks of the re-creation of reality through a cultural and political act which he calls "the creative act"; in it imagination plays an active part and incarnates both love and hope for the building of the future.

For Míguez faith provides the reorientation of reality, and its signs are incarnate love in commitment and in solidarity with the oppressed. They both point to the creation of new values, new criteria for judgment and reasoning. Alves explores the meaning of the new time and new space, Míguez of a relocation of the new creation. The former specifies the reconstruction of cultural structures, the latter the reorientation of political structures. Yet they both aim at the same project, a new reality that is essentially a new socio-political and economic order in which the Christian takes an active part. In Alves's terminology, the prophet and the poet must take the place of the banker and the technician in shaping the future.

In *The Theology of Human Hope* Alves has used two terms to describe the language and action of liberation: *humanistic Messianism* as a strictly human task, and *Messianic humanism* as God's action manifested in his acts of deliverance, breaking the bonds of human oppression, opening up new possibilities of free life for the future. If exodus and deliverance are the basic themes in his first writings, the themes of exile and hope describe more accurately his last work, *Tomorrow's Child*, where he analyzes the culture of oppression. What are the bases of our present hope? What is the meaning of captivity? What is our present task toward liberation?

He answers by asserting that the reality of oppression and repression is not the last word, just as it was not in Habakkuk's prayer (3:17), or in Jeremiah's symbolic and prophetic action of buying a piece of land in the time of exile and captivity (32:15). "One hopes for the future because one has already seen the creative event [God's deliverance; that is why Habakkuk rejoices in spite of the existential situation] taking place in the past."[27]

The problem of captivity is how to concretize the hope that helps shape the future of liberation, and this he finds in a political task of sowing, of conceiving the future. How do we start the creative act? he asks.

The Bible does not tell *how* it happens but *that* it happens. It seems to me that this is what the "sociology of liberation" that is articulated through the biblical symbols, myths, and stories is all about. It does not explain; it describes. It does not provide recipes, but it points to the *signs* or the *fruits* of the Spirit. In traditional theological language, we are not saved by works: *we cannot produce the creative event.* We are saved by grace. . . .

The Bible answers the question as to the historical shape of the creative act by pointing to a community. The "community of faith" is that social reality where creativity is incarnated. It gains flesh and bones. In this community the future takes on space in the time still present: it is the "objectification of the Spirit," *the place where the creative insight and the creative intention become creative power.* . . .

Our task is thus simply to be able to recognize the social marks of the creative event. What is its physiognomy? How does it look?

The biblical answer is quite disturbing. Only the oppressed can be creative. Why? Because only the oppressed have the will to abolish the power presuppositions which are at the root of their oppression. . . .

What the Biblical sociology of liberation tells through the symbol of the community is thus unequivocal: the creative event cuts its way through the social inertia by creating a *counter-culture.* In the Old Testament, the community of Israel was a counter-culture. Its life-style, values and patterns of human interrelatedness were radically different from and opposed to the dominant cultural patterns of its environment. The early Christian community was a counter-culture. Or more precisely, an *underground* counter-culture. The reason it was so ruthlessly persecuted was because the dominant powers perceived it as a basically dysfunctional and subversive social reality. The values it wanted to realize and live out implied in the long run the abolition of the very foundations of the Roman Empire. . . .

The air all around us is filled with sorrow and pain. How can love close its ears to this, and plunge itself into the oblivion of immediate experience? Love looks for effectiveness. Love demands power. The gifts of the future enjoyed in community must function like the preliminaries of *love:* they must create the excitement that prepares one for the great experience still to come. They are its *sacrament,* the *aperitif* of the absent, of the possible, of that which does not yet exist. And therefore they contain *the ethical and political imperative of creative love.* [28]

Two themes that are a kind of leitmotif in Míguez's works are the ethics of the kingdom and the mission of the church. Love is a key word in his speeches and writings, the concretization of love in the human community and specifically in terms of the Latin American historical situation. Related to the first theme, Míguez points out the necessary *mediations* that exist between our understanding of the kingdom and our obedience. He affirms that these mediations are of two types. The first is our understanding of the Scripture, of the gospel, and the "rationality" or theological-hermeneutical tool that we utilize. The second is our understanding of the historical context. Under this second aspect, our actions—whether individual, collective, political, or economic, or our interpersonal relationships—synthesize a certain understanding of reality, of man, and of the future—in other words, an ideology—and all those actions, insofar as they pertain to a Christian or to the Christian community also synthesize an understanding of the gospel. I believe that it is particularly urgent today for us to realize this fact and to discern these mediations, examining them critically and accepting them consciously, for without them there is no true obedience.

He states as a way of summary that

(1) the kingdom can be discerned only within history through the obedience of faith; (2) this obedience cannot and should not endeavor to escape the tension created by its double historical reference—that of naming and demonstrating the eschatological reality that we await; (3) this obedience is made history through mediations (both doctrinal and ideological) that we must recognize, analyze, and accept critically. . . . A number of Latin American Christians utilize the concept of liberation as a contemporary historical expression of that quality of life which can be translated into significant action. I believe that the term is a legitimate one (a biblical study would show this to be so), so that we may use it as a core for our reflection. From this core flow two closely connected yet distinguishable processes which relate not only to a discussion of the meaning of the term liberation, but also to a critique of the historical action of Christians in Latin America today. The first process consists of confronting the practice with the biblical teaching about the quality of life that we call liberation. We may provisionally describe it as justice, solidarity, the real possibility to assume responsibility, access to the creation that God has given to man, freedom to form a community based on one's own work and love, opportunity to worship the Lord. Although these elements are still somewhat abstract, they together describe a certain texture of human life. The second process extends to the conditions which structure our life in Latin America: how they govern the relationship of man to his neighbor, of man to the world in which he lives—the transmission of culture, the production and consumption of goods, determining and satisfying needs, resolving conflicts, ordering life. In this process we have at our disposal scientific instruments; although relative and capable of improvement, they are indispensable for a contemporary analysis.

This double process has convinced me—and others on our continent and elsewhere—that liberal capitalism marked by the current monopolistic international system is not a viable structure for promoting the incarnation of the quality of life which has a future in the kingdom. . . . It is an anti-liberation: In terms of the kingdom it means oppression and slavery. For this reason, the term liberation aligns me—however ambiguous the relationship may be—with those who are struggling for the elimination of that slavery.[29]

If captivity and exodus, deliverance and hope, are recurring themes in Alves, Míguez's themes are incarnate love and the mission of the church, the kingdom and history. All engagement against oppression and injustice has a future because it is an act of love, and love is never left without a future. Two of his latest books edited in Spanish, *Love and Do as You Please* and *Space to Be Humans*, are the product of a search for how to express existentially the new humanity offered by Christ. The London lectures on contemporary Christianity, published in English as *Christians and Marxists: The Mutual Challenge to Revolution*, present probably the clearest and most thorough confrontation between Marxist ideology and Christian faith that has been produced so far. The chapter dedicated to the God in history is centered in the power and efficacy of solidary love, which is, as we said, his leitmotif in other reflections.

Based on a triple interpretation of the trinitarian doctrine, the covenant relationship, and the unity of creation and redemption, he asserts the ontologically ultimate nature of love, its concrete historical nature, and its power to unify the totality of human relationships. Again his main interest in a solid biblical criticism and ethics recurs in several sections, drawing the ethical consequences of the whole argument at the end. Love is the expression of Christian availability for the other, a commitment even unto death since there is suffering inherent in ethical action, "especially in a realistic understanding of the revolutionary situation." And he continues:

To be a believer means to participate in the movement of love which brought Jesus Christ to share our human life, emptying himself of his power and glory and assuming the fragility, the temptation and even the guilt of man, giving his own life even unto the death of the cross. What is here at stake is not a mere "imitation" but a participation in the lot of solidary love, the only thing that can really create a possibility of new life for man. . . . Not every suffering has this character: it is that suffering which results from taking in love responsibility for others. . . . It is the inevitable suffering that comes with service. Why? Because we live in a world which has turned its back to love, the world of injustice, the world which accepts the norms of the anti-Kingdom.[30]

As in Alves, love, hope, and suffering are main themes related to concrete engagement for revolutionary change.

As a final word, I would say that Latin American theology is moving to a center: Christology.[31] I would venture to say that it will move us from the stress on history and the kingdom to a new interpretation of the meaning of exile and suffering, of the cross and resurrection. I believe that we need a fresh understanding of the meaning of Christian suffering, which in its turn would continue to give consistency to our hope and to the struggle toward the liberation of all oppressed people. Otherwise the theme of exile might become a dead-end road with no possibility of leading us beyond the present impasse in our society. It could lead us to accept with resignation the apparent hopelessness of oppression and repression on our continent and lead the Christian community to fall into a static, suicidal attitude.

What the gospel demands of us is not a suicide vocation, nor a masochistic or naive kind of self-inflicted suffering. The gospel is calling us to the vocation of witness ("martyr" in the etymological sense). To live a vocation means to assume it, in this case to assume the suffering of others and one's own for the sake of others. This involves a free decision that will express Christian responsibility as a response to the existential situation. It means a de-centering of one's egocentrism to assume one's suffering for the cause of "the other," because Christ did it first. This is the meaning of assuming Christ's suffering in the world today. From the experience of the "fiery ordeal" and the situation of "exile" of which Peter speaks in his letters, hope is born out of a shared suffering, hope that is the experience of the resurrection itself as a new living reality; therefore it provides vision and true joy.

CONCLUSION

By way of summary, let me draw attention to two historical facts, and to three tasks that lie ahead of us.

In the first place, we should keep in mind the origin of the Protestant Latin American theology of liberation. Its development has been a slow and painful process of critical awareness of the Latin American historical situation in its many and complex dimensions. The raising of this critical awareness was bound up with the search for the meaning of faithfulness to a Lord of history, a God of justice and mercy, of judgment and redemption, on a continent where the vast majority of its people survive or simply succumb to subhuman conditions of existence. Because the very nature of the gospel is world-judging and world-transforming, the appeal for the concretization of Christian witness in relation to our particular historical context begins with the reckoning of the need for an incarnate reflection that would take seriously the problematic of our continent and assume it as an act of obedience.

We have seen appear in the course of more than twenty-five years different types of theological reflection and of ecclesiastical approaches to mission. We have seen it move in this direction: from a call to a relevant or incarnate theology *to* a theology of development *to* an ecumenical theology *to* a theology of history *to* a theology of liberation. These different names are descriptive of the direction that reflection and action took in successive steps of a search; they refer to essays, church declarations, and working papers that give a certain coherence and unity to each step of the way. They do not represent a complete, finished product of a definite theological position; they are simply steps in a movement toward both an increasingly critical social awareness of the historical context and a theological search to illuminate it.

This process has in its background a philosophical counterpart that can be schematized as follows: liberal idealism (process of desacralization of society) *to* pragmatism (developmental interest) *to* utopian socialism.

In the second place, we should bear in mind another historical fact. The Committee on Church and Society in Latin America has been a catalyst and a ferment in the search for and development of Protestant Latin American theology. Yet it has been violently criticized and rejected by the church, mainly for its stand on social analysis (Marxist type) and political commitment, especially during the late sixties and early seventies. Whether we agree or not as individuals or as churches with the tools it used to analyze the socio-economic context, or with its strategy in terms of action, or with the results of its theological reflection, it stands as a significant challenge in its effort to make theology an instrument for the renewal of Latin American society. Even though it would be unfair to circumscribe the ferment in theology to the members and collaborators of this committee, no doubt its publications and their reflection born of concrete social and political engagement have had a far-reaching influence on the laity and clergy of an ample spectrum of Protestants and—I would venture to say—Roman Catholics.

There are at least three tasks that lie ahead of us. The first is the continual purification of our hermeneutical tools. The *hermeneutics of suspicion* must be related to the methods used in the interpretation of reality to sharpen the vision and serve as a corrective element in epistemology.[32] The theologians from Africa as well as the black theologians from the United States have poignantly unmasked the ideology of racism, which divides people according to their race and therefore serves as a means of social discrimination and economic exploitation. The feminist theologians from the North Atlantic have brought to light another oppressive theology that discriminates on the basis of sex. Gustavo Gutiérrez has recently given a symbol of the interrelation between different types of oppression. He said that "the spinal column of oppression is the economic and political system of exploitation; the flesh and blood of that body are racial and sexual oppressions. We cannot understand the body without the bones that give a framework to support the flesh and blood."[33]

As we share our insights as a community of Third World theologians, we may learn from each other and move toward a more holistic type of liberation theology that will include the liberation of all oppressed people in their many different kinds of oppression. Together with the political and economic system that produces masters and slaves, there are other types of alienation suffered by human beings, types that produce masters and slaves as well. Cultural anthropology will probably be a necessary tool to use in the future hermeneutical circle as one turns to the interpretation of reality.

Also, other types of social analysis, such as the one best exemplified by Emile Durkheim, will help in the understanding of symbols and values originated by culture and embodied in our social institutions.[34] Max Weber's analysis of power alienation can also provide a useful critique for both capitalist and socialist societies.

Also, we may need to be suspicious of possible methodological aberrations in approaching the Scriptures, to be aware of prejudices, preconditioning, internalized images, etc. This has already been done by unmasking our false conscience and the ideological coverture used during centuries of biblical interpretation. The hermeneutics of suspicion is only the counterpart of a *hermeneutics of hope*, born from the commitment to collaborate with our Savior as ambassadors of the kingdom, as agents of liberation.

A second task that lies ahead of us is to rethink some fundamental theological themes so as not to fall into reductionism but rather to embrace the totality of the biblical scope. This places us before an urgent demand to reformulate themes such as sin, the church, and Christology. Here it is interesting to note that so far only Juan Luis Segundo, a Uruguayan Jesuit, has covered a wide spectrum of traditional doctrinal subject matter.[35]

In brief, we are confronted with the *hermeneutical* task of a continual purification of tools and the *theological* challenge of broadening of themes treated.

Finally, we continue to have before us what can be called the *existential* dimension of liberation theology in a third task, that is, to continue to *explore* and *live* the literal enterprise of liberation that the Bible so clearly demands as an act of obedience to God—especially through the prophets and through Jesus Christ himself. To enter into or to continue with this type of discipline and discipleship cannot be done without paying a corresponding high price. The joy in the readiness to pay the price is a matter of faith in the unshakable certainty of his promises.

> Is not this the sort of fast that pleases me
> —it is the Lord Yahweh who speaks—
> to break unjust fetters
> and undo the thongs of the yoke,
>
> to let the oppressed go free,
> and break every yoke,
> to share your bread with the hungry,
> and shelter the homeless poor,

to clothe the man you see to be naked,
and not turn from your own kin?
Then will your light shine like the dawn
and your wound be quickly healed over.

If you do away with the yoke,
the clenched fist, the wicked word,
if you give your bread to the hungry,
and relief to the oppressed,

your light will rise in the darkness,
and your shadows become like noon.
Yahweh will always guide you,
giving you relief in desert places.

He will give strength to your bones
and you shall be like a watered garden,
like a spring of water
whose waters never run dry.

You will rebuild the ancient ruins,
build up on the old foundations.
You will be called "Breach-mender,"
"Restorer of ruined houses" (Isa. 58:6–12).

NOTES

1. In the proposed program of the meeting of the Ecumenical Dialogue of Third World Theologians two papers were to be presented by Latin American Protestants, as well as another two on the same themes by Roman Catholic thinkers from Latin America. Since Dr. Rubem Alves was unable to attend and he was responsible for the historical theme on the "Presence of the Church," I was asked to assume his task in addition to the one assigned to me concerning the "Outline of the New Theological Approaches and New Visions of the Church." I present my double assignment in only one essay, trying to work on the double task, historical and theological, and this I do for two reasons. I believe that in this way we can perceive more easily their unity; secondly, I am not by training a historian.

I assume full responsibility for the translations into English of quotations from Spanish books and articles, as well as a literal translation of titles, themes of conferences, etc. If, without my knowing, any of these are already translated into other languages, the wording may be slightly different. I have tried to use a descriptive methodology rather than to take an apologetic or polemic attitude toward the development of Protestant theology on our continent. It represents a process of growth of which I feel very much a part as a Christian and as a Latin American. The future will judge this type of reflection and action.

2. José Míguez Bonino, "Visión del cambio social y sus tareas desde las iglesias cristianas no-católicas," in *Fe cristiana y cambio social en América Latina* (Salamanca: Sígueme, 1973), pp. 179–202.

3. Protestant churches were established between 1850 and 1870, some years after these countries gained their political independence from Spain and Portugal.

4. The case of Pentecostalism would deserve a study in itself. The phenomenon of cultural "uprootedness" is transformed into a kind of new "social rootedness" in the sense that the marginated classes of society find a new identity in the church precisely because they have experienced margination, and the church offers them acceptance and inclusion. The Swiss sociologist Christian Lalive d'Epinay calls the Latin American (and more precisely the Chilean) Pentecostal church a "substitute society." What I called "uprootedness" is specifically expressed in this case not in relation to culture (their liturgy incorporates popular culture) but in relation to history and to social struggles. Lalive calls their retreat from the "world's struggles" a "social strike." Cf. Christian Lalive d'Epinay, *Haven of the Masses: A Study of the Pentecostal Movement in Chile* (London: Lutterworth, 1969).

5. Enrique Dussel, *América Latina, Dependencia y liberación* (Buenos Aires: Fernando García Cambeiro, 1973) pp. 37–48.

6. Primera Conferencia Evangélica Latinoamericana, Buenos Aires, 1949, p. 11.

7. Míguez, "Visión," pp. 189–91.

8. Ibid., p. 191.

9. Dussel, *América Latina*, p. 30. Míguez Bonino mentions five types of churches in Latin America, following Christian Lalive d'Epinay's typology, using two paradigms: the sociological type of the mother church (ecclesia, denomination, established sect, conversionist sect) and the form and place of penetration (basically groups of immigrants and native population). The five types are (*a*) the transplanted Protestant ecclesia of immigration; (*b*) denominations established among Protestant immigrants (or "injected" immigrants' churches); (*c*) missionary denominations (or "traditional Protestant-

ism" according to Latin American connotations); (*d*) established conversionist sects ("Protestantism of sanctification"); and (*e*) conversionist sects. Cf. Míguez, "Visión," pp. 179–80.

10. The names of John Mackey (Scot Presbyterian) and D. Foster Stockwell (U.S.A. Methodist) are intimately related to this fact. Both were deeply acquainted with the Spanish mystics and the former was a disciple of Miguel de Unamuno. They were visionaries whose impulse stimulated the ecumenical movement, theological education, and the whole enterprise of publication and production of indigenous literature in Latin America.

11. Emilio Castro, "La situación teológica de América Latina y la teología de Karl Barth," *Cuadernos Teológicos* (Buenos Aires), May 1956. Castro points out that it is Miguel de Unamuno, the Spanish philosopher, who discovered Barth for the Spanish world, mentioning him in his articles and other publications that reached Latin America. Also, Barth is known because of a famous Spanish philosophical magazine, the *Revista de Occidente*, which circulated among university students publications of Ortega y Gasset, who comments on Barth, and because of a philosophical evangelical magazine in Mexico, *Luminar*, which by 1938 (!) had already discovered the "new theologian."

12. Ibid., p. 13.

13. This fact is denounced especially in Latin American literature. A typical example is represented by the Peruvian novelist Ciro Alegría. He takes up the problem of the distribution of land and the Indian population in *The World is Wide and Alien*. He belonged to the Aprista party (socialist) and was persecuted for his political militancy. His poems and short stories denounced also the injustices of white supremacy and the exploitation of the Indian. In a pathetic and realistic style he portrays how the world is wide, yet alien, to the native population who does not have a minimum to survive and is continually displaced by the privileged class. Also from Peru, the writer José María Argüedas in *Los ríos profundos* (The Deep Rivers), portrays political persecution and the Indian problem.

14. Castro, *Cuadernos Teológicos*, no. 38, April–June, 1961, p. 98.

15. Ibid., p. 100.

16. Cf. *América Hoy* (Montevideo: ISAL, 1966).

17. Julio de Santa Ana, *Protestantismo: Cultura y Sociedad* (Buenos Aires: La Aurora, 1970), pp. 168–69.

18. The main lectures and findings of small study groups were published under the same title a year later in Uruguay.

19. The Roman Catholic liberation historian and theologian Enrique Dussel has produced some material on the Latin American marginalization of women, calling them the "oppressed of the oppressed." (Cf. "The Metaphysics of Femininity. Woman: An Oppressed Being," chapter in *América Latina: Dependencia y liberación* [Buenos Aires: Cambeiro, 1973], pp. 90–107.) The author of the present essay has published some material and lectured widely since the early 1960s on this theme, inscribing it in the liberation of *all* peoples, not as a separate agenda, but as a fundamental part of liberation and humanization in the search for the "new humanity."

20. Rubem Alves, *Tomorrow's Child* (New York: Harper and Row, 1972), p. 189 (Reinhold Niebuhr quoted from *Christian Realism and Political Problems*, 1953, pp. 5–6).

21. It is important to recall that this phenomenon of polarization was present at CELA III (Buenos Aires, 1970), which stressed on the one hand a "theory of develop-

ment" concerning social change and the relativity of any political option, and on the other hand the need for political revolutionary engagement.

22. Míguez, "Visión," p. 201.

23. See the publications of the Latin American Theological Fraternity: *Fe cristiana y Latinoamérica hoy* (Buenos Aires: Certeza, 1974); *El reino de Dios y la historia*, (El Paso: Casa Bautista de Publicaciones, 1975).

24. Míguez, "Visión," pp. 201–2.

25. Renee Padilla, *Fe Cristiana*, pp. 146–47.

26. Míguez, "Visión" p. 193.

27. Rubem Alves, *Tomorrow's Child* (New York: Harper and Row, 1972), |p. 196.

28. Ibid., pp. 197–203.

29. José Míguez Bonino, in *El Reino de Dios y la historia*, pp. 86 ff.

30. Míguez Bonino, *Christians and Marxists—the Mutual Challenge to Revolution* (Grand Rapids: Eerdmans, 1976), p. 139.

31. See the two issues of the magazine *Cristianismo y Sociedad* (1975), vols. 1 and 2, whose theme is "Who is Jesus Christ in Latin America?" with contributions of Roman Catholic and Protestant theologians.

32. We have to be aware when we approach the Scriptures that we are already conditioned by some kind of philosophical, ethical, political, and social background. The hermeneutics of the theology of liberation starts with what we may call the "hermeneutics of suspicion." As I see it, we should begin with two considerations: the first one is the suspicion about our own ideas as we approach the Scriptures. The second is suspicion about our methods. There are no innocent methods; every method presupposes a theory with its own limitations and within its own purposes.

33. Quoted from a discussion in the meeting of the Ecumenical Dialogue of Third World Theologians.

34. There are certain dimensions of human existence—such as the tragic aspect of evil—that cannot be reduced to conceptual language; symbolism takes hold of reality in a way that is not possible through philosophical or scientific thought. The revealing power of the symbol is closely related to the hermeneutical task and both symbolism and its intepretation are closely related to the understanding of the depths of the self through the way it projects its finitude and its transcendence in art, institutions, rites, beliefs, dreams, symbols, etc.

35. Cf. Juan Luis Segundo, *A Theology for Artisans of a New Humanity*, 5 vols. (Maryknoll, New York: Orbis Books, 1973–74).

16

Two Theological Perspectives: Liberation Theology and Progressivist Theology

Gustavo Gutiérrez (Peru)

For many Christians active involvement in popular liberation struggles has created a wholly new way of living, celebrating, and communicating their faith. Poor or rich, they have deliberately and explicitly identified with the oppressed on our continent. They have come to that commitment by different paths, determined by class origin and personal philosophy, and have broken with their pasts in different ways. This is *the major fact* in the recent life of the Christian community in Latin America. It is the source and matrix of the effort at theological clarification that led to liberation theology, which can only be understood in relation to liberation practice. The popular liberation movement poses new questions, theological as well as socio-political, and these questions, rooted in liberation practice, are both starting point and ultimate criteria for liberation theology.

Its roots in liberation practice go far to explain the varied responses to liberation theology. These range from total hostility to mistrust to flattering efforts to neutralize it by co-option into the existing system. Different from all of these has been the reaction of the most advanced wing of progressivist theology.

To understand the criticisms, we must be clear about their origins. The most aggressive attacks on liberation theology urge orthodoxy and fidelity to the magisterium, but they originate in a reactionary social order that feels shaken to its foundation and that is appealing to religion to shore up its position. These attacks are relentless, monotonous, mindless; they are launched by liberation's most cruel, powerful, and implacable enemies. But they have nothing to do with theology.

Other criticisms, however, have come from other currents in contemporary theology. While avoiding useless, hair-splitting polemics, liberation theologians must answer these criticisms. In the process they will have reassessed their roots in liberation practice and clarified their differences from other contemporary theological currents.

In the following pages I shall consider two different theological outlooks—progressivist theology and liberation theology—and the differences between them. (The reader should bear in mind, however, the real-life implications of reactionary hostility to both outlooks.)

To understand these theological currents, I think one must understand their historical contexts, and these I propose most briefly to outline.

POINT OF VIEW OF THE DOMINANT CLASSES

The Coming of the Modern Age

The modern age emerged from a radical and overall transmutation of Europe that "began" in the sixteenth century and culminated (though by no means terminated) in the eighteenth. The free exercise of human reason was gradually admitted and its astounding capacity to transform the physical environment quickly recognized. These transformations, perceived as ameliorative, generated an optimistic empiricism, whose conjunction with revived emphasis on mathematics and invention of adequate measuring and testing devices was most notably embodied in the work of Galileo. Rational questioning, observation, and empirical proof replaced dogmatic assertion and deduction from First Principles. *"Sapere aude!"* Kant said, "Dare to use your own mind! . . . All that is required for Enlightenment is . . . the most inoffensive sort of freedom: the freedom to make public use of one's own reason in any and every domain."

In addition to transforming the environment, the new empiricism bore three noteworthy consequences. First, science is "methodologically atheistic"; it has no need of the "God hypothesis," and this realization gave significant impetus to secularizing tendencies. Mathematics, which in Newton's work superseded philosophy as "queen of sciences," revealed natural laws of such universal validity that it became logical to envision God as master mathematician, with whom a personal relationship was unthinkable. The disappearance of a personal God, or Divine Providence, also provided stimulus for secularization. Second, individual disciplines replaced the search for Universal Truth, and efforts to impose various universal truths, by force if necessary, fell into desuetude. Third, if human reason could by discovering the laws of nature so triumphantly improve the physical environment, who could doubt that applied to human relationships it could also transform society. The search for a social or "practical" philosophy replaced the search for the City of God. This amounted to a radical secularization of hope, with Reason replacing the Second Coming and heaven achievable on earth.

Simultaneous political changes of equal magnitude were occurring. Nationalism on the one hand and individualism on the other replaced "Christendom" with nation-states and their citizens. The nation-states, though each maintained—some most rigidly—an established religion, were for all practical purposes secular, operating independently of religious considerations and according to purely political principles, as Machiavelli had taught. Divine-right monarchy obtained, but not unchallenged and not for long: If God is a mathematician and Divine Providence nonexistent in a universe of immutable laws, then the philosophical basis of the "divine right of kings" disappears, to be replaced by the "rights of man" and the "social contract."

Rationalism and empiricism are both expressions of individualism;[1] the one deals with ideas and the other with experience, but both affirm that individual consciousness is the starting point of cognition and action. Truth is not vouchsafed by authority, divine or human, but can be reached by the exercise of critical reason. With truth accessible to reason, people can master the world and themselves; the search for a "practical philosophy" is rationalism's corollary, as rationalism and empiricism are corollaries of individualism. In the free exercise of human reason Hegel saw the defining characteristic of the Enlightenment.[2] Modern science and politics obviously required a new theory of knowledge, and that need was filled by a new epistemology (Kant) and new theories of ethics (Kant) and of history (Hegel).

Individualism, beginning as the Renaissance's call to reason for the sake of knowledge, received powerful stimulus from the Reformation, which deposed universal religious authority in favor of individual reason applied to Holy Writ. "This is the essential content of the Reformation: man is left on his own, determined to be free.
. . . Henceforth each individual was to find enlightenment and form his conscience by starting off from the Bible. . . . The whole tradition and structure of the church became problematical, since the principle of church authority was now toppled."[3]

Thus far we have spoken of the transforming power of new ideas. But accelerating technological innovation throughout the seventeenth and eighteenth centuries was an equally potent agent of change. The industrial revolution, beginning as unsystematic empiricism applied to production, culminated in the bourgeois ascendancy. And the right to private property, particularly ownership of the means of production, is fundamental in bourgeois society. A liberal historian states that "the freedom of industry is the child of modern individualism, indeed its favorite child,"[4] but industry is more nearly individualism's mother than its child. To the bourgeois mind the individual is the autonomous center of decision-making and the motivating force of economic activity, and free interplay of individual decisions achieves the general good. Where individualism is paramount, capitalism seems the natural economic order.

Individualism also governs the organization of bourgeois society. Individual liberty is primary; society is based on freedom of association; and a prerequisite of freedom of association is social equality. Social equality is also a precondition of the bourgeois economy: In the marketplace people must be equal.[5]

The light of events quickly faded the bright optimism of the Enlightenment as human relations proved less amenable to Reason than the material world to scientific empiricism; Hegel spoke of the unfulfilled Enlightenment. Nevertheless Enlightenment ideals, notably the "rights of man," mold the modern mind and spirit to this day. They form the temper and ideology of the new dominant class: the bourgeoisie.

Intellectual, political, religious, technological, and economic agents of change—jostling, altering, and reinforcing one another —dissolved the Old Regime and created modern bourgeois society. From its equivocal status as medieval townspeople, the bourgeoisie has become subject and agent of the modern temper and master of the modern world. As both agent and beneficiary of the industrial revolution and private enterprise, its economic—and thence political —dominance is based on maximal exploitation of Europe's working class and the colonial and neocolonial poor. To consider modern ideology (individualism in all its ramifications) apart from its historical agent (the bourgeoisie) would falsify sociology, philosophy, and theological as well as secular history.

The Modern Critique of Premodern Christianity

The modern age and premodern Christianity were natural antagonists. One Truth precluded religious tolerance; dogma was inimical to science; Divine Providence was as clearly inimical to individual autonomy, liberty, and initiative, and hence profoundly immoral. Intelligent and subtle people resolved this painful schism in various ways: Some kept intellectual freedom and belief in a personal God in separate mental compartments; atheists denied God's existence; eighteenth-century Deists tried to formulate a rational religion, free of dogma and authoritarianism and hence universally acceptable to enlightened minds but also completely tolerant of dissent—religion for an intellectual elite.

The market economy was no less an enemy of premodern Christianity, despite links between Protestantism and capitalism; buying and selling would not be fettered by religious sanctions and did not require commonality of belief. Gradually bourgeois Europe unraveled Christianity from its social fabric and made it a personal and private matter.[6] Nevertheless criticism intensified and increased: Critics like Feuerbach placed modern theology permanently on the defensive before skepticism or atheism.

Theological Response to Modern Criticisms

While the Old Regime remained politically intact, conservative Christianity responded to modernity with total and fervent antagonism. When the Old Regime—and with it the hope of restoring medieval Christendom—shattered, and the bourgeoisie was perceived to be firmly in power, Catholicism began a reluctant accommodation. The bourgeoisie, shaken by the first attacks of the masses, was looking for allies. The way was paved for compromise.

Protestantism accorded far better than traditional Catholicism with the modern world, and liberal Protestant theology became the most significant Christian theology of the modern age. Its center, like modern philosophy's, was Germany, and its spokesmen were "enlightened" *and* Christian. Kant and Hegel were both advocates and acute critics of Enlightenment principles, and both sought to "prove" and define God's being—Kant by reference to ethics ("practical philosophy") and Hegel by reference to human history.

Schleiermacher, more theologian than the others mentioned above, also addressed himself to the modern critique of religion; all his writings were markedly apologetic. His main defense of religion against rationalism was to posit an essential religiousness, the "religious sentiment," in every person. Religion's existence and value, he said, were unassailable by human reason, whose proper function regarding religion was to define its essence—more particularly the essence of that higher form of religion known as Christianity.

Liberal theology, more a point of view than a strictly defined body of doctrine, has antecedents in Hegel's and Schleiermacher's great syntheses and emphasizes Kant's epistemological and ethical questions. It is the product of strenuous efforts to construct a theology compatible intellectually with the Enlightenment and socially with modern bourgeois society. Its application of historical and textual criticism to religion marks its acceptance of—some would say its capitulation to—intellectual modernity.

Liberal Theology Called in Question: Faith or Religion?

The charge of capitulation to modernity came in the twentieth century and dislodged liberal theology from its ascendancy. Barth, Bultmann, and Tillich, Protestant theologians of enormous influence on contemporary Christianity, asked: How could rationalism and modernity be criteria for authentic Christianity?

The challenge to liberal theology occurred in a new historical context that also challenged Enlightenment and bourgeois values. The *belle époque* and bourgeois society's facile optimism ended together in 1914. Socialism, frightening as a movement, became terrifying as the Russian regime. Soon after, fascism joined the attack on bourgeois ideology.

In his prison diary Bonhoeffer evaluated the new theological approach. Tillich, following Schleiermacher, expounded a religious worldview that the modern world found extrinsic and superfluous. Barth attempted a rapprochement with secularism by situating faith in God's word gratuitously revealed rather than in human religiousness, but this emphasis on revelation and consequent neglect of the world failed to extricate him from liberal theology. Bultmann espoused liberal theology even more explicitly. His "demythologization" is a typical liberal attempt—ultimately useless and impossible —to reduce Christianity to its "essence."

Bonhoeffer perceived modernity's challenge to Christianity thus: "How are we to talk of God in a world come of age?" In other words, can the Christian *faith* be dissociated from religiousness? His secularized theology is now considered too reductive, too eviscerating, but Bonhoeffer apparently identified religiousness with belief in an omniscient and omnipotent God—and this belief he found untenable in the modern world. Faith, on the other hand, he related to the weak, suffering God of the Bible: "God allows himself to be edged out of the world and on to the cross. God is weak and powerless in the world, and that is exactly the way, the only way, in which he can be with us and help us. Matthew 8:17 makes it crystal clear that it is not by his omnipotence that Christ helps us, but by his weakness and suffering."[7] As a victim of Nazism, Bonhoeffer reached that insight through personal suffering and witness to God's impotence.

"How are we to talk of God in a world come of age?" Bonhoeffer is not asking whether people are inherently religious or whether people are capable of belief in God. He is asking: Who is God? Who is Jesus Christ for us today? The latter question suggested a possible answer to the former: The God of Christian faith is the God who suffers in Jesus Christ.[8] The Christian living in a world come of age—meaning a world without God—must share God's suffering.

Bonhoeffer was the first to reply so penetratingly to modernity's challenge. His questioning, though originating in the modern world, did much to free theology from the fetters of modern assumptions.

Political Theology

As early as the nineteenth century a liberal Catholic minority was challenging official Catholicism's authoritarian rejection of the modern world and seeking dialogue with bourgeois society. Finally Leo XIII sanctioned its more moderate political opinions. Still later, in its attempt to engage the contemporary mind, Catholic theology came to accept certain nonpolitical modern values as well. These openings to modernity, initially peripheral to church teaching, were reinforced by social and political developments.

Accommodation proceeded from both sides, though conflicts occasionally flared and never wholly subsided. The bourgeoisie, finding religion no longer much threat and increasingly uneasy about the gathering protests of the poor, gradually abated its hostility to religion, in practice if not in rhetoric.

Vatican II, the culmination of nineteenth-century nascent Catholic liberalism and bourgeois moderation, reflected a new political theology. It embodied Catholicism's acknowledgement of the modern world's values and disregard of its defects. Human autonomy, reason, rights, liberty, and progress received explicit sanction, while poverty, injustice, inequality, and class conflict were barely touched on. "The possibility of a new political theology," says Metz, "arose when people began to consider the possibility of a theology related to the modern world and Enlightenment, secularization, and emancipation. The ultimate question is whether theology and theological reasoning are possible in the modern world. This basic question of theology and of theological theory provides the locus for a new political theology."[9]

Moltmann prefers to call political theology the "political theology of hope,"[10] and his definition of it excludes Luther's doctrine of two realms or kingdoms as well as Barth's political ethics. Moltmann finds political theology equally applicable to Catholicism and Protestantism because "both churches are faced with the same problem (the growing irrelevance of their doctrines for modern life) and cannot find any key to a solution in their respective traditions." The key, Moltmann says, lies in the modern world's concern for the future. This means that the experience of transcendence is not metaphysical but eschatological. "Political theology," says Moltmann, "finds its roots buried in the theology of hope."[11]

This is a new and fruitful approach to the issues raised by humanity's coming of age, although, like earlier theological revisions, it owes its historical context to the Enlightenment and the bourgeois ascendancy. Now, however, political theology is beginning to take cognizance, albeit uneasily, of the questions raised by liberation theology.[12] The cause of its uneasiness may be liberation theology's unfamiliar context. That context—though it undoubtedly follows on and has in a sense grown out of the triumphs of individualism, rationalism, and the bourgeoisie—is not the historical culmination or even the present phase of these developments; it is their converse, their dark underside.

POINT OF VIEW OF THE OPPRESSED

Colonialism and Neocolonialism

For nascent bourgeois society in fifteenth- and sixteenth-century Europe, the discovery of new worlds catalyzed the development of capitalism. The bourgeoisie participated eagerly in the conquest and colonization of Latin America.

Nowhere is it clearer than in Latin America that the emergence of the modern world has meant very different conditions in different places. In Western Europe the modern process engendered political freedom and individual liberty. Elsewhere that same process meant new and more refined forms of exploitation of the common people. Their liberty will consist in liberation from oppression and spoliation inflicted in the name of "modern freedoms and democracy" and by its bearers.

The faith of poor peoples is nourished by hope of that liberation. In its context they are trying to create a new theology that will not be an opiate for their sufferings or a corollary of the prevailing ideology. The makers of this new theology are increasingly aware of its differences from currently dominant conservative and progressivist theologies.

Democratic Principles and Economic Exploitation

The industrial revolution increased the European bourgeoisie's power and extended it beyond Europe's boundaries. Latin America was born a dependent continent, its history contingent on events in Europe. As Spain weakened during the eighteenth century, England achieved maritime and commercial supremacy. By the end of the eighteenth century England was trading to the Spanish colonies, though still subject to certain restraints. Political independence from Spain only replaced Spanish colonialism with English-dominated "neocolonialism": The nations of the New World would sell raw materials to and buy manufactured goods from the industrialized nations—both on the latter's terms. With the complicity of local ruling classes the former colonies had entered the capitalist system—as victims.

Utopian liberals dreamed of political liberty and modernity for the new nations and vaguely liberal ideology flavored their political constitutions. Political independence and the subsequent neocolonialism were accomplished by a predominantly white and creole elite. The poor—the native Indians, blacks, and mestizos—participated passively or sporadically, if at all. The freedom guaranteed by the new constitutions did not free everyone; it simply reinforced the privileges of local elite who served the interests of international capitalists. Many of the poor were worse off even than under colonialism.

As in Europe, the local elite were initially split into liberal and conservative blocs. The liberals espoused the political and intellectual values of post-Enlightenment Europe, together with a somewhat reformist and benevolent bourgeois capitalism modeled after contemporary England's. The conservative bloc comprised the great landowners, the bureaucracy (relatively unchanged since colonial days), and the Catholic church; it sought to retain the economic perquisites of the colonial era. Again as in Europe, incipient populism's threat to both parties' privileges conduced to their rapprochement.

The system that meant intellectual and political freedom and economic opportunity for Europe and the United States (to which the preponderance of economic power was shifting by the end of the nineteenth century) brought only new forms of oppression and exploitation to the common people of Latin America. That is why the sacred principles of bourgeois democracy are not above question here.[13]

Social-Doctrine Christianity in Latin America

The international depression of the 1930s, besides generating political and economic changes (like the beginnings of native industry), opened the way for the introduction of liberal European Catholic social doctrine into Latin America. In its perspective the wretched of Latin America were no longer seen as pawns of ineluctable fate or as objects of charity, but as victims of human, therefore remediable, social injustice. Individual Christians now felt committed, as Christians, to remedying injustice but failed to see that injustice called in question their society's whole structure and value system. The nebulous aim of this Christian humanism was a society devoted to Christian values, human dignity, democracy, and moderate social justice.

The flaws in this benign vision are not hard to find: One was its failure to recognize the extent to which social inequity is a prime mover in the body politic and moral—the extent to which it subverts liberal institutions and values. Another was its assumption that social and political committment and action are necessarily religious-affiliated.

Gradually, and more in some countries (e.g., Peru, Brazil, Uruguay) than in others, some Christians dissociated politics from faith, cooperating politically with non-Christians and professing common faith with Christians of differing political views. Where religion was dissociated from politics, Christians were quickly radicalized politically; furthermore their politics did not evolve directly or primarily in opposition to Christian temporal institutions. In countries where politics and Christianity remained entwined, opposition to the conservative past naturally involved opposition to its Christian component.

Beginnings of the People's Struggle: The World of the Downtrodden

From the start of the Iberian conquest the native Americans rebelled against their new overlords as did the imported black slaves against their masters,[14] although till recently our history books said little about those struggles for liberation. Gradually Christian motifs began to appear in these rebellions. The Indians, blacks, and mestizos who had accepted the gospel message found in it reasons to reject their oppression. Their interpretations of the gospel in light of their own situation and culture diverged from traditional orthodoxy but coincided with the Bible's definition of justice.[15] The ideologies of their revolts often took the form of politico-religious messianism,[16] and a study of these messianic movements would be useful for liberation history.

Some of the poor fought in the wars for national independence, but the victories incorporated few traces of their aspirations. The first currents of French socialism, which acknowledged the plight of the new proletarian class, reached our shores in the latter half of the nineteenth century engendering protests and *pronunciamentos* against poverty but little action. The poor were mostly peasants: there were as yet few miners or urban laborers. Toward the end of the nineteenth century came the first stirrings of the labor-union movement and of syndicalist struggles marked by anarchist ideology. At the start of the century, as the workers began to form political parties, the socialism of the Second International contributed to the organization of workers' Centrals. After 1920 Latin American socialism split into moderate and revolutionary movements.

The revolutionary camp's greatest leader and theoretician was the Peruvian, José Carlos Mariátegui, who tried to interpret Latin American realities in Marxist terms as the basis for changing those realities for the better.

With few exceptions, among them Clotario Blest, founder of Chile's Central Unica de Trabajadores (CUT, Unified Workers' Central), these early efforts to politicize and organize the working class were not under specifically Christian auspices. Where there was a tradition of Christian social thought, there was also a tendency to form specifically Christian labor organizations alongside secular ones.

The dissociation of socio-political activity from religion did not begin until much later.

In recent decades Latin America has been made increasingly aware of the "other"—its poor, oppressed, and exploited. Exploited classes, cultures, and races are awakening to both their distress and its gratuitousness. They have begun to cry out for justice and to retaliate directly against the minority that benefits from and perpetuates the social order that afflicts them. They have begun to reject both charity and the self-serving manipulations of demagogues. They seek to become agents of their own history and to forge a radically different society.

This awakening was heralded by the popular content of revolutionary efforts in Mexico, Bolivia, and Guatemala. It acquired new perspectives from the socialist revolution in Cuba. Armed struggle reached a high point in 1965, hastening the political radicalization even of those who would have preferred other means toward a just society. Camilo Torres and Che Guevara, incandescent symbols of countless unknown rebels, indelibly marked Latin American history and powerfully influenced many Christian movements.

During these years a growing number of Christians, first in Brazil then elsewhere, began taking active part in Latin American politics, discovering in the process the fact of exploitation and even, sometimes, that they were themselves the exploited. This committed involvement is the major event in the recent life of the Christian community here and the major bond between Christians whose participation in the liberation process varies in form, expression, and radicality. It produced a new way of living, a new way of pondering and practicing the faith, and a new vision of what it means to be an ecclesia. It has created a new epoch in Latin America and in the life of the Latin American church, which now encompasses two utterly different worlds, idioms, and kinds of experience.

Latin America has always been a continent of repression and oppression, and protest movements have caused the repression to increase in refinement and ferocity.[17] Governments have extended their systematic violations of elemental human rights by indiscriminate use of terror—summary arrests, torture, assassinations. These tactics, which the Medellín Conference aptly termed "institutional violence," are employed to silence the demand for justice but defended as the means to keep movements of the masses "orderly."[18] Government repression and terror notwithstanding, however, the populist movements are increasing in numbers and political maturity. They have not experienced uninterrupted triumphs, but they have learned even from their mistakes and setbacks, and they are characterized by a political realism and a hopeful resilience bewildering to the established order and even to revolutionary elite of the recent past whom failure reduced to frustrated quiescence.

In this context the theology of liberation arose. It could not have arisen before the populist movement and its historical praxis of liberation had reached a certain level of maturity. The struggles of the common people for liberation provide the matrix for a new life and a new faith, both to be achieved through a new kind of encounter with God and our fellow human beings. This spiritual experience, which Paul described as "living according to the Spirit," occurs amid social conflict and in solidarity with the downtrodden of history. It is the wellspring of the new theological effort in Latin America.[19]

The Philosophy of People's Struggle and the Theology of Liberation

When the wretched of the earth awake, their first challenge is not to religion but to the social, economic, and political order oppressing them and to the ideology supporting it.

The Latin American poor seek to eradicate their misery, not ameliorate it; hence they choose social revolution rather than reform, liberation rather than development, and socialism rather than liberalization. These options, which seem to the ruling classes utopian, are utterly rational to the oppressed. Dependence on external powers and domination by internal minorities typify the social structures of Latin America. But this theory as first propounded may not have emphasized adequately that the primary confrontation is not between powerful ("developed") nations or continents and weak ("underdeveloped") ones, but between different social classes. Nationalism and racism are more clearly understood in the context of class inequity; so too the economic and political control of multinational corporations over poor countries.[20]

The challenge of the poor to the prevailing order that oppresses them is actual, not theoretical, and it brings together Marxism, social-scientific analysis, and popular movements within the historical process. Similarly the challenge of the poor juxtaposes Marxism and the social sciences with liberation theology in the present moment of history.[21] Liberation envisions not only a new society but a new kind of person, one increasingly free of the bonds preventing us from shaping our own lives. This implies defects in the prevailing ideologies that have shaped our societies and ourselves, and since religious elements are present in those ideologies, religion must be criticized insofar as it generates or reinforces oppression. For such criticism to be sound, however, religion must be seen in the context of the social order as a whole: Our thinking and actions as Christians are to a great extent socially conditioned, and in creating a theology of liberation we must be aware of the pervasive connection between ideology and theology.[22]

A new society and a new kind of person can only be fashioned by the oppressed themselves, grounded in their values. An authentic social and cultural revolution can only be created by its subjects, never for them.

Given that fact, liberation theology's first question cannot be the same one that progressivist theology has asked since Bonhoeffer. The question is not how we are to talk about God in a world come of age, but how we are to tell people who are scarcely human that God is love and that God's love makes us one family. The interlocutors of liberation theology are the nonpersons, the humans who are not considered human by the dominant social order—the poor, the exploited classes, the marginalized races, all the despised cultures.[23] Liberation theology categorizes people not as believers or unbelievers but as oppressors or oppressed. And the oppressors include people who "call themselves Christians," in the words of Bartolomé de Las Casas.

Note the contrast between the interlocutors of progressivist and of liberation theology: The interlocutors of progressivist theology question faith; the interlocutors of liberation theology "share" the same faith as their oppressors, but they do not share the same economic, social, or political life. But in light of God's word, faith cannot be separated from historical reality ("real life"); in order to exist faith must be lived—though for a long time persons claiming to be Christians have falsely contended otherwise.

We must not forget that the common people have their own,

popular religion. It is incomprehensible to the bourgeoisie, despised by them, yet manipulated by them to defend their own privileges. It is also true that popular religion contains elements of the dominant ideology. Nevertheless the concrete religious experiences of the common people also contain valuable elements of protest, resistance, and liberation.[24]

The differences between traditional or progressivist theology and liberation theology are not merely geographical (the former being European and the latter indigenous in origin)[25] or merely theological; the primary difference is political, grounded in social inequity. Both traditional and progressivist theology persist in Latin America as the theologies of the conservative and liberal sectors, respectively, of the ruling class. The locus of liberation theology is the common people seeking to be agents of their own history and expressing their faith and hope in the poor Christ through their efforts for liberation.

Salvation and Social Justice: Bartolomé de Las Casas and the "Scourged Christs" of the Indies

The conquest and colonization of Latin America quickly became a missionary enterprise. Spain's self-imputed motive was the salvation by conversion of these new-found infidels. This Christian motive might have justified an ideal colonial enterprise but it rebuked the real one. That discrepancy was the heart of the "controversy over the Indies."

Salvation was Bartolomé de Las Casas's passion and the motive of his missionary work. But in his eyes salvation was so closely associated with social justice that he inverted the usual hierarchy of missionary principles in two respects. First, Las Casas pointed out, the Spaniards' gratuitous or exploitative cruelty toward the Indians was endangering their own salvation: "It is impossible for someone to be saved if he does not observe justice."[26] Second, with deep prophetic insight Las Casas saw the Indians more as "poor" persons in the gospel sense than as infidels. He did not hesitate to write to the emperor that the destruction and death of the Indians was too high a price to pay for their conversion.

Many shared Las Casas's opinion, and worked hard and cohesively to defend the Indians.[27] But their opinion had determined enemies. One of the most renowned champions of the Spanish conquest and colonization was Juan Ginés de Sepúlveda, whose central argument was that Indians were by nature inferior to Europeans and hence ought to be their slaves. This distinction between naturally superior and inferior people was based on a famous passage in the writings of Aristotle and on some ambiguous comments by Thomas Aquinas on slavery. Their inferiority justified the Indians' enslavement, and to enslave them—as well as convert them—it was necessary to conquer them.

Sepúlveda's argument is brilliantly expounded and abundantly buttressed with quotations from traditional authority. Naturally the *encomenderos* applauded this theological defense of their oppression-based privileges. We have had many such Sepúlvedas in Latin America since, all of them advocating or justifying the exploitation or enslavement of the majority in the name of "western Christian civilization." But only Sepúlveda's more recent disciples have approached the candor with which he justified oppression and murder.

Las Casas's ideas are familiar and need not be recapitulated in toto. I should like to summarize those elements of his theology, however, that prefigure current liberation theology.

In his controversy with Sepúlveda, Las Casas precedes his abundant careful rebuttals based on doctrine with one overwhelming confutation from life: The wars of conquest and the *encomienda* system defended by Sepúlveda have brought about "the perdition of countless people and the depopulation of more than two thousand leagues of land."[28] Las Casas repeatedly emphasizes that the criteria of any theology are its practical consequences, not its theoretical assumptions, and he repeatedly criticizes the Spaniards for their intellectualism, their ignorance of the Indies, and the concrete consequences of their theology. Las Casas himself was a man of action, and his theology served his active defense of the Indians.

Las Casas was less tradition bound and academic than any other theologian of his day. Francisco de Vitoria, also a Dominican and the most famous theologian of his era, author of advanced opinions on the rights of nations and international law, was not nearly as advanced as

Las Casas on the question of the Indies. He vigorously rejected Sepúlveda's reasons for conquering and enslaving the Indians but claimed that certain hypothetical motives and situations could justify such wars. His centrist theology represented the most enlightened opinion of the ruling class of his day.

Las Casas respected Vitoria greatly, but his own standpoint was very different. His starting point was not the hypothetical case but the actual Indians, exploited members of a despised race. That is why Las Casas rarely cited Vitoria's work and often criticized his intellectualist views as too far removed from concrete experience. All centrism, political or theological, opens the door to ultraconservatism. Vitoria's centrism would have justified "moderate" warfare against the Indians.

It has been charged that a theology of active witness to faith, of practice, of involvement in liberation struggles, must be intellectually less rigorous, and therefore less valid, than an academic, theoretical theology. But is Las Casas's theology less valid than Vitoria's? I think not. Reasoning from a concrete situation is quite different from (but no less rigorous than) reasoning from a priori "first principles" —unfamiliar though the ruling classes and their ideological dependents may have found it. Furthermore participation in a concrete historical process—such as the lives of the oppressed—enables one to perceive aspects of the Christian message that theorizing fails to reveal. Las Casas's insight into the relationship between salvation and justice proves the point. It derived from seeing the Indians not primarily as infidels to be evangelized, which abstracts them from their humanity, but rather as poor human beings in the gospel sense of the term. The poor Indian was the "other" who was challenging the truths of Christendom. Las Casas carried this insight further when he realized that Christ was speaking to him and his contemporaries through the Indians. His account of his own conversion tells us this, and he repeated it often: "In the Indies I left behind Jesus Christ, our God, suffering affliction, scourging, and crucifixion not once but a million times over."[29]

Sepúlveda would have found such an identification of Christ with the Indians inconceivable, but Las Casas and those who followed in his footsteps, though trained in traditional theology, saw that in and through the "scourged Christs of the Indies" Jesus is denouncing exploitation, denying the Christianity of the exploiters, and calling people to understand and heed his gospel message.[30]

Liberation Theology's Modern Antecedents

Intellectual modernity did not produce an innovative or even characteristic Latin American theology. In the nineteenth and early twentieth centuries Latin American theology pallidly reflected the European liberal-conservative division. Protestantism was closer to the modern spirit than Catholicism, but being less indigenous it was even less theologically significant.

From about 1930 to Vatican II Latin American theological liberals were content to follow French theology, enthusiastically if not creatively, for French theology then represented the Catholic avant-garde. Social-doctrine Catholicism was followed by theology based on the distinction of planes. Social-doctrine Christianity was a version of social reformism, acknowledging modern reality and, with reservations, liberal ideology, and seeking an alternative to capitalism and socialism. But its timid social concern could not transcend the search for a political alternative or see Christ in the oppressed. Hence it is not really surprising that in Chile, for example, social-doctrine Christianity ended as the ally of ultraconservatism.

The theology based on the distinction of planes had greater theological breadth and sensitivity to modern values. It advocated democracy and social justice and stressed the church's presence in the world and the possible diversity of Christian political commitments. Even prior to Vatican II, from which it derived great impetus, it had led certain groups into progressivist theology.

After Vatican II the liberal element of the Latin American church turned briefly to the theology of development, which combined positive evaluation of human progress with increased social concern for poor peoples and nations. Its optimism, and dynamism, however, could not conceal its superficial explanation of the underlying causes of poverty and injustice or its paucity of concrete Christian experience.

The theology of revolution sought to escape bourgeois assumptions and embrace radical political commitments, but its perspective was limited. It tended to consecrate the idea of revolution and broaden it so that it lost all meaning, and it tended to lack theory based on concrete praxis.

Liberation Theology

The years 1965–1968 were decisive for the popular movement in Latin America and for the Christian participation in that movement. Liberation theology struck deep roots in those years, and we cannot understand what happened at the Medellín Episcopal Conference without reference to the life of Christian communities at that time.

Medellín expressed the experiences of Christians personally involved in the liberation process. It offered them acceptance and support and it pointed new directions for thought and action. Medellín took on a task assigned to Vatican II but not carried out: the task of proposing solutions to contemporary world poverty. Medellín's stated theme was "Latin America in the light of Vatican II"; its aim was to examine Latin American realities from the conciliar point of view. Concrete contact with those realities, however, reversed the theme, and Medellín considered "Vatican II in the light of Latin American reality." That reversal reflected the maturity of the Christian community in Latin America. More important, it expressed the wretchedness, hope, and commitment of the oppressed and their allies. Advocates of social justice were galvanized by Medellín's reversal of theme, while opponents have tried but failed to expunge that conference from Latin America's memory. Once the Christian community has committed itself to the reality of the poor and their achievement of God's promised justice, it can only move forward.

In Latin America today human rights and social justice are nearly nonexistent. This has generated nostalgic misrepresentation of the years 1965–68 as halcyon times, and a corresponding false claim that liberation theology was an evanescent product of enthusiasm and euphoria. But though the socio-political context was indeed more favorable then, those were years of conflict, struggle, failure; 1968, when liberation theology was first tentatively formulated, was hardly a time of easy optimism, let alone euphoria.[31] Moreover, though the times have worsened, our motives for hope remain unchanged. We must bear in mind that whatever the external situation, the people of Latin America are moving toward liberation. To bear witness to a life of authentic faith and hope in the Lord, we must go with them.

Two intuitions are central to liberation theology. They came first chronologically, and they continue first in importance. One is methodological; the other is its frame of reference.

From the start liberation theology has maintained that active commitment to liberation comes first and theology develops from it. Theology is critical reflection on and from within historical praxis, and the historical praxis of liberation theology is to accept and live the word of God through faith. We fashion and alter our faith according to frequently ambiguous historical mediations, but liberation theology does not merely replace the deductive with the inductive method.[32] Rather, liberation theology reflects on and from within the complex and fruitful relationship between theory and practice.

Liberation theology's second central intuition is that God is a liberating God, revealed only in the concrete historical context of liberation of the poor and oppressed. This second point is inseparable from the first: If theology is reflection on and from within concrete praxis, the concrete praxis in question is the liberation praxis of the oppressed. It is not enough to know that praxis must precede reflection; we must also realize that the historical subject of that praxis is the poor—the people who have been excluded from the pages of history. Without the poor as subject, theology degenerates into academic exercise. Theological discourse becomes true—is verified—in and through its engagement in the liberation of the poor.

The inseparability of these two intuitions explains why liberation theology must begin with the hopes of the poor, expressed in their own words from within their own world. Speaking for the poor might hasten, initially, the illusion of progress but could not produce real qualitative change, only the old reality tricked out in new phrases. The poor, who have never been allowed to speak for themselves, must now begin.

This will initiate vast historical changes. If liberation theology, with its admitted deficiencies, contributes to those changes and to a new understanding of the faith, then it will have fulfilled its role in this transitional period. Like all theology, it simply expresses how certain Christians interpret their faith in light of their times. The present generation has scarcely begun to cut its ties, conscious and subconscious, to the prevailing system and has only begun to discover the world of the "other" and the Lord's presence there.

History is the concrete locale of human encounter with the Father of Jesus Christ. In Jesus Christ we proclaim the Father's love for all human beings, but till now we have interpreted history from the standpoint of the "winners," or rulers, or upper classes. The perspective of the "losers" is very different, and we must reinterpret history in terms of their hopes and struggles. The "winners" have done their best to strip the "losers" of their historical consciousness in order to eradicate their will and thereby lull their rebelliousness. Now the downtrodden are trying to recover their past in order to found on it a fitting present.

The history of Christianity has also been written by white, western, bourgeois hands.[33] We must recover the memory of the "scourged Christs of the Indies," of the victims of this world. That memory lives on in elements of our culture, in popular religion, in resistance to ecclesiastical high-handedness. It is the memory that Christ is present in all who are hungry, thirsty, or humiliated (Matt. 25), and that he has set us free to be free (Gal. 5:1).

Reinterpreting history might be mistaken for purely an intellectual exercise, but it is not. It is a necessary part of the active effort to *remake history*. We cannot reinterpret history without being actively engaged in the liberation struggle. To remake history is to subvert it, to channel its course from the standpoint of those on the bottom. The established order has taught us to attach a pejorative connotation to the word "subversive," but in subversive history we find a new experience of the faith, a new spirituality, and a new proclamation of the gospel message.

Throughout history the "winners" have never wholly suppressed their victims' historical memory and attempts to remake their history. We find traces of them in groping expressions of impatience with "the system," in treatises that were ignored or suppressed, in movements put down in blood. Throughout history we can also detect a theology born out of the struggles of the poor and suppressed or subverted by those in power. Liberation theology must trace the course of the poor in Christian history in order to maintain its historical continuity. It must analyze the great landmarks: the primitive Christian commu-

nity; the church fathers; the Franciscan movement and Joachim of
Fiore in the twelfth and thirteenth centuries; the Hussite movement
in the fifteenth century; the German peasant wars and the figure of
Thomas Münzer in the sixteenth century; the defense of the American Indians by Las Casas, Juan del Valle, and others; Juan Santos
Atahualpa in seventeenth-century Peru; the peasant uprisings and the
course of popular piety in our more recent history.

That stream was forced underground most of the time, surfacing—frequently tinged with mysticism—when the poor adverted to
the reality of their liberating God. Welling up periodically in the
desert of academic theology, it engendered surprising new lines of
thought: the rights of the poor hinted at in scholastic theology's
discussion of tyranny and the property of others; the first stirrings of
social-doctrine Catholicism in eighteenth-century France; religious
socialism in twentieth-century Germany and Switzerland; in the
United States certain aspects of the "social gospel" and the writings of
Niebuhr.

It is instructive in this context to contrast the theologies of Barth
and Bultmann. Barth, the theologian primarily of God's transcendence, seemingly theologically unconcerned with the human hearers
of God's word, was pastor in a working-class milieu. His experiences
there led him to a well-defined and lifelong socialism.[34] However his
politics may have influenced his theology, he remained sensitive to
the evil of human exploitation. Bultmann, on the contrary, concerned
with the great questions of contemporary life and with modern
humanity's incomprehension of the gospel message, was nevertheless
limited by bourgeois ideology: His theology is oblivious to the oppression created by and for the very people who were the objects of
his theological concern.[35] So the theologian who started from
"heaven" was deeply aware of those who lived in "hell on earth,"
whereas the theologian who started from "earth" seemed oblivious to
human exploitation. There is no real paradox here. An authentic and
profound sense of God does not preclude awareness of the poor and
the questions they raise. "Spirituality" does not preclude "social
conscience." The real incompatibility is between bourgeois individualism and spirituality.

In Bonhoeffer too we find both concerns present.[36] Like Barth,
Bonhoeffer's profound sense of God showed him the importance of

interpreting reality from the standpoint of the oppressed: "There remains an experience of incomparable value. We have for once learned to see the great events of world history from below, from the perspective of the outcasts, the suspects, the maltreated, the powerless, the oppressed, the reviled—in short, from the perspective of those who suffer."[37] This never became Bonhoeffer's main theme, but personal experiences had certainly turned his thoughts in this new and potentially fruitful direction.[38]

A new historical situation is gradually taking shape as the exploited classes and peoples of the world recognize their centuries-long oppression. Local historical variations (nature and degree of oppression, composition of oppressed and oppressing groups) naturally produce variations in liberation theology (e.g., the theology of black power, feminist theology).[39] All liberation theology originates among the world's anonymous, whoever may write the books or the declarations articulating it. The subterranean stream of liberation theology is surfacing, fed by the rain of current events and the underground springs of past history. It separates into rivulets according to local topography, but then, gradually, the rivulets flow together again, and the stream gains power.

This, then, is the historical and theological context of Latin American liberation theology. It could not have arisen before the popular movement had attained a certain maturity, but its roots reach far into the past and its significance transcends Latin America. Despite the effect of differing national contexts on Christian life and thought, one fact is becoming universally apparent to the oppressed: The God of the lords and masters is not the same God in whom the poor and exploited believe. Local variations and resulting intramural polemics in liberation theology help clarify our postulates, principles, and methods.[40]

The popular movement, and therefore liberation theology, is still in process. The people's struggle is not yet victorious, not even on the high road to victory. Suffering and bondage still exist; the poor are still in exile.[41] But exodus has begun, and hope and rebelliousness against the powers that be remain alive, despite fascism and increased oppression. Liberation theology has arisen from this ongoing tension between a moribund but tenacious past and a future that must be created.

Of late new dimensions have been added to captivity and exile, however, and it would be suicidally unrealistic to ignore them. At the same time we must not overestimate their potency. New and creative efforts are being made despite harsh conditions now prevalent on the continent. They may be less glamorous and less well known than efforts of the recent past. They may have been initiated by people whose names are unfamiliar to "Latin-America-watchers," but that does not diminish their reality or their significance for the common people.

More than ever before in our history the exodus must be lived, not preached. Beyond their own willingness to suffer, and the compassion of outsiders, the oppressed need a strong spirit of self-affirmation and self-assertion in the face of a life that denies their very humanity. They need to hold fast the knowledge that Christ came to establish not bondage but liberation from bondage. The core of his message is the Father's saving and liberative love. It must also be the core of our Christian life and our theology.

NOTES

1. L. Goldmann, *La ilustración y la sociedad actual* (Caracas, 1968). On this work is based much of my discussion of Enlightenment mentality and capitalist economy.

2. G.W.F. Hegel, French translation, *Leçons sur la philosophie de l'histoire* (Paris, 1967), pp. 336–37.

3. Ibid., p. 320.

4. G. de Ruggiero, *Storic del liberalismo europeo* (Milan, 1966), p. 43.

5. This point Marx would summarily reject. He saw a real inequality between buying and selling once the majority of people were forced to sell their own labor in exchange for a salary.

6. The situation in the United States seems to have differed. Individualism may have been even more deeply rooted and pervasive in the U.S., but religion was not relegated to private life. On the contrary, it had an important public and political function. Individualism and stress on the private sector are not the same; the former need not rule out a public function for religion. In that context the issue is not the privatization of faith but the individualistic interpretation of it. Here proponents of political theology have much food for thought.

7. Bonhoeffer, *Letters and Papers From Prison* (New York: Macmillan Paperback, 1962), pp. 219–20.

8. Bonhoeffer's insight opened up new perspectives for some currents of contemporary theology. See J. Moltmann, *The Crucified God*, Eng. trans. (New York: Harper and Row, 1974); and K. Kitamori, *El Sufrimiento de Dios*, Spanish trans. (Salamanca: Sígueme); in English see *Theology of the Pain of God* (Richmond, Virginia: John Knox, 1965).

9. J.B. Metz, *Questioni seelte e prospective*, Italian trans. (Brescia: Queriniana).

10. See the excellent work on Moltmann's theology by R. Gibellini, *La teologia di Jürgen Moltmann* (Brescia: Queriniana, 1975).

11. Moltmann, "Fe y política," *Diálogo Ecuménico*, 1974.

12. In their introduction to the published lectures of Moltmann and Metz, A. Alvarez Bolado and J. Gómez Caffarena point out that the audience as well as the two lecturers confronted liberation theology. Caffarena writes: "It could be said that liberation theology served as the backdrop for many of the participants as they came to grips with the new thoughts proposed by the two German-speaking theologians. . . . The novel aspect of their two approaches might be summed up in the following terms. Moltmann sought to provide a clearer and more nuanced systematic statement of his theology, which could confront situations such as those existing in Latin America and Spain but which would do that in a more mature way than liberation theology does. Metz, on the other hand, sought to put strong stress on an aspect of his theology which he had not brought out before: i.e., importance of the people as an active agent and subject of history. Thus his theology would try to confront such situations as those of Latin America and Spain in a more authentic way than liberation theology does" *(Dios y la ciudad* [Madrid: Cristiandad, 1975], pp. 14–15).

13. In his open letter to Míguez Bonino, Moltmann does not seem to understand the perspective from the losing side of history. Moltmann is worried by liberation theology's seemingly slight interest in liberty and democracy. The point is that our historical experience has made us wary of bourgeois society's lies and concerned about how the common people can win real democracy and liberty. This process is part of what we call "liberation." Moltmann's incomprehension is also evident in his comments on liberation theology's references to historical events or to European thinkers. Given the historical and cultural situation of Latin America, such references are necessary for an understanding of our present, but their importance lies in the perspective from which we view and interpret them. That perspective is the subject of this article.

14. We in Latin America have no work equivalent to H. Aptheker's *American Negro Slave Revolts* (New York: International Publishers, new edition, 1974). It would be instructive to follow the history of this movement among the oppressed people of Latin America. Some data and bibliographical references can be found in Ann M. Pescatello, *The African in Latin America* (New York: Knopf, 1975).

15. Among such rebels we find, for example, Juan Santos Atahualpa, who led a native rebellion in the middle of the eighteenth century; also Tupac Amaru, who led a rebellion toward the end of that century.

16. We should re-examine the history of the *Cristeros* movement in Mexico from this point of view.

17. See the important works of Comblin on the whole national security system. Dom Candido Padim called attention to it some years ago: "La doctrina de la seguridad nacional a la luz de la doctrina de la Iglesia," in *Sedoc*, Petropolis, 1968, vol. 1, col. 432–34. See also Germán Arriagada, José Manuel Santos, et al., *Seguridad nacional y bien común*, Santiago, Chile, 1976. The same theme, but with greater stress on economic factors, is addressed in Gerald and Patricia Mische, *Toward a Human World Order: Beyond the National Security Straitjacket* (New York: Paulist Press, 1977). More will certainly be written on the subject in the coming years.

We must realize that the "state" did not fall fullblown from heaven nor was it decreed in heaven. It is a political structure created largely to serve certain economic and social interests and must be so understood. For example, to understand the political regimes now being established in Latin America one must consider the role of multinational corporations and the present situation of international capitalism.

18. These tactics have been clearly and forthrightly denounced in documents issued by the bishops of Paraguay and Brazil, for example.

19. Concrete spiritual experience is of major importance for liberation theology. Intellectuals accustomed to an outworn scholastic rationalism and comfortable only with abstract hypotheses may find it distasteful or discomforting. But many other Christians have begun to experience what Frei Betto longed for in his Brazilian prison cell: "Finding some way to live the gospel message in terms of the Latin American reality also presupposes a spirituality of its own. We must find some concrete way of being docile to the Spirit that will lead us to communion with God and with human beings in the history of our exploited and oppressed people" (Letter of January 15, 1973; see Carlos Alberto ["Betto"] Libanio Christo, *Against Principalities and Powers: Letters from a Brazilian Jail* [Maryknoll, New York: Orbis Books, 1977]).

20. See the analyses offered by the Christians for Socialism movement in *Christians and Socialism* (Maryknoll, New York: Orbis Books, 1975).

21. See the important book by J. Míguez Bonino, *Christians and Marxists: The Mutual Challenge to Revolution* (Grand Rapids, Michigan: Eerdmans, 1976). Note particularly the author's viewpoint (p. 7) and his presentation of the book's main thesis (p. 19).

22. See J.L. Segundo, *The Liberation of Theology* (Maryknoll, New York: Orbis Books, 1976); and James H. Cone, *The God of the Oppressed* (New York: Seabury Press, 1975).

23. The women of these groups are doubly exploited, alienated, and oppressed.

24. About three years ago we began to study "popular religiosity and liberative evangelization" at the Bartolomé de Las Casas Center in Lima. The theoretical context of the project is contained in the first publication: Raul Vidales and Tokihiro Kudo, *Práctica religiosa y proyecto histórico* (Lima: CEP, 1975). The importance of the issue must be re-emphasized since it has been subjected to some very cavalier treatment. I tried to emphasize its importance in *A Theology of Liberation*, Eng. trans. (Maryknoll, New York: Orbis Books, 1973). After noting that "the relationship between evangelization and popular religiosity is beginning to appear in a different light," I offered a brief bibliography on the subject (p. 74, note 20). This concern resulted from our refusal to accept unquestioningly the validity of secularization for Latin America, though secularization was then intellectually fashionable.

25. This has been clearly pointed out in an excellent article by J.P. Richard, "Teología de la liberación latinoamericana. Un aporte crítico a la teología europea," *Páginas* (Lima, July 1976).

26. *Del único modo de atraer a todos los pueblos a la verdadera religión* (Mexico City: Fondo de Cultura Económica, 1942), p. 545.

27. J. Friede (*Bartolomé de Las Casas: Precursor del Anticolonialismo* (Mexico City: Siglo XXI, 1974) has stressed this aspect of his work and challenged the "idealistic" appraisal of it. On the bishops of that era, see E. Dussel, *Les évêques hispano-américains, défenseurs et évangélisateurs de l'indien, 1504–1620* (Wiesbaden: Steiner, 1970). Also the same author's *Historia de la Iglesia en América Latina* (Barcelona: Nova Terra, 1974).

28. *Aquí se contiene una disputa o controversia*, 1552, reprinted in *Obras Escogidas*, 5:293.

29. *Historia de las Indias*, reprinted in *Obras Escogidas*, 2:356. It is worth noting that Las Casas does not restrict his defense to the Indians. He also defends the poorer Spaniards, who were at the mercy of those in power in the Indies. See Friede, *Precursor*, p. 105.

30. Las Casas's well-known suggestion that black slaves be imported into the Indies has aroused criticism that makes necesssary a summary of the historical facts. In 1516 he did accept and promote the idea that black slaves be imported to alleviate the plight

of the native Indians. But he did not initiate or implement that idea. A royal decree of 1501 had already authorized it. More important, Las Casas soon repented of this suggestion and retracted it on numerous occasions. In a later work, which he pondered long and hard before writing, he says: "Blacks have the same right to freedom that Indians do." Elsewhere he states that he is not sure his ignorance and good intentions will "pardon him before God" for having made the earlier proposal (*Historia de las Indias* [Mexico City, 1951], 3:117 and 275). This change in attitude is noted by a well-known historian of black slavery in the United States: see J.H. Franklin, *From Slavery to Freedom: A History of Negro Americans*, 3rd ed. (New York: Knopf, 1967), p. 36.

31. That year the repressiveness of the Brazilian dictatorship greatly increased. Argentina had a military dictatorship rather than Campora or Peron; Chile had Frei rather than Allende. In Mexico City hundreds of students were slain. Peru went through a difficult and depressing year. The rest of Latin America, except for Uruguay, was then much as it is now. Che Guevara's death a year earlier shook the armed resistance movement. Most significant of all, the common people at the bottom experienced little change in these years. In some countries political repression became more cruel and refined, but economic repression in Latin America is hard to qualify. The poor are so inescapably badly off that better and worse are imperceptible differences. At a CICOP meeting in Washington, D.C., in 1970, I pointed out that conditions were so bad that Latin Americans had to "hope against hope" (G. Gutiérrez, "De la Iglesia Colonial a Medellín," *Víspera*, April 1970, pp. 3–8). It is hardly a view redolent of euphoria.

32. On the whole issue of methodology in relation to liberation theology see especially J.L. Segundo, *The Liberation of Theology*. See also H. Assmann, *Teologia desde la praxis de liberación* (Salamanca: Sígueme, 1973); in English see his *Theology for a Nomad Church* (Maryknoll, New York: Orbis, 1975); see also the series *Estudios Centroamericanos* (San Salvador), issue of August-September 1975, devoted to "Método teológico y cristología latinoamericana," with articles by I. Ellacuria, J. Sobrino, and J. Hernández Pico; R. Vidales, "Cuestiones en torno al método en la teología de la liberación" (Lima: MIEC-JECI, 1974); J.P. Richard, see note 38 of this paper; and the statement by Beatriz Melano Couch in *Theology in the Americas*, edited by Torres and Eagleson (Maryknoll, New York: Orbis Books, 1976), pp. 304–8. On the idea of praxis see F. Castillo, *El problema de la praxis en la teología de la liberación* (Münster, 1976).

33. Leonardo Boff uses the expression "white hands" in discussing the history of Brazil in *Teología do cativerio e da libertação* (Lisbon: Multinova, 1976).

34. See the challenging study of F.W. Marquart, *Theologie und Sozialismus: Das Beispiel Karl Barth* (Munich: Kaiser Verlag, 1972). An article by the same author, with passages from Barth and other contributions, can be found in the volume edited by G. Husinger, *Karl Barth and Radical Politics* (Philadelphia: Westminster Press, 1976). Henry Mottu spells out the extent of Barth's socialism in an excellent article, "Le pasteur rouge de Safenwill: Réflexions sur le socialisme du premier Barth," in *Bulletin du Centre Protestant d'Etudes*, Geneva, August 1972, pp. 15–30.

35. Dorothee Sölle (*Politische Theologie* [Stuttgart: Kreuz Verlag, 1971]) detected the similarity between Bultmann's theology and political theology. Both are framed in the context of the Enlightenment. Her work corroborates my view that both derive from the political consciousness of the modern bourgeoisie, not from that of the oppressed.

36. Tillich's work should be reconsidered from this viewpoint. His involvement with "religious socialism" in the early part of this century is well known. See the anthology of his writings entitled *Political Expectations* (New York: Harper & Row, 1971).

37. Bonhoeffer, *Letters and Papers from Prison*, expanded edition, Eng. trans. (New York: 1971), p. 17. In an excellent article Robert McAfee Brown calls attention to this text, stressing that North American theology should not be too quick to break its ties to European theology, since the latter realized the need for radical social change (R. M. Brown, "A Preface and a Conclusion," *Theology in the Americas*, p. xxii).

38. Making use of Gramsci's analysis, Henry Mottu has shed new light on Bonhoeffer's critique of religion by relating it to his political experience. He shows that Bonhoeffer was capable of "taking into account the sound nucleus in popular religion" ("Theologische Kritik der Religion und Religion des Volkes," in *Genf 76: Ein Bonhoeffer-Symposium* [Munich: Kaiser Verlag, 1976], pp. 68–97). On the importance of Bonhoeffer in Latin American Christian circles see Julio Santana, "Bonhoeffer und die Theologie der Befreiung," ibid., pp. 151–70

39. See "Statement of the Ecumenical Dialogue of Third World Theologians," Dar es Salaam, August 5–12, 1976. document 17 of this volume. Also see the papers and discussions from the Detroit Conference of 1975 reproduced in *Theology in the Americas*.

40. Juan Carlos Scannone has dealt with this topic systematically, clearly, and in depth (see his articles anthologized in *Teología de la liberación y praxis popular* (Salamanca: Sígueme, 1976). But I disagree with his distinction between two "main lines of thinking" in liberation theology (see his chapter "Teología de la liberación, cultural popular y discernimiento," n ibid. Scannone vitiates one of these lines by excluding certain elements from it, e.g., popular movements, popular religiosity, pastoral efforts among the common people. Though there may well be some difference between these two lines of thought the difference does not lie in the inclusion or exclusion of populist elements but in varying approaches to and emphases on them.

41. See the work of Leonard Boff cited earlier: *Teología do cativerio e da libertação*. As I said elsewhere: "The spirituality of the Exile is as important today in Latin America as that which is nurtured in the paschal experience of the Exodus. The joy of the resurrection calls for death on the cross in one way or another" (Gutiérrez, course on liberation praxis and Christian faith given at the Mexican-American Cultural Center in San Antonio, Texas).

CONCLUSION

17

Final Statement

*Ecumenical Dialogue of Third World Theologians,
Dar es Salaam, Tanzania, August 5–12, 1976*

We, a group of theologians of the Third World gathered at Dar es Salaam, August 5–12, 1976, having spent a week together in common study of our role in the contemporary world, are convinced that those who bear the name of Christ have a special service to render to the people of the whole world who are now in an agonizing search for a new world order based on justice, fraternity, and freedom.

We have reflected from our life experience as belonging to the oppressed men and women of the human race. We seriously take cognizance of the cultural and religious heritage of the peoples of the continents of Asia, Africa, and Latin America. We have expressed our view of history, our perspective on the churches, and our expectations for the future. We invite all persons doing theology in the churches to consider our presentations and participate with us and with all those who are struggling to build a more just world in order that the believers in Christ may truly be involved in the struggle toward the realization of a new world order and a new humanity.

The Third World Political, Social, Economic, Cultural, Racial, and Religious Background

As we are increasingly aware of the impact of the political, social, economic, cultural, racial, and religious conditions on theology, we

259

wish to analyze the background of our countries as one point of reference for our theological reflection.

The concept of the "Third World" is a recent one, referring to the countries outside the industrialized capitalist countries of Europe, North America, Japan, Australia, and New Zealand, and the socialist countries of Europe, including the U.S.S.R.

The economic standard of living of these countries is low. They are technologically less advanced and are mainly agricultural in production. Their terms of trade are unfavorable and deteriorating; capital accumulation is small and external debt is large and growing. The "Third World" is divided into the free enterprise countries under the western powers and the socialist countries, which generally cut themselves off or have been cut off by the capitalist powers.

The Third World countries are rich in natural resources as well as in their cultural and religious traditions, which have given a deep meaning to their peoples' lives. These countries have been historically slow and late in technological development, in modernizing education, health, and transportation, and in the general growth of their countries. Traditionally the masses have been subject to long-term exploitation by their rulers and chiefs or aristocracy. However, prior to colonization by the western powers they had a rather self-reliant economy, with a strong sense of communal solidarity. In certain respects some of these areas were superior to the West in science, technology, agricultural and industrial methods, architecture, and the arts. Religion, profound philosophies of life, and cultures have been the soul of these peoples for many generations.

The principal cause for the modern phenomenon of the underdevelopment of the peoples of the Third World is the systematic exploitation of their peoples and countries by the European peoples. From the end of the fifteenth century, a large-scale and unprecedented expansion of the European peoples brought most of the rest of the world under their military, economic, political, cultural, and religious domination. For them it was a triumph of military technology, adventure, and a zeal to "civilize" and "Christianize the pagans." While they contributed a process of modernization in the colonized countries, they reaped enormous material benefits in the process. They plundered the riches of the Americas, Asia, and Africa. Gold, silver, precious stones, and raw materials were taken to add enormously to their capital accumulation. Their countries grew in wealth and power by the underdevelopment of these conquered and colonized countries.

The western powers took over all the temperate lands that they could populate with their own peoples. Where the numbers were few and relatively weak militarily, they nearly exterminated the native populations—as in North America, parts of South America, Australia, and New Zealand. This was a simple solution, with only a few people left to remind us of this most heinous genocide of human history.

In other areas the Europeans settled down alongside the local populations, subjugating the latter to their domination as in southern America, Central America, and southern Africa. In South America intermarriage has produced a large mestizo population, still dominated by the settlers.

In most of the countries that were thickly populated, imperial power was established following the penetration by traders and sometimes by missionaries. Only a few countries like Thailand and the hinterland of China escaped this process. The Russians, on the other hand, expanded southward and eastward up to Alaska.

In the process the western powers allocated to themselves the free or freed land spaces of the earth and established new sovereign states in them to preserve the land base of raw materials and power for themselves. Everywhere they established a pattern of economic exploitation in their favor. They exterminated entire peoples, enslaved millions, colonized others, and marginalized all, thus laying the base of their development and the underdevelopment of the Third World.

The colonizers undermined the economy of the colonies for their advantage. They made their colonies suppliers of raw materials based on cheap labor and markets for their finished goods. They forcibly expropriated fertile lands of the oppressed peoples, set up plantations of sugar, coffee, tea, rubber, etc. They transported millions of peoples from one country to another to serve as slaves or indentured labor. Thus we have the black population in the Americas and Indians in Africa, Malaysia, Sri Lanka and the Pacific and Caribbean islands. Paying a mere subsistence wage to the workers and charging high prices for their exports, the colonial powers were able to add further to their capital stock. They continued the pillage of the raw materials of these countries: oil, tin, bauxite, copper, timber, gold, silver, diamonds.

Hence for centuries the Western European peoples had a free hand in Asia, Africa, and South and Central America. North America, having become independent, joined the race for colonial power, along with Germany, Italy, and Japan.

As political independence was gained by these colonies, beginning with the Latin American countries in the last century, a new form of exploitation consolidated itself. In Latin America, Spain and Portugal lost their dominance to be replaced by the United States, Britain, and other Western European countries as the economic colonizers.

In Asia and Africa too the gaining of political independence led generally to the transfer of power to the local elite that continued the economic system established by the colonial powers. Since the 1950s the mode of economic exploitation of Third World countries by the United States, Western Europe, and Japan has been further strengthened by the horizontal and vertical integration of companies. We have thus the growth of giant multinational corporations (MNCs), based generally in the United States, Western Europe, and Japan, that have enormous economic, political, and cultural power of domination over entire lines of production and commerce. The MNCs have made the exploitation of the poor countries such a fine art, with the advantage of the most developed technology, that the gap between the rich and the poor in the world and within the countries has continued to grow.

As we have spoken of imperialistic and political domination, it is also necessary to emphasize racial and sexist domination. The oppression of blacks and other races in different areas has been brutal and constant.

Women have been discriminated against and oppressed on all levels of both society and the church. Their condition has not changed in the new independent countries of the Third World. The different forms of oppression (political, economic, racial, sexist) have their own identity. They are interrelated and interwoven in a complex system of domination.

In this centennial exploitation of the Third World by the Euro-American people, the cultural subjugation of the weak has been an important tool of oppression. The languages, arts, and social life of the peoples of Asia, Africa, and the Americas were cruelly attacked by the colonizers.

Unfortunately the Christian churches were in a large measure an accomplice in the process. The very sense of spiritual superiority of Christians gave a legitimation for conquest and sometimes even extinction of "pagans." The theology of the colonizers in most cases was thus attuned to the justification of this inhumanity; and is this not substantially what has passed for Christian theology during many centuries in its relationship to the oppressed peoples?

The People's Republic of China has entered a path of self-reliant growth based on socialism and the people's participation in the direction of agriculture and industry. By cutting themselves off from the capitalistic system they have been able to reverse the trend of continuing underdevelopment that characterized the colonies and the newly independent "free enterprise" countries. North Korea, North Vietnam, and Cuba took similar lines with appreciable results. In recent months South Vietnam, Cambodia, and Laos in Asia, and Mozambique, Guinea Bissau, and Angola in Africa, have opted for self-reliant socialist development. Tanzania is attempting a socialist approach without going the whole way of eliminating free enterprise. Other countries in the Third World have varying degrees of socialist experimentation: e.g., Burma, Algeria, Sri Lanka, Ethiopia.

The Soviet Union and Eastern Europe, considered the Second World, often render assistance to the oppressed peoples of other countries in their struggles for liberation—as in Cuba, Vietnam, and Angola. They are a valuable counterbalance against imperialist domination by the North Atlantic powers, along with China and the nonaligned powers of the Third World.

However socialism too has its own problems to resolve—especially in relation to the safeguarding of human freedom and the very price of the revolutionary process in terms of human lives. The "aid" given by the socialistic countries, while being generally on better terms than that given by capitalist countries, is also not altogether without strings and disadvantages to the recipients. The foreign policies of the socialist countries tend sometimes to be according to their national self-interest and thereby even to divide the anti-imperialist cause. Further, our information concerning socialist countries is rather limited, due to the barriers of communication.

In recent years, the very sharpening of the contradictions of capitalism has increased the tensions in the dependent, free enterprise countries of the Third World. The rising expectations of the peoples have led to much unrest and revolt. The response of beneficiaries of privileges has been generally in collaboration with foreign powers —to set up military dictatorships and to declare martial law or emergency rule as in most countries of Latin America, Asia, and Africa. We witness today a growing repression of people's movements, imprisonment without trial of political dissidents, and a trend toward sophisticated and inhuman torture in these countries. Human freedom is a victim in most parts of the Third World. Conflicts among Third World countries further worsen the condition of the masses of the people. Tribalism, caste, and other forms of religious, racial, and sex discrimination are further lines of exploitation.

In international affairs desperate efforts are being made by the Third World leaders to obtain better prices for their exports, ensure integrated commodity agreements, reschedule external debt, control or eliminate MNCs and military bases, and regulate the transfer of technology as through UNCTAD IV. From within the capitalist framework the OPEC countries, mainly of the Middle East, have been able to obtain for themselves enormous quantities of petrol dollars by the method of confrontation against the consumers of petrol. This has greatly harmed the development plans of petrol-importing poor countries.

A theology of the Third World has to take into account this historical situation. It has to ask: What role has the church been playing throughout these developments at each stage and in every situation? How did Christians react to this phenomenon of the western invasion of other peoples? What was the prevailing theology? How does Christian theology relate to today's continued exploitation in the world? What is its contribution to the building of a just world society? What contribution will the church make to the liberation of the oppressed peoples who have long suffered due to sexist, racial, and class domination?

The Presence and Role of the Church in Third World Countries

The Christian churches, while taking their origin from Jesus Christ, the word of God, and the Scriptures, are institutions composed of human beings and hence are subject to human weakness and conditioned by their socio-cultural environment.

Christianity was born in Asia and reached Africa before it spread in Europe. According to reliable tradition the Oriental churches in India trace their origin to the work of the apostle Thomas, and the church in Egypt was begun by the evangelist Mark at the dawn of the Christian era. Christianity flourished in Ethiopia, North Africa, and parts of Asia in the early centuries after Christ.

However the present-day churches of Asia, Africa, Latin America, and the Caribbean have their source in the missionary zeal of the European and North American churches. The Christianization of Latin America and parts of Asia and Africa was mainly the task of the Spanish and Portuguese missionaries. In a later phase, missionaries from the other European countries spread the Christian faith—both Catholic and Protestant—to the corners of the earth. In Korea, lay Christians from China made the first converts and developed Christian groups for several decades without a clergy or European missionaries.

Missionaries who left their countries to propagate the faith in the continents of Asia, Africa, and Latin America were persons generally dedicated to the spiritual welfare of humanity. They often underwent severe hardships of a physical and psychological nature. Their labors have given birth to the Christian communities of these continents and these are a testimony to their zeal and devotion.

All the same the missionaries could not avoid the historical ambiguities of their situation. Oftentimes and in most countries they went hand in hand with the colonizers—both traders and soldiers. Hence they could not but be, at least partially, tainted by the designs of the searchers for gold, spices, lands, slaves, and colonies. While they were zealous for souls, they tended to think that the commercial and military expansion of western peoples was a providential opportunity for the salvation of souls and the spread of the evangelical message. Thus they collaborated in the colonial enterprise, even when their Christian consciences sometimes felt revolted by the atrocities of the brutal colonizing process. Hence it is necessary to distinguish their good will and the substance of the Christian gospel from the actual impact of the Christian missions in these countries.

The missionaries could think of the spread of Christianity in terms of transplanting the institutions of their Euro-American churches, within, of course, the framework of imperial destination. Thus the new Christians were segregrated from their fellow human beings and alienated from the traditional religious and cultural heritage and their community way of life. This process strengthened their hold on the new believers. The liturgy was imported wholesale from the "mother churches"; so were the ecclesiastical structures and theologies. A pietistic and legalistic spirituality common in Europe at the time was introduced in the new churches also. In later times, the western educational system was instituted in the colonized countries largely through the services of the churches. We have thus the establishment of Christian churches in these continents more or less as carbon copies of European Christianity, adapted however to the subject situation of the colonized.

In the early phases of western expansion the churches were allies in the colonization process. They spread under the aegis of colonial powers; they benefited from the expansion of empire. In return they rendered a special service to western imperialism by legitimizing it and accustoming their new adherents to accept compensatory expectations of an eternal reward for terrestrial misfortunes, including colonial exploitation. The crafty merchants and soldiers of the West were not slow to see and take advantage of the presence of missionaries among their captive peoples. The gospel was thus used as an agency for a softening of national resistance to the plunder by the foreigners and a domestication of the minds and cultures of the dominated converts. In fact, the foreign powers often gave the Christians a privileged position of confidence within their arrangements for the administration of the countries. In the process Christian teaching got badly tainted by the search for selfish gain of the peoples who called themselves Christian and exercised power in the name of emperors and spiritual rulers.

The theology of the Christian churches at this time not only suited the colonization process but was also fed by it. The sense of military and commercial superiority of the European peoples was underpinned with the view that Christianity was superior to other religions, which had to be replaced by "the truth." For centuries theology did not seriously contest the plunder of continents and even the extermination of whole peoples and civilizations. The meaning of the message of Jesus Christ was so blunted as not to be sensitive to the agony of whole races. These are not merely sad historical realities, but the immediate predecessors of contemporary western theologies. For these latter have not yet learned to contest the successors of the colonizers—viz., the powerful countries of Europe, North America, and Japan. Nor have they evolved a theology to counteract the abuses of the heirs of the colonial merchants, viz., the giant predatory multinational corporations of today.

The Christian churches in the tri-continental colonial situation fostered educational and social sciences that helped improve the conditions of the population of these countries. Unfortunately their value patterns were such as to fit into capitalistic domination and hence were largely academic and individualistic, with the result that the leadership to whom independence was granted in the colonies (except after a revolutionary struggle) were generally persons schooled in the western capitalistic tradition. In this way the churches—perhaps unwittingly—contributed to the formation of the local elites that were to be the subsequent collaborators in the on-going exploitation of the masses of the people even after political independence. The social services too, while relieving immediate needs, failed to generate a critical social conscience or support the radical movements for social justice. The churches thus generally continued to be a sort of ideological ally of the local middle classes, which joined the power elite and shared economic privileges with the foreign companies that continued even after political independence.

We see in the churches on the three continents the growth of a "liberal" trend in more recent decades, as a successor to the traditional "conservative" position. The liberal trends are in favor of the adapta-tion of the churches to the indigenous cultures and to the operation of parliamentary democracy within the framework of free enterprise capitalism. Local religious, priests, and bishops have replaced the foreign ones. The theology was thus adapted to suit the post-independence situation. However, there was not yet a fundamental alliance of the churches with the masses struggling for radical social justice.

In more recent years there are groups of Christians all over the world beginning to understand the situation of the exploited peoples more sensitively and more correctly. The leaderships of the churches, such as the Second Vatican Council and the World Council of

Churches, have given an impetus to the commitment of Christians for the building up of a just world and for openness to the other religions and ideologies in the world. Several local churches, regional conferences, and episcopates have supported this trend (e.g., the Bishops' Conference of Medellín, 1968). The movements of liberation of the peoples from foreign domination now receive more support from the churches, as in the World Council of Churches' contribution to combat racism. The church groups are beginning to be more conscious of the injustices in the economic system. Human rights are now being defended by Christian groups, including some church leaders, in many countries of Asia, Africa, and Latin America.

The Orthodox churches have struggled for many centuries against different forms of oppression and have preserved their religious and cultural identity. Orthodox theologians share in the process of renewal as they address themselves to the task undertaken by the early fathers of the church, namely, to find the relevant expression of their faith in struggling against alienating forces and finding renewed meaning for the Christian faith in the present world.

A new vision of a theology committed to the integral liberation of persons and structures is now being developed in the very process of participation in the struggles of the people. This takes different forms in different regions. In Latin America, the "theology of liberation" expresses this analysis and commitment. In Cuba and Vietnam, Angola, Mozambique, and Guinea Bissau, groups of Christians have been involved in the revolutionary struggles. In southern Africa some Christians are also in the center of the struggle for liberation. Christian rulers in countries like Tanzania and Zambia search for new ways of realizing the gospel ideals in the contemporary world. In Asia Christian groups have been in the forefront of the struggle for human rights, especially in South Korea and the Philippines.

The study of the traditional religions and the promotion of indigenous spirituality are preoccupations of Christian groups in Asia and African countries. In several parts of Africa and Asia serious efforts are being made toward the development of indigenous theologies and liturgies, especially theology of religions. The constitution of truly authentic local churches is a major preoccupation of many theologians in these countries. Latin America has generated new groups of witnesses to the radical gospel of liberation in almost every country of the continent. Various groups such as women, youth, students, workers, and peasants are now contributing much to the renewal of the churches and of a theology relevant to their situations.

There are thus signs of hope in the presence of the churches in these countries. The search for self-reliance, the participation in the peoples' struggles, the indigenized liturgies, the emerging relevant theologies, the modern ecumenical movement, renewal efforts in many churches, and the relative openness to socialistic changes are harbingers of a more radical Christianity.

However, a deep challenge remains to be faced. The churches are still burdened by the traditions, theologies, and institutions of a colonial past, while the countries want to move rapidly into the modern world and peoples clamor for radical changes in favor of justice and freedom, all-round inculturation, and increased interreligious dialogue and collaboration.

Toward a Theological Approach in the Third World

We affirm our faith in Christ our Lord, whom we celebrate with joy, and without whose strength and wisdom our theology would be valueless and even destructive. In doing theology we are trying to make the gospel relevant to all people, and to rejoice in being his collaborators, unworthy as we are, in fulfilling God's plan for the world.

The theologies from Europe and North America are dominant today in our churches and represent one form of cultural domination. They must be understood to have arisen out of situations related to those countries, and therefore must not be uncritically adopted without our raising the question of their relevance in the context of our countries. Indeed, we must, in order to be faithful to the gospel and to our peoples, reflect on the realities of our own situations and interpret the word of God in relation to these realities. We reject as irrelevant an academic type of theology that is divorced from action. We are prepared for a radical break in epistemology which makes commitment the first act of theology and engages in critical reflection on the praxis of the reality of the Third World.

The interdisciplinary approach in theology and the dialectical interrelationship between theology and the social, political, and psychological analyses need to be recognized. While affirming the basic goodness of creation and the continued presence of God's Spirit in our world and history, it is important to bear in mind the complex mystery of evil, which manifests itself in human sinfulness and the socio-economic structures. The inequities are diverse, and account for many forms of human degradation; they necessitate our making the gospel the "good news to the poor" that it is.

The church, the body of Christ, needs to become aware of its role in today's reality. Not only should it not remain insensitive to needs and aspirations, but also it must fearlessly announce the gospel of Jesus Christ, recognizing that God speaks in and through our human needs and aspirations. Jesus identified himself with the victims of oppression, thus exposing the reality of sin. Liberating them from the power of sin and reconciling them with God and with one another, he restored them to the fullness of their humanity. Therefore the church's mission is for the realization of the wholeness of the human person.

We recognize also as part of the reality of the Third World the influence of religions and cultures and the need for Christianity to enter in humility into a dialogue with them. We believe that these religions and cultures have a place in God's universal plan and the Holy Spirit is actively at work among them.

We call for an active commitment to the promotion of justice and the prevention of exploitation, the accumulation of wealth in the hands of a few, racism, sexism, and all other forms of oppression, discrimination, and dehumanization. Our conviction is that the theologian should have a fuller understanding of living in the Holy Spirit, for this also means being committed to a lifestyle of solidarity with the poor and the oppressed and involvement in action with them. Theology is not neutral. In a sense all theology is committed, conditioned notably by the socio-cultural context in which it is developed. The Christian theological task in our countries is to be self-critical of the theologians' conditioning by the value system of their environment. It has to be seen in relation to the need to live and work with those who cannot help themselves, and to be with them in their struggle for liberation.

There was a considerable measure of agreement in the area of the need to do theology in context as described above; furthermore, we recognize that our countries have common problems. The analysis of the social, economic, political, cultural, racial, and psychological stiuations showed clearly that the countries of the Third World have had similar experiences of which account should be taken in the task of theologizing. Nevertheless, obvious differences in situations and consequent variations in theology were also noted. Thus, while the need for economic and political liberation was felt to offer a vital basis for theologizing in some areas of the Third World, theologians from other areas tended to think that the presence of other religions and cultures, racial discrimination and domination, and related situations such as the presence of Christian minorities in predominantly non-Christian societies, reveal other equally challenging dimensions of the theological task. We are enriched by our common sharing and hopefully look forward to the deepening of our commitment as Third World theologians.

As we began, so we must end. Our prayer is that God make us faithful in our work and do his will through us, and that God continually unfold before our eyes the full dimension of the meaning of our commitment to the gospel of Jesus Christ.

Conclusion

Our encounter has been brief but dynamic. We are, however, conscious of having shared in a historic session. The president of Tanzania, Julius K. Nyerere, added light and warmth to our conference by his presence at several of our sessions. We are convinced that what we have gone through these days is a unique experience of theologizing from, as it were, the other side of the earth and of human history. Rarely, if ever, have theologians of our three continents and solely from among the oppressed peoples of the world met together to reevaluate their thought, their work, and their lives. From it certain creative insights have come forth. As we share them with others we humbly pledge to continue our work together to try to comprehend better the plan of God in Jesus Christ for the men and women of our time.

We have spoken from the depths of our lived experience. We kindly request all to accept our statement as a sincere expression of our consensus from our knowledge of what our peoples have gone through over centuries. We hope it will be of some service in spreading genuine and frank understanding among the peoples of the world.

18

Communiqué

Ecumenical Dialogue of
Third World Theologians,
Dar es Salaam, August 12, 1976

The first meeting of the Ecumenical Dialogue of Third World Theologians was held at Assembly Hall of the University of Dar es Salaam, August 5 to 12, 1976. There were twenty-two participants, of whom seven were from Africa, seven from Asia, six from Latin America, one from black America, and one from the Caribbean. There were eleven Roman Catholics, ten Protestants, and one Coptic Orthodox.

The conference program consisted of three parts:

1. socio-political and cultural analysis of the background of each continent,
2. an evaluation of the presence of the church on the three continents,
3. efforts toward a theological approach in the Third World.

For each part position papers were presented by different participants following which the issues raised were discussed.

The experience of fellowship as well as the common concern for doing theology in the Third World context gave the theologians a sense of belonging together in spite of the differences of their theological orientation.

They found this experience and the consensus in their discussions so worthwhile that they decided that more ecumenical gatherings of the Third World theologians would be highly desirable for promoting the doing of theology in the context of Third World social, political, economic, religious, and cultural realities. Accordingly they decided to form an *Ecumenical Association of Third World Theologians* after adopting a provisional constitution. They have defined the aims of the association as "the continuing development of Third World Christian theologies which will serve the church's mission in the world and witness to the new humanity in Christ expressed in the struggle for a just society."

Objectives

1. Sharing with one another the present trends of interpretation of the gospel in the different Third World countries, particularly bearing in mind the roles of theology in relation to other faiths and ideologies as well as the struggle for a just society;
2. promoting the exchange of theological views through writings in the books and periodicals of Third World countries;
3. promoting the mutual interaction between theological formulation and social analysis;
4. keeping close contacts as well as being involved with action-oriented movements for social change.

The membership of the association is for those born and normally serving in one of the Third World countries and for members of the dispersion from Africa, Asia, and Latin America involved in some form of doing theology.

The association will have an Executive Committee consisting of a President, a Vice-President, and an Executive Secretary; and an Advisory Committee consisting of four members from each continent.

They elected Dr. J. Russell Chandran of India as President, Bishop Patrick Kalilombe of Malawi as Vice-President, and Fr. Sergio Torres of Chile as Executive Secretary for the next four-year period.

The discussion at the meeting concluded with the adoption of a statement which expresses their convictions about the directions toward which the interpretation of the gospel of Jesus Christ should move in the Third World situation today.

This first consultation will be followed by an All-Africa Consultation of Theologians and other Christians, planned to take place in Accra, Ghana, in December 1977. This consultation will be considered as the second meeting of the Third World theologians and will be focused on the African reality.

Contributors

1. SERGIO TORRES: Roman Catholic priest from Chile, Executive Secretary of the Theology in the Americas program and of the Association of Third World Theologians.

2. PATRICK MASANJA: Lecturer in Sociology at the University of Dar es Salaam, Tanzania.

3. PATRICK A. KALILOMBE: Catholic Bishop from Malawi, East Africa, and on leave in the U.S.A.

4. CHARLES NYAMITI: Professor of Theology at the Seminary of Kipalapala, Tanzania.

5. KWESI A. DICKSON: Professor of Theology at the University of Accra, Ghana.

6. NGINDU MUSHETE: Professor of Theology and Ethics, National University of Kinshasa, Zaire.

7. MANAS BUTHELEZI: Bishop of the Evangelical Lutheran Church in Southern Africa.

8. ALLAN BOESAK: Chaplain of student movement in Bellville South, Republic of South Africa.

9. ORLANDO CARVAJAL: Executive Secretary of the Secretariat for Social Action, Mindanao, Philippines.

10. CARLOS H. ABESAMIS: Professor of Scripture and Theology at the Loyola School of Theology, Manila.

11. PETER K.H. LEE: Director of the Christian Study Centre on Chinese Religion and Culture, Hong Kong.

12. D.S. AMALORPAVADASS: Director of the National Biblical, Catechetical and Liturgical Centre of the Catholic Bishops' Conference of India, Bangalore.

13. J.R. CHANDRAN: Principal of the United Theological College, Bangalore, India.

14. ENRIQUE DUSSEL: President of CEHILA (Comisión de estudios de historia de la Iglesia en América Latina), Mexico City.

15. BEATRIZ MELANO COUCH: Professor of Theology, Union Theological Seminary, Buenos Aires.

16. GUSTAVO GUTIERREZ: Professor of Theology, Catholic University, Lima.

OTHER ORBIS TITLES

THE COMING
OF THE THIRD CHURCH:

An Analysis of the Present and Future of the Church

Walbert Buhlmann

"Not a systematic treatment of contemporary ecclesiology but a popular narrative analogous to Alvin Toffler's Future Shock." America

ISBN 0-88344-069-5 CIP
ISBN 0-88344-070-9

Cloth $12.95
Paper $6.95

FREEDOM MADE FLESH

Ignacio Ellacuria

"Ellacuria's main thesis is that God's saving message and revelation are historical, that is, that the proclamation of the gospel message must possess the same historical character that revelation and salvation history do and that, for this reason, it must be carried out in history and in a historical way." Cross and Crown

ISBN 0-88344-140-3
ISBN 0-88344-141-1

Cloth $8.95
Paper $4.95

CHRISTIAN POLITICAL THEOLOGY
A MARXIAN GUIDE

Joseph Petulla

"Petulla presents a fresh look at Marxian thought for the benefit of Catholic theologians in the light of the interest in this subject which was spurred by Vatican II which saw the need for new relationships with men of all political positions." Journal of Economic Literature

ISBN 0-88344-060-1

Paper $3.95

CHRISTIANS AND SOCIALISM
Documentation of the Christians for
Socialism Movement in Latin America

edited by John Eagleson

"Compelling in its clear presentation of the issue of Christian commitment in a revolutionary world." The Review of Books and Religion

ISBN 0-88344-059-8   *Cloth $7.95*

ISBN 0-88344-058-X   *Paper $4.95*

THE CHURCH AND
THIRD WORLD REVOLUTION
Pierre Bigo

"Heavily documented, provocative yet reasonable, this is a testament, demanding but impressive." Publishers Weekly

ISBN 0-88344-071-7 CIP   *Cloth $8.95*

ISBN 0-88344-072-5   *Paper $4.95*

CHRISTIANS, POLITICS
AND VIOLENT REVOLUTION
J.G. Davies

"Davies argues that violence and revolution are on the agenda the world presents to the Church and that consequently the Church must reflect on such problems. This is a first-rate presentation, with Davies examining the question from every conceivable angle." National Catholic News Service

ISBN 0-88344-061-X   *Paper $4.95*

THEOLOGY FOR A NOMAD CHURCH
Hugo Assmann

"A new challenge to contemporary theology which attempts to show that the theology of liberation is not just a fad, but a new political dimension which touches every aspect of Christian existence." Publisher's Weekly

ISBN 0-88344-493-3   *Cloth $7.95*

ISBN 0-88344-494-1   *Paper $4.95*

THE GOSPEL IN SOLENTINAME

Ernesto Cardenal

"Upon reading this book, I want to do so many things—burn all my other books which at best seem like hay, soggy with mildew. I now know who (not what) is the church and how to celebrate church in the eucharist. The dialogues are intense, profound, radical. The Gospel in Solentiname calls us home."
Carroll Stuhlmueller, *National Catholic Reporter*

ISBN 0-88344-168-3 CIP *Cloth $6.95*

THE CHURCH AND POWER IN BRAZIL

Charles Antoine

"This is a book which should serve as a basis of discussion and further study by all who are interested in the relationship of the Church to contemporary governments, and all who believe that the Church has a vital role to play in the quest for social justice." *Worldmission*

ISBN 0-88344-062-8 *Paper $4.95*

HISTORY AND
THE THEOLOGY OF LIBERATION

Enrique Dussel

"The book is easy reading. It is a brilliant study of what may well be or should be the future course of theological methodology." *Religious Media Today*

ISBN 0-88344-179-9 *Cloth $8.95*

ISBN 0-88344-180-2 *Paper $4.95*

LOVE AND STRUGGLE
IN MAO'S THOUGHT

Raymond L. Whitehead

"Mao's thoughts have forced Whitehead to reassess his own philosophy and to find himself more fully as a Christian. His well documented and meticulously expounded philosophy of Mao's love and struggle-thought might do as much for many a searching reader." *Prairie Messenger*

ISBN 0-88344-289-2 CIP *Cloth $8.95*

ISBN 0-88344-290-6 *Paper $3.95*

WATERBUFFALO THEOLOGY

Kosuke Koyama

"This book with its vivid metaphors, fresh imagination and creative symbolism is a 'must' for anyone desiring to gain a glimpse into the Asian mind." Evangelical Missions Quarterly

ISBN 0-88344-702-9   *Paper $4.95*

ASIAN VOICES
IN CHRISTIAN THEOLOGY

Edited by Gerald H. Anderson

"A basic sourcebook for anyone interested in the state of Protestant theology in Asia today. I am aware of no other book in English that treats this matter more completely." National Catholic Reporter

ISBN 0-88344-017-2   *Cloth $15.00*

ISBN 0-88344-016-4   *Paper $7.95*

THE PRAYERS
OF AFRICAN RELIGION

John S. Mbiti

"We owe a debt of gratitude to Mbiti for this excellent anthology which so well illuminates African traditional religious life and illustrates so beautifully man as the one who prays." Sisters Today

ISBN 0-88344-394-5 CIP   *Cloth $7.95*

POLYGAMY RECONSIDERED

Eugene Hillman

"This is by all odds the most careful consideration of polygamy and the attitude of Christian Churches toward it which it has been my privilege to see." Missiology

ISBN 0-88344-391-0   *Cloth $15.00*

ISBN 0-88344-392-2   *Paper $7.95*